Steaming Through the War Years

Reminiscences on the Ex-GER Lines in London

by
Reg Robertson

GW00535859

THE OAKWOOD PRESS

© Oakwood Press and Reg Robertson 1996

British Library Cataloguing in Publication Data
A Record for this book is available from the British Library
ISBN 0 85361

Typeset by Oakwood Graphics.

Printed by Alpha Print (Oxford) Ltd, Witney, Oxon.

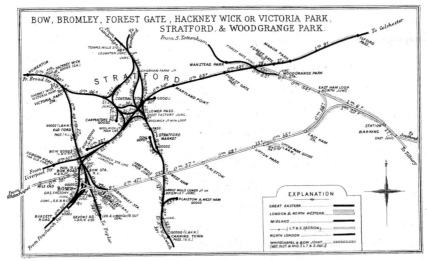

The lines around Stratford, taken from the Railway Clearing House's *Railway Junction
Diagrams, 1914.*

Published by
The Oakwood Press
P.O. Box 122, Headington, Oxford

Contents

Preface

The reasons for writing this book were twofold. Firstly it is a chronicle of the earlier part of my life and an historical background for any of my family who may be interested.

Secondly, and more importantly for those who research the history of our civilisation and its advancement through the centuries, it is a record of an industry and way of life that no longer exists in many of the advanced nations. When the steam locomotive was relegated to the scrap iron merchant in the 1960s, and superseded by dieselisation or electrification, a form of transport disappeared forever.

There is nothing to match the power, the beauty and the challenge of the steam locomotive and man's battle to control its untamed strength. As the steam locomotive was withdrawn from service a chapter of engineering prowess closed. As the men who worked those iron horses die so dies their knowledge of how to operate a steam locomotive. It becomes a closed book on man's historical achievements.

I feel it is essential that the facts of the steam days of rail be recorded for future generations to read and ponder upon. All too often this kind of insight into a past way of life is lost because nobody troubled to record it. There is a growing movement called industrial archaeology and this book fits in well with the scheme of things.

Reg Robertson
Prospect
Tasmania

Publisher's Note

The publisher would like to thank John Watling and Lyn Brooks of the Great Eastern Railway Society for their help with checking the manuscript and with picture research for this book.

The Great Eastern Railway Society was formed in 1973 in order to promote a widespread interest in the GER; to encourage and coordinate research into its history; and to provide a permanent record of the results. As well as studying the life span of the GER the Society encompasses its constituent Companies and its successors up to the present day, plus other independent and joint railways in the Eastern Counties.

Membership is open to all, and offers scope for a wide range of interests; archivists, historians, modellers and general railway enthusiasts.

Two general meetings are held each year, visits are arranged to places of GER interest and several local area groups meet regularly. The *Great Eastern Journal* and *Great Eastern News* are both published quarterly and are supplied to members only, whilst some 400 Information Sheets covering all aspects of the railway are also available.

A prospectus and membership application form is available from the Membership Secretary, 9, Clare Road, Leytonstone, London, E11 1JU.

Chapter One

A Family Affair

It is often said that a lot of good comes from wars. If one accepts that argument I suppose the 'good' that came from World War II, from my point of view, was that I joined the London and North Eastern Railway (LNER) at Stratford in the Greater London area. Until the war began in 1939, getting a job with any private railway company in England was as unlikely as winning the football pools. This especially applied to the traffic grades.

The railways were like big private families. To stand any chance of a job you had to come from a family that already had the breadwinner working for the company. If you were not that fortunate but were related to a railway employee, your application was given a second thought. If, on the other hand, you were a complete outsider you could give the idea away.

This policy was never explained to me but, after serving eight years with the LNER on the footplate at the Stratford locomotive depot, I felt that the attitude of the company was based on the fact that railway work was a world of its own. It had a language of its own, a line of promotion and times of its own that made service within its framework unbearable unless you had the required aptitude of seeing yourself as a servant of the company, for the company.

Those who lived in families whose well being was governed by a father who worked on the railway grew up to realise that it was no ordinary job. They realised the awkward shifts, the sudden change of shifts and the fact that the majority of railway work was done when other people were asleep or enjoying a relaxing time.

This background was natural to them and so the application for a job meant that they automatically accepted the world of the social outcast. It saved the company the expense of training new employees for a month or so, only to have them leave because work interfered with the Saturday night dance or the soccer match.

In 1939 the war changed all that and, with the associated manpower problems, the private railways found themselves in a cleft stick. Firstly, to obtain essential recruits to keep the services running, they had to call on the open market. Secondly, they came under government control as part of the British defence system and ran as the prototype of British Railways in the interest of England's security.

It was late in 1940 when I answered an advertisement in the *Brentwood Gazette* for engine cleaners at Stratford depot. My knowledge of railways at the time was limited to the occasional cycle ride to Shenfield station to watch the railway activities at that busy junction, where the Southend-on-Sea branch line left the main east coast line of the old Great Eastern Railway.

The roar of the steam locomotives on the express trains, as they thundered through the station and over the steel bridges, always fascinated me. At Shenfield there were so many comparisons of train working to watch. Apart from the expresses that did their 80 miles an hour on the up main there were the busy little tank engines on the Shenfield to Liverpool Street suburban run.

There were also the lumbering, clanking freight trains and the fussingly important Southend-on-Sea branch connections.

I was not sure of the work of an engine cleaner. It was the wage that I found interesting. It was more than three pounds a week when one included the adult rate of pay received for labouring work around the depot due to manpower shortages. Cleaners would be called upon to load ashes from the disposal pits into wagons or load coal from the stockpiles near the Jubilee Shed outlet roads into wagons for transfer to the coal stage. After shovelling twelve tons with a number eight shovel into wagons with the floor shoulder high, you didn't need 'keep fit' classes. At that time, I was earning 17 shillings a week as delivery boy for a Brentwood chemist.

My next door neighbour was a platelayer with a Special Gang at Stratford. He told me the job was very dirty. He also said that one could get promotion to fireman and then driver, but he never really encouraged me to take the job. After joining the LNER and experiencing the friction between the sections I soon realised why he, as a platelayer, was not very interested. The track maintenance men were very hostile toward train crews. They felt that the maintenance of the track was equally as important as running trains and yet their wage was about a third of the train crews.

The recruiting offices were in the smoke grimed buildings that frowned over the platforms of Liverpool Street station, on the Bishopsgate Road side. The whole atmosphere within the building was that of austerity and decadence. The seedy paintwork of chocolate brown and cream was grubby with the rub marks made by people going up and down the bare boarded staircase. The corridors were long and tall and empty of comfort. Regularly spaced doors would display signwritten boards in gold lettering stating 'Loco. Superintendent' or 'Loco. Running Officer' or 'Roster Clerk'.

I later discovered that the run-down appearance was nothing to do with the war, which was entering its second year. It was an example of private industry letting itself run down with the firm belief that, after the war, the whole railway system in England would be nationalised.

I took my medical and educational exams in various rooms within the building and was told that I would be advised of my success or otherwise by post. Two weeks later I received a departmental memo which tersely stated that I had been successful in obtaining a position as supernumerary engine cleaner at Stratford locomotive department and to report for duty at 8.0 am the following Monday. So started a 36 mile round trip to and from work which was to last for the next eight years.

Stratford station was being rebuilt prior to the beginning of the war. The steam train services were planned to link with an extension of the London Transport underground railway services. This suddenly stopped and left Stratford station with a series of entrances and tunnels that led to nowhere most of the time. It was through one of these subways that one reached the Loco. Department. The vast, sprawling complex of workshops and engine sheds hid under a constant pall of smoke and ash on the southern side of the main line.

I had never seen so many railway lines in all my life. There were trucks and carriages everywhere. Engines seemed to come from nowhere and the noise, at times, was unbelievable. About ten of us started that morning. We were all shown where to sign on, given a rule book that had to be studied rigorously, two sets of bib and brace overalls and told to report to the shed foreman.

He told us to call him Joe. Short and stocky, with a face like a prize fighter, he watched us with keen eyes from beneath the peak of his greasy cloth cap. He spoke in short, rapid bursts of pure Cockney.

Joe's office was an old freight box wagon, taken off its wheels and put on the ground opposite the loco. crib room and dormitory for country crews. It was next to the oil and tool store, sandwiched between a line servicing the disposal pits and the coal stage and No. 1 Road of the Jubilee Shed. The end result was that all conversations took place at a shouting level due to engines rumbling by for coal or standing outside the main shed with a full head of steam, now and then roaring off through the Ross safety valves as they waited to depart for the day's work.

Joe was a man of few words but you could trust him. If you transgressed the lines of duty Joe would give you a lecture, maybe a clump, and that was it. His relief was a more smartly dressed man with smooth ways and no greater love than reporting the slightest misdemeanour to higher authority. We liked Joe best. When he said 'All I want is the work done what I gives yer an' no bleedin' backchat', we all knew where we stood.

There would be about five of us in a gang, depending on the size of the engine to be cleaned. If it was only a tank engine then two would be given the job. The main shed at Stratford was called the Jubilee Shed. It had 12 roads and was about 200 metres in length. Imagine 12 roads with either 15 to 20 tank engines, or about 10 tender engines to each road and you can imagine the effect of such a sight on the novice.

Some would be belching thick, acrid smoke after being lit up to come into traffic later that day. Others would be hot but just holding a good head of steam, waiting for the next crew to come on duty. Then there would be the cold locomotives, with no steam or fire, waiting repairs, boiler washout or just not required. In this atmosphere, dim with smoke and steam, with skylights blackened due to wartime requirements, we had to scramble over engines and get the bodywork spotless. It reminded me of the scenes Dickens painted of the Industrial Revolution. I suppose, with more than 400 locomotives being stabled at Stratford loco. depot, one could not really expect anything else.

Not being accustomed to the work, and being boys, we were soon as black as the engines we were cleaning. Cleaning engines was not a task being done just for the look of the thing. The motions, wheels and frames had to be cleaned of grime, ash and dirt so that engine crews could oil up without getting filthy. It also helped the fitters to examine the working parts of the locomotive for defects and breakages in vital areas.

The underframe, axle boxes, springs, motions and footplates were cleaned with paraffin oil. 'Motions' was the term used for the connecting rods, pistons, big and small ends, straps, siderods and eccentrics that, together, converted the steam power from the cylinders to the movement of the wheels to drive the engine. 'Inside motions' was the term for all this machinery when housed under the boiler of the engine which had its cylinders directly under the smoke box. 'Outside motions' was the name for all those flashing rods that one saw as an express engine rushed by with its cylinders outside the main frame and directly below the smokebox. The famous *Flying Scotsman* would be one of them.

No one liked doing the inside motions because of danger to life and limb. The engines would stand in a line over inspection pits that ran the whole length of the Jubilee Shed. When cleaners were working they had warning boards which fitted on each end of the engine. The boards had brackets which clamped onto the fittings which held the engine's headlamps. The boards then projected about a metre into the walkway between the roads with an oil lamp that flickered behind a red aspect glass so that, in the smoky gloom, those working round the shed could see that cleaners were working on an engine. The red light also indicated to shunters that the engine could not be moved because cleaners were working on, under and around it.

Unfortunately red lights do not stop moving objects, neither do they stop accidents. Shunters would often be working the shed, placing engines for future shifts, or taking out 'dead' ones from running roads to put on workshop roads. It only needed a rough shunt and the locomotive being cleaned could jolt backwards or forwards. Maybe it would be less than a metre but it would be sufficient to take off a cleaner's hand or crush him against the boiler as he straddled the big ends.

This was our constant fear as we cleaned the motions. You stood with one foot each side of the inspection pit, on the brick edge which carried the rail, and your body would be braced against the steel connecting rods which connected the massive big ends to the pistons. If you were silly enough to stand on the rail and not the brick edging, because it was far more comfortable, you could easily lose a foot as 90 tons of engine rolled forward in a shunting movement. Such things did happen and many men on shed duties were there through injuries sustained during footplate duties.

The boiler, tanks, tenders and cabs were cleaned with a white creamy substance called splonk. Nobody knew its real name but it did an excellent job and soon removed the grime and grease of a few days running from the green livery of the passenger engines. It also made the all black boilers of the mixed traffic engines and freight locomotives shine like a well polished boot. The wheels were finished off with splonk to get a fine shine.

The smokebox and chimney were cleaned with a substance known as smokebox jelly. This was dark green in colour and something like a thick vaseline. It did a very good job on the business end of the locomotive and, when finished, it would shine like new. It was best if the smokebox was hot as the jelly would then melt and work into the solid metal walls.

Cleaning locomotives was not as tedious as it sounds, depending on where your interest was focused. If you were only there for the money, waiting for a better job or call up for the armed forces, then I suppose the grime and depressing surroundings were unacceptable. If however you were there with the hope that one day you would be a member of a crew that would try to tame the steam monster in motion, then cleaning engines was chapter one in the book of knowledge.

Swabbing the moving parts with paraffin made you aware of the slide valves, the eccentric straps and the connecting pins. Stephenson's Link and Walschaert's gearing began to mean something. The square design of the

Belpaire firebox and boiler emphasised its different lines under the splonk filled cloth. We only cleaned the outside of the engines. The interior of the cab was the crew's responsibility.

You could tell the characters of the crews by the way they cleaned their cabs. Some would just polish the boiler front and the collection of brass fittings and copper pipes. Others would be equally meticulous but would also do the cab roof and walls. It was easy to pick the engine that had regular crews and the locomotive that was used in a common pool. On one you could eat off the footplate, so to speak. The other was like a chimney sweep's bag.

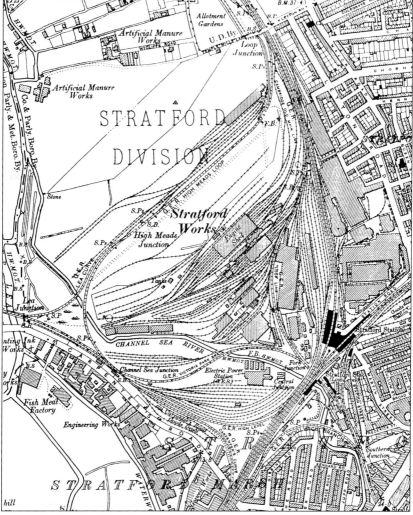

Stratford Works and station. *Reproduced from the 6", 1920 Ordnance Survey Map*

Chapter Two

First Steps on the Ladder

Engine cleaning was the base grade in the Loco. branch. Depending on your ability, the road led to locomotive superintendent but many years and problems stood between that dream and reality. The first step on the lengthy ladder was to Lamps and Boards boy. There was no extra pay except that it took you from day work to shift work, with the necessary compensating rate of pay.

Every locomotive had to carry a set of headlamps. Three lamps were the set and they were an essential part of the equipment as well as being linked with railway operations in general. Seen from today's standard of electric headlamps on locomotives, the oil burning headlamp of pre-war years was very antiquated. It was all metal and stood about 300 mm high with a metal handle on top for carrying purposes. The front glass was very thick and convexed to magnify the light from the flickering oil fed wick that sat in a porcelain holder held by a tinplated reservoir.

All lamps had one red slide that could be flicked over the glass inside the lamp container which held the paraffin reservoir. Others had both red and violet coloured slides. The lamps were painted white and had brackets on the back with which they were attached to upright steel prongs on the engine's footplate.

The coloured slides enabled the crews to work to the requirements of the company's headlamp codes. The red aspect gave the red light that always had to be on the rear of the engine when running 'light' or engine only. The violet slides enabled crews on the LNER suburban service, and local freight trains, to use the destination codes for guidance of signalmen and others involved in traffic movements. It must be remembered that at this period of time the use of telephones on the railways was still very primitive. Much of the work on country lines was in morse code or bell code form. The headlamp codes assisted this form of communication.

A signalman would receive the bell code for a train in his section and, working with the timetables, he would know the train he was expecting. If the train coming towards him at night did not have a headlamp code that linked with his timetable or bell code he knew that the train was off course. For instance, if his bell had indicated a fast through train he would expect a train with one white light on the bracket on the smoke box, directly under the chimney. If the train that came had a white light over the left hand buffer he would know it was a local goods train.

The lamps were predominantly for night operations but they could be used during the day in place of boards. They were never intended to be a means by which the driver could see his way. Night driving was a blind operation and relied purely on a good sense of judgement, signals and the handlamp signals from a shunter or guard. If anything went wrong during a night shift the only form of illumination was the slush lamp.

Day operations were covered by the use of boards. These were circular metal discs about 380 mm in diameter with a bracket on the back by which you could place them on the same steel prong used for the oil lamps. They were all white on one side, and violet with a white border on the reverse. They were carried by the sausage shaped hole cut in the top of the disc. The only time the lamp had to be used during daylight hours was when the engine was travelling light. The lamp on the rear bracket indicated to the signalman that the train was complete.

The lamp boy's duties were to collect the lamps and boards from incoming engines on the disposal pits and store them in an area near the tool stores. Crews coming on duty would then pick them up as they collected their tools from the store and take them to the engine which was booked for their job.

At the Stratford depot railway lines ran everywhere and much of the work area had engines running through it. Looking back, it was a miracle that many were not killed by engine movements through areas where crews walked to sign on, collect tools, go home or go about some other railway business. Perhaps it was because most railwaymen studied the safety of others that the accident rate was low.

I always remember how an old driver taught me a lesson in safety during my early days at the depot. I was doing Lamps and Boards at the time. I was carrying some lamps from the Tank Road to the stores. It was a murky day, the winter fog mixing with the Stratford smoke and covering the whole area with a yellowy green cloud. In front of the stores was the line that ran from the turntable road to the coal stage. The lines were like tramways with the surface filled in to facilitate walking and pushing barrows around the area.

I was walking near the line in the fog and it was very quiet. Fog always seemed to blanket the normal sounds round the sheds. I felt a nudge between the shoulder blades and thought one of my mates had crept up on me in the fog. The nudge came from the solid buffer of a 'J' class local goods engine. It was right behind me and I had not allowed sufficient clearance from the track.

The old driver smiled as he saw my look of horror.

'Just to let you know, boy, you can't dream round here. Could have run you down - just like that.'

His fireman was leaning over the side enjoying the proceedings. "E wasn't really worried about running yer down, son,' he said. 'It's just that wreaths is a little expensive this time o' year.'

The remark was typical of the railway humour that I was to encounter during my service with the railway. The driver sucked on his stumpy pipe, gave the engine a little steam and they glided into the gloom. It's amazing how quietly 90 tons of steel can be when coasting on a wet rail. I never forgot that lesson.

The next promotion for an engine cleaner, and next lesson in Loco. Shed working, was firelighting. Stratford had a regular gang of firelighters. They were usually footplate men who had fallen by the wayside with health problems or through accidents. They worked three shifts round the clock, seven days a week. When they went on leave or were off due to sickness the senior engine cleaner, who was not being rostered as spare fireman, was rostered to relieve as firelighter. This was relished because we immediately received the adult rate of pay.

If locomotives were not required for a period of time, were in for major repair or boiler washout, the fire was dropped and the engine was stored in the running sheds or workshops. When next required for work the engine had to be lit up. This called for the firebox to be coaled in a certain manner with firelighters to ignite the coal.

A firelighter was a simple device consisting of four sticks about 150 mm long, which formed the corner pieces of a bundle of glued wood shavings soaked in napthalene. The lot was wired together and about four would be used to get a fire going. The firelighter's tools were a fireman's shovel, a packet of firelighters and a slush lamp. The slush lamp was the name of an all purpose torch consisting of a galvanized container with a spout that carried a wick of worsted yarn feeding into the paraffin held in the container at one end and a handle the other end. The end of the yarn protruded about 40 mm from the spout. When lit it flared well to give an oily, smoky light. This was both for illumination and lighting firelighters.

When lighting up tank engines the coal was placed all round the firebox, leaving the centre for the firelighters. After lighting one and placing it in the box with the others, coal would be placed over them and the firebox door was shut. The ashpan door had to be open to allow a draught of air to feed the firelighters.

As the engine had no steam the blower could not be used to create a false draught and so extract smoke and fumes through the chimney. This meant that most fumes came through the firebox door into the cab. The acrid smoke would cause eyes to water and lungs to be violently irritated by the sulphur in the smoke. You would choke and gasp for breath and the only way to work was to be bent double as the purest air was near the floor.

When sufficient steam had been raised the blower could be used and this would speed up proceedings. The blower was a steeel tube which sat over the top of the exhaust outlet from the cylinders in the smoke box. It was about the same dimension as the superheating steam pipes that went through the boiler and it was circular, with small holes drilled in the upper surface. As the blower control handle was pulled in the cab, steam entered the pipe and blew through the holes and out of the chimney. This forced current of air drew fumes from the firebox through the boiler tubes and out through the chimney.

It was an essential part of the steam engine's equipment and used constantly when on the run. When a locomotive was in motion the exhaust from the cylinders roaring through the smokebox created the necessary draught to take the firebox fumes and flames through the boiler tubes, and so heat the water to create the necessary steam for operations. If the driver shut off steam to allow the engine to coast along, and failed to pull the blower on to counteract the lack of draught through the smokebox, there was an immediate blowback from the firebox into the cab. Terrific heat with flames and fumes would fill the cab. It was extremely dangerous, especially if the fireman happened to be firing up at the time with the firebox door open.

A situation similar to this existed on the engine that had been 'lit up' for service. The fire built up in heat and fumes but, until steam was available, there was no way of forcing it from the cab. The result was a smut filled cab with all working parts too hot to touch.

When lighting tender engines, which normally had a greater firebox area, only half the box was coaled. After getting a good fire going it was then pushed over the box and built up so that the entire grate was covered. This kept the cold air off the boiler plates. It was normally looked upon as having a engine in steam, from completely cold, in about two to three hours.

There were other essentials that the firelighter had to check before lighting the fire. Firstly that there was sufficient water in the boiler. Secondly that the engine had water in the tank or tender with which to fill the boiler when steam was raised. Thirdly, that ashpan dampers and firebox doors were working correctly, as well as the smokebox door being closed properly.

Fitted in with this work on the eight hour shift was the maintenance of fires in engines which had been placed in the shed ready for their next shift requirements. This could involve the firelighter in being responsible for more than 20 engines during the shift.

By the time the engine cleaner had experienced these first 'promotions' he had become acquainted with the mechanism of locomotives, the requirements in the shape of equipment when an engine was on the run and the basic knowledge required by a locomotive fireman. If he had not gained this knowledge he was in for a great shock when first out as spare fireman because, typical of most industries, there was no training given to the new entrant. Everything was self taught.

Chapter Three

Apprenticeship on the Shovel

After rotating on these jobs for a period of time quite a lot of general knowledge was gained regarding engines and the duties that existed in getting those engines ready for work before the crew signed on. At the same time, with lads starting and leaving, one soon learned the importance of seniority. The cleaners with the longest service became the first for relief as firemen with the locomotive running staff. They were known as spare firemen or 'spare irons'. Those on the bottom then moved up for relief in the grades that carried the adult rate of pay and the new entrant became the raw recruit for engine cleaning. This did not just happen and neither was it through any benevolence of the employer. It was a fair and square method planned by the union representing locomotive grades and removed any possibilities for favouritism by management.

Having reached the hallowed ranks of spare fireman one entered an entirely new world. It was also the old grind all over again, all the menial jobs, the dirty jobs. The only consolation was the knowledge that all firemen started that way and it was a start towards getting the first stage of a rate of pay that went up with yearly service. Firemen and drivers went about seven years before they reached their top rate of pay for the job. Each year gave an increase but, if you were a spare fireman, your year was calculated as 313 firing turns in not more than five years.

This was a good scheme because, when the spare fireman first started his career on the footplate, he might only get two firing turns a week. The rest of the week would be cleaning duties or other tasks. It could take three years to get those first 313 firing turns but, once you reached that stage, you automatically received second year fireman's rate of pay for your next 313 turns of firing.

One was also introduced to the Link rostering system which, when fully appreciated, was the best and fairest rostering system in any industry. The top roster at Stratford was the express and intermediate express passenger trains. There was also the express freight link; not a lot of difference in maximum speeds attained but a lot of difference in the work and driving techniques. In my opinion the express freight driver was more of an expert than the express passenger driver.

The links, or gangs, then came down in prestige to suburban passenger trains. These, in turn, were graduated in importance with the length of run and semi-fast runs being seen as of greater importance than the short run with all-station work. The suburban run from Liverpool Street to Shenfield or Chelmsford was more important than the Chingford run. Wood Street and Epping were of higher importance than Palace Gates to North Woolwich. There was no difference in the work. It was just a point of view that had gained control with management over the years.

All suburban passenger work was based on split second timing to and from

Liverpool Street. In the rush hours a suburban train entered or left one of the 18 platforms every three minutes, with main line expresses using platforms eight to eleven. It did not matter whether you were Gidea Park, Chingford or Hertford bound, the tussle for steam and water was just the same.

Below the suburban passenger links were the local goods rosters, then the shunting gangs in the various marshalling yards such as Temple Mills, Northumberland Park, Stratford Market and the docks. Equal to them were the shunting crews of the various carriage sidings. The lowest of the low were the crews manning the shunting shifts within the loco. running sections, such as Coal Road Pilot, Loco. Shunter, Carriage Shed Pilot and Workshop Mike.

Each link had an area where knowledge was gained that would be useful in the higher links. Each link automatically supplied relief crews for the higher links so that, overall, the whole system was an integrated part of increased knowledge and efficiency for both employer and employee. As an example, if a driver or fireman was absent in the suburban passenger links due to sickness the relief would come from the senior men in the local goods link, rostered in a 'spare' position. Each roster carried about five to eight spare weeks to cover the various relief jobs within the gangs. In turn the spare shifts in the local goods links would be filled by the senior men in the shunting links and the shunting vacancy would be filled by the senior engine cleaner, now classified as 'spare fireman'. In this way the engine cleaner took his first step towards that coveted spot on the footplate.

There was not a lot of movement in the locomotive and workshops links as they were mainly staffed by men who were off the track due to some disability received during their service with the company. The only time the spare fireman relieved on those engines was in the event of holidays or sickness. They were some of the most boring jobs on the railway. The locos in the various carriage shops were midget 0-4-0 tanks that could have come straight out of toytown. Affectionately called 'coffee pots', you could only get into the cabs by standing sideways. The officially-classed 'Y5', had a 3 ft 7 in. driving wheel and a spark arrester on the end of a tall chimney.

The one I remember was No. 7230, built in 1903. The firing shovel was about three feet long from handle to the end of the blade and the coal bunker, which was beside the miniature tank, would be lucky to hold two hundredweight. Smoke was prohibited in carriage shops. Work was spasmodic so it was a case of nearly letting the fire out, then building it up for an hour's work, without smoke, then quietening down the little boiler until the next shunting spell.

Drivers were mainly from the old brigade, in their late fifties and very uncommunicative with youngsters. They resented us because we were not from railway families like themselves. The would tell us of the days when drivers reported for work wearing top hats; when those same drivers would refuse to take an engine out of the shed if it had so much as a smear of grease behind the spokes of the wheels. Although we felt that some of this had reached the realms of fantasy over the years, we did know that the position of railwaymen in the early 20th century was one of high esteem in any community.

Up to the commencement of the war the engine driver carried a great deal of respect and came somewhere between the vicar and the Justice of the Peace in many townships. His name on a legal document was accepted in court as something of an honourable degree. The war, nationalisation and the rapid advance of the internal combustion engine changed all that. By 1970, with the diesel locomotive making the job look more like a bus driver, the social status of the railwayman slipped from the top five in the community to a base grade. The relegation to something like a second class citizen really hurt many of the fine men whose work effort in the hectic years of steam helped make England the industrial nation that the world respected.

These elderly drivers were also part of a 'closed shop' complex, created by their restriction to one location due to illness or other reasons. They were restricted to one regular fireman, one work area and one regular shunter. It was a cosy setup of three or four people and anyone entering from outside was like someone coming from outer space.

The work of the Loco. Shunter was not as restrictive or boring mainly because there was always a chance of driving an engine yourself. The work of the Loco. Shunter was to place engines on the various shed roads ready for turns of duty as planned by the Running Department. The shifts were seven days a week on the 6.0 am to 2.0 pm, 2.0 pm to 10.0 pm and 10.0 pm to 6.0 am basis for both engine and shunting crews. The mess room and headquarters was an old 'humpy' made from disused rolling stock, situated at the western end on the main shed and near the smelly River Lea which meandered its murky way through the many railway yards at Stratford. It was smelly and murky because most industries on its banks used the river as an industrial sewer.

The 'humpies' always fascinated me as they were living relics of an age and industry that was peculiar to itself. Sometimes the 'humpy' would be a disused carriage from the six-wheeled stock that was the pride of the track before World War I. The wooden floors were well scrubbed by brush and constant mopping and the mess tables would often have lino on top, obtained by questionable means from the local carriage shop. To the crews that used them the converted carriages or wagons were home for the best part of their lives and so they tried to make life as comfortable as possible. This was understandable when one realised that, due to lack of staff, sick or holiday leave was only obtained by the three shifts combining and turning three shifts of eight hours into two shifts of twelve hours. We are also talking of a time when the working week was 48 hours, annual leave was one week a year and Sunday work was part of the shift.

Often there would be an old carriage bench seat against the wall in place of the company issue of hard wooden chairs. Lighting was by oil lamp only and could well be supplied by the acquisition of an old oil lamp on hand in the stores, brought in from some country station where it once sat in a cast iron filigreed lamp standard and blinked over the ticket collector's hut.

Heating was by a coal fired kitchen stove, commonly known as a kitchener. The stove would shine like the well cared for boiler fronts in the cabs of express engines. Every day the cast iron would be rubbed down with lubricating oil obtained from the shunting mike. It would work its way into the ironwork with the heat of the stove and a final rub with a dry cloth would bring the stove up better than any in Mrs Beaton's kitchen. Mind you, the smell of the hot oil was a bit overpowering but the job was done after breakfast on the morning shift, when everyone was out in the yard. Loco. crew and shunting staff shared this housework and most gangs were proud of their humpies. Woe betide those who entered without wiping their boots!

As the work location never moved from the 12 roads that spread from the river end of the depot, disappearing like some giant hand into the blackness of the smoky Jubilee Shed, crews would often cook their meals on the stove. A big black kettle always sat on top of the stove, gently singing all the time and the billy of tea was a constant piece of the scenery. Nothing went down better in those days than a couple of slices of hot buttered toast, done in front of the fire, and an enamel mug of hot, strong tea, sweetened with condensed milk. It would be too sweet now but, in those days of strict rationing, that tea helped to replace other foods that we never saw.

I found the kettle was a must at all depots and was told by many drivers that it was an unwritten law that hot water should be available at all times for medical as well as refreshment reasons. Often the water was used to clean wounds from various accidents. On the other hand there was always the train crew that would steam into a depot in the country, or stop at a signal box, and look for the hot water with which to make a billy of tea. It could be their first drink from many hours. Believe me, it went down well if you had just clocked up about 10 hours and no sign of relief.

The end result of this 'humpy' complex for me was the fascination of 'humpy' smells in a world of harsh industrial noise and bustle. How wonderful it was, especially in wartime, to walk into a 'humpy' about six in the morning and be greeted with the smell of fried bacon, warm toast and steaming tea in the billy. The background of paraffin oil, coal fire smoke and carbolic soap only seemed to add to the flavour.

Shunting locomotives was very different from shunting rolling stock. There is nothing quite as immobile as a 'dead' engine. 'Dead' in locomotive terms refers to the engine that has no steam with which to move itself. The worst roads to shunt were those where engines had been idle, waiting for repairs or boiler washouts. The Running Department would give a list of engines coming into service from repairs or washouts and they would have to be placed on the running roads in departure time order. This sometimes meant coupling up a rake of dead locomotives, maybe six or seven at a time. They would average 70 to 100 tons each.

Before starting to pull them the shunter had to make sure the handbrakes were off, the gears were at mid-gear position and the cylinder cocks were open. If the latter were shut air pressure would build up in the cylinder and movement would be impossible. Handbrakes could also be a problem, depending how they were put on by the last crew. If the engine had been placed with plenty of steam and the steam brake had been used to hold the blocks on the wheels while the fireman screwed the hand brake on, it meant that the blocks were on the wheels at the pressure of the steam and not hand pressure. Sometimes it was impossible to unwind the hand brake in these conditions. It usually meant hammering the handle to get a start or, in extreme cases, a fitter would have to uncouple the rods.

The work horse of the shunting yards, an 0-6-0 tank affectionately known as the 'Buck Jumper', was used for this work. The official classification of this Victorian piece of equipment was 'J67' and 'J69', they were built between 1886 and 1904. They weighed 42 tons. It was a wet steam locomotive with a boiler pressure of either 160 or 180 psi. It had great strength for its size and its small wheels of four feet in diameter had wonderful traction. It had taken troops to the Boer War and was now fighting Hitler's 20th century war machine.

It was full regulator most of the time when shunting locomotives and the firebox was filled to the door to maintain steam. The deep fire would dance to the beat of the engine and the dead locos would grind on the rails as they left the shed with cylinders hissing through the open cocks. There was quite a cross section of rhythms in the shunt as engines of different lengths of valve travel would hiss round the yard during shunting operations, with the three cylinder engine interspersing with something like a tango beat.

Sometimes a dead engine had to be pulled out of a road which also had locomotives under steam. This was the time when, to save on shunt moves and loco. power, the fireman could assist by driving the 'live' engine back into the shed. The promoted engine cleaner sometimes found himself at the controls of an express engine, just in from a long run through East Anglia, still warm with the heat of the journey. It was an indescribable thrill as he coaxed the dormant monster into its stable. Hand on regulator, slightly eased open. A 'pop' through the snifter valve as steam went to the cylinders, a rumbling forward as the sleek pistons thrust their shiny rods into the cylinders and a hushed 'choof' would come from the stumpy chimney. A little more steam, hand on the steam brake to test it for power. The brake blocks clamp on to the steel tyres of the 6 ft 8 in. driving wheels with a resounding 'chonk'.

What dreams went through the young lad's mind as he placed the locomotive for its next job! The Hook of Holland boat train thundering through the night, snaking its 12 shining coaches of varnished teak through sleepy hamlets at nearly one hundred miles an hour. The people in the dining cars oblivious of the battle going on between man and machine for supremacy.

Engine placed, the cleaner would return to his cheeky, snorting 0-6-0 that had not seen a cleaner's rag for years and get down to the task of maintaining steam. It was surprising how much water and coal went into an eight hour shift, pulling and pushing dead engines around.

Chapter Four

The Slice, the Pricker and the Bent Dart

As engines came into the depot at the end of a shift they would go over the disposal pits and the crews would clean the fire, ashpan and smokebox, ready for the next turn of duty. After coaling they would leave the engine at the end of the Coal Road, ready for placement in the sheds. This was the work of the Coal Road Pilot. He was a driver mainly on a spare shift, whose fireman had been rostered for another job. The senior spare fireman from the cleaners' roster would become his mate.

They would receive a list of engine numbers from the Loco. Foreman and would then place the engines in the appropriate roads for their next job. The engines would be under steam so it was a simple matter of driving them to the back end of the Jubilee Shed and then placing them on the correct road. Tank engines invariably went on roads 1 to 6, with tender engines going on roads 7 to 12. Roads 11 and 12 were mainly used for engines that were to be repaired or washed out.

Quite often, when crews reached the depot, they would be on overtime. This meant that they could leave the engine on the disposal pit roads for others to put away. The allowance for disposal was 30 minutes for tanks and 45 minutes to an hour for tender engines. By having relief crews the company reduced overtime in a substantial manner.

There was a good relief system at Stratford and crews would be coming on duty every two hours, from midnight to midnight, seven days a week, just as stand-bys. They would originate from the spare shifts on the main rosters and would cover all absenteeism on rostered jobs, or become relief for crews on excessive overtime. If none of this was required they sat in the mess room and became disposal pit relief. Quite often the fireman would be called for a job on the road and the driver would become spare. This made a job for the senior engine cleaner and he went on disposal pit duties with the driver when an engine arrived with the crew on overtime.

It was a thankless job. It was a case of doing other people's dirty work but at least you were learning the art of cleaning a fire. The tools needed for fire cleaning were the slice, pricker and bent dart. On tank engines these tools lay on top of the tank, fireman's side, and were reached through the porthole type window in the cab front. On tender engines they were in a tray built on the side of the tender, inside the main bodywork and on the fireman's side.

The slice was a steel shovel and handle forged as one piece, in any length from six feet to about seventeen feet long. It could weigh up to 50 pounds without any fire on it. The pricker was of the same steel and from six feet to 20 feet in length. It was a long rod with a pointed end.

At about 12 inches from the end there was a piece of steel sticking out at right angles. It was about eight inches long. This would get under the clinker on the firebars and release it for the slice to pick up.

The bent dart was another steel rod about six feet long with a dart shaped head. It was used to dislodge clinker from the firebars directly under the firebox door. As fireboxes differed in depth the fireman had to bend the dart to the required depth, after heating it in the fire. This is how the name came about.

There is always a certain amount of dross in coal and, during the burning of this fossil fuel, the foreign matter is left on the bars of the firebox grate. It depended on the fireman's ability and interest in his job as to how dirty a fire could get. The proper use of the dampers, combined with intelligent firing, played a major part in keeping clinker to a minimum.

When the day's work was over it was the usual practice to run the locomotive to the depot with a light fire. This would save having to handle too many live coals. On commencing to 'dispose' of an engine the first move was to clean the smokebox. It depended on how much footplate the designer of the engine had given you at the front end as to how easy was the task of unscrewing the handles that held the large door tight against the main frame.

In the firebricked area around the exhaust stack would be found the fine black ash that had been sucked through the boiler tubes by the beat of the engine. It was more like minute particles of unburnt coal. This had to be shovelled out and the area swept clean.

Everything on a locomotive was balanced in its working and, if the smokebox was not kept clean, the restricted air space in the box would reduce the suction created by the beat of the engine. This in turn reduced the lift given to the fire by the exhaust beat in motion and, as a consequence, the fire became lifeless. The restricted movement allowed dross to settle on the firebars and so clinker started to form and choke the fire still further.

Another problem created by lack of cleanliness in the smokebox was that, if the packing round the door had the slightest air leak, the build up of ash would ignite with the suction of air through the door. The intense heat from such a fire was not only detrimental to the exhaust stack but the door itself would eventually buckle. I have seen freight trains at night coming towards me with what seemed to be a large red light on the front. As they got closer it could be seen that the smokebox door was red hot, the burning ash creating the effect of a bright red half moon on its back above the buffers.

The next step was to clean the fire. The firebox was normally oblong in shape, varying from six feet to 12 feet in length and always about four feet in width. All the 'clean' fire was scooped up with the slice from one side of the box and placed on the other side. The pricker would then be used to ease the clinker off the bars on the side with no fire. The clinker was shovelled up with the slice, lifted out of the firebox and tipped onto the slag heap beside the engine on the disposal pit.

This was a work of art in itself as cabs were restricted in room and many cab doorways were only as wide as the slice blade. It was not too bad on tank engines as the slice would only be about six feet long. On tender engines it was a different story even though you did not have to contend with the back wall, as on tanks. It took careful manoeuvring to pull a 16 feet slice out of a 12 feet firebox without hitting the roof of the cab and shooting red hot clinker on the wooden floor instead of the slag heap.

The slice handle would be very hot, being worked in a firebox over live fire all the time. Engine crews were supplied with thick, woollen yarn cloths on each trip. These were for wiping down cabs, cleaning various parts and headlamps and handling fire irons; there was no such thing as safety gloves in those days. The cloths were essential and had to be folded double to avoid serious burns. Many cloths became badly scorched by the end of a trip or shift. Replacements were only available if the old cloth was handed in at the tool stores. The old cloths were then issued to cleaners for cleaning purposes.

After cleaning one side of the firebox the clean fire was placed back on the clean bars and the remaining clinker was shovelled out. Coal was then shovelled into the box to create the new fire ready for stabling purposes or the fresh crew.

This left the ashpan to be emptied. The ashpan was the worst of the lot. Much of the problem was solved if the wind was blowing in the right direction. The ashpan was under the firebox and caught all the fine ash from the fire while the engine was in motion. It also served the double purpose of controlling draught to the fire.

On tender engines the ashpan only had one door at the smokebox end. With tank engines the ashpan had doors both ends as the engine was designed to run both engine and bunker first. Tender engines also ran tender first on short distances and limited occasions but, when doing so, there was a speed restriction on their movement.

Cleaning tank engine ashpans was always preferable to tenders for the obvious reason that it did not matter which way the wind was blowing, you could always rake the ash out with the wind behind you. Tender engines gave you no choice. To compensate for this most disposal pits had hoses fitted on the walls so that you could dampen down the ash before raking. This was all right in theory but it did not allow for manpower shortages when pits were not cleaned out and became filled with clinker and ash. Using the hose in that situation only flooded the pit where you were standing.

After cleaning the ashpan of a tender engine in adverse conditions you would emerge from the pit like some grey ghost. The very process of going through these jobs sorted the men from the boys and the experienced drivers knew that when they had a spare fireman rostered with them he would be one that had come up the hard way and accepted the knocks as part of the job.

Chapter Five

Outstation Outcasts

'Outstation' was a term given to a locomotive depot that operated on its own, as far as work management was concerned, but had Stratford as the parent depot. An outstation would have its own staff, engines and set working. It would draw its supplies, replacement engines and relief crews from the parent depot. Major outstations supplied by Stratford were Chelmsford, Colchester, Harwich, Southend-on-Sea, Maldon and Bishops Stortford.

In the suburban area of operations in the London district there were a multitude of smaller depots, all fed from Stratford in time of need. To name a few there were Brentwood, Ilford, Woodford, Epping, Ongar, Wood Street, Hertford, Palace Gates, Enfield, Spitalfields, Millwall, Canning Town and Goodmayes.

I spent some time at most of the suburban outstations, working as coalman, labourer and spare fireman. The outstations in the London area were good to work at because there was a common bond. Going to the country stations was a very different thing. There always seemed an air of dislike about anything or anyone who came from London. Country people in England were very clannish and parochial in their ways and it took a long time to make friends. Sometimes it never happened.

Three depots always remained unhappy memories for me as a spare fireman. They were Maldon, Hertford and Bishops Stortford. All had a rural background. This did not worry me as I came from a country town. What did concern me was their obvious dislike of my presence. One felt like an alien and, coupled with the fact that one was new to the business of loco. management, the hours seemed to drag and you never knew if you were doing the right thing.

Maldon was a small town on the Essex coastline and the terminus of the Witham to Maldon branch line that connected with the main line from London to Norwich. It was a legacy of the old private company days when branch lines ran everywhere. It never paid for itself during the war years. The loco. depot was like a step into the past. The buildings were low with small windows set in the massive stone walls. The old tank engine that was stabled there must have been retired from the main line years before because I had never seen its like at Stratford. It was a class 'G5', an 0-4-4T with 5 ft 1 in. driving wheels. All I knew was that it had a very hungry firebox as the five ton bunker was always empty. There was also an old 'J15' class tender engine for local goods work.

The coal stage was a solid timber affair and situated next to the reedy banks of the estuary. The waterways were full of wildlife and the white swan was predominant. They were no lovers of strangers who shattered their nocturnal peace. The only shift I ever worked at Maldon was at night, from ten o'clock to eight the next morning. A note would be left on the mess room table telling me what to do and the only people I saw were the crew of the early morning passenger train which I caught home.

If the moon was up at night it helped me to see what I was doing on the coal stage as the only lighting was the slush lamp which I would put on the bunker's edge. Even this was not possible during air raid alerts. The added moonlight was a help in one way but also a hindrance as it enabled the swans to find the person who was intruding into their night. Often they would sweep over the reeds in vee formation, wings beating the air with great power, to carry out a dive bombing attack on the coal stage. I started to retaliate by throwing coal at them but soon found that it was best to get in the engine's cab and wait for the swans to tire of the operation. I had heard that a swan could break a man's arm with a blow from its wing.

Hertford was another place where friendship was an unknown word. It was also obvious from the work done at outstations that the man from Stratford had the worst shift. It was always the night shift involving the coaling of locomotives, looking after them in the shed under steam and being the relief standby. This meant that you could have your work done by four in the morning. You would have two hours to go before completing the shift and somebody would sleep in. By six o'clock, instead of finishing work, you could be firing on an 'N7' tank to Liverpool Street, starting another day's work with no relief in sight until you returned to Hertford some three hours later.

Hertford was the terminus of the branch line which joined the main Liverpool Street to Cambridge line after leaving Broxbourne. There was also a connecting line from Hertford to the main Great Northern line from Kings Cross. It was rarely used in peace time but, during the war, was a vital link for freight and troop movements. Also on the Broxbourne to Hertford branch was another minor branch line from St Margaret's to Buntingford.

Freight and passenger requirements for the Buntingford branch were worked by the Hertford depot. An early morning freight train would leave Hertford, pick up transfer freight at St Margaret's, and take it to Buntingford. On one occasion the fireman slept in and I became the fireman on a freight train to a place I had never seen. Luckily I had fired on the type of goods engine they had for the job and so did not feel a complete stranger to the task.

The engine was a 'J17' class 0-6-0 tender engine with the Belpaire type firebox which gave the square appearance to the boiler front. It was superheated and the controls were very simple. Two gauge glasses on the boiler front, two boiler feeds with large brass wheels on the boiler and a steel water control handle nearly flush with the wooden topped cupboards over the rear driving wheels that also served as the fireman's seat. The regulator was the simple type that was pushed from about forty-five degrees to ninety for first port and then another forty-five degrees for second port.

The engine was a two cylinder, inside motion type and worked on a boiler pressure of 180 psi. The only brake on the engine was the steam brake, a simple lever with movements similar to the regulator for applying the brake.

The driver was elderly, a man from the era which only spoke to the fireman when they had to and he never said a word as we prepared for the trip. The Buntingford line was single line working, with the necessary staff being carried on the engine in a special holder. Single line working was new to me and every so often I would get a grunt to change the staff at some unattended station or wayside halt.

We only had about 10 wagons from St Margaret's and, as we turned on to the branch line, the driver put his feet up on the boiler casing as though he were going to sleep. The regulator was set at a steady beat and we trundled along at a steady 15 to 20 miles an hour. I was getting quite worried because, here we were, on a single line, chugging round bends, up hill and down dale with a driver asleep and a fireman who didn't know the road! At the top of one incline we rumbled over a wooden bridge. It was like an alarm clock to my driver. He sat up, shut off steam and warmed up the steam brake. We rolled into an empty station, shunted the siding and chugged on to the next stop, with the driver settling down again for his snooze.

I discovered by this that he knew the road by sounds and so the next few miles didn't worry me. The Buntingford line was very picturesque, winding through the countryside and past sleepy farms and villages. It also had some steep inclines but the old engine took them in her stride. She knew the road as much as the driver! The main freight was sugar beet for the Cambridge line.

Bishops Stortford was different from the other outstations in that it was not a terminus. It was situated on the main line between Liverpool Street and Cambridge. The main duties involved relieving crews on long distance freight trains between March and London, working local passenger trains from Bishops Stortford to Liverpool Street and freight work on the local branch lines. Once again my main work at that station was the night shift, disposing of engines, coaling and cleaning the shed area.

Relief work in the London area was more interesting and friendly. I spent many months at Palace Gates in north London, working as coalman and spare fireman. It was an old depot and terminus of the Palace Gates to North Woolwich line. Although part of the old Great Eastern system it had a branch link with the Great Northern line which passed nearby from Kings Cross. This was another handy connection during the war for freight from the industrial north to the docks in the eastern region when main transfer routes were disrupted by German air raids.

The main work at the depot was passenger trains from Palace Gates to North Woolwich via Stratford Low Level station. There was also the push-and-pull service between the Gates and Seven Sisters junction on the Enfield line. The engines stationed there were 'Gobblers', or 'F5s', and 'N7s'. The 'N7' was the predominant work horse of the LNER suburban service both pre- and post- war years. A sturdy little 0-6-2 tank, it steamed well, was economic on coal and water and had a superheated boiler with a working pressure of 180 psi.

The 'Gobbler' was our nickname for the old tank engine that had been replaced by the 'N7' but was still used on the less demanding suburban runs such as Palace Gates to North Woolwich, Liverpool Street to Woodford and Liverpool Street to Enfield. Sometimes they were rostered on the Liverpool Street to Gidea Park run but that usually meant late running. If something went wrong and the 'Gobbler' ended up on a Liverpool Street to Shenfield train, it was a certainty that five to ten minutes would be lost at Harold Wood station while the crew built up sufficient steam and water for the Brentwood bank. The old girl just could not take it. She had a bigger driving wheel than the 'N7', 5 ft 4 in. compared with 4 ft 10 in. and slipped that much more when coupled to the standard eight coach suburban set. The 2-4-2 wheel arrangement was powered by 180 psi wet steam power and, with more than three-quarters water level in the gauge glass, she would prime at every start.

Palace Gates derived its name from Alexandra Palace which sat on the hill near the railway station. It was quite a hilly part of London and the station and locomotive depot were situated at the top of the last hill. In its heyday the line had been very busy but, after the war with the extension of the London transport bus and underground services, the traditional patronage fell.

I quite enjoyed the companionship of the railwaymen at that depot and was encouraged by them to apply for a transfer to Palace Gates as engine cleaner, for which there was a vacancy. The logic of the move was that I would avoid being pushed around other depots from Stratford and gain greater firing experience because I would be first in line for local relief work. This proved to be correct and often I would be firing for weeks at a time at Palace Gates. I also learned much more of engine management as it was a more compact depot with only about seven tank engines on roster, with some 14 crew members, two coalmen and a foreman.

The engines were housed in an old brick running shed and everything about Palace Gates-North Woolwich line was characteristic of the railways in their prime years of the 1900s. The shed was a solid structure with arched windows in the sides between sturdy buttresses and a blackened slate roof that had the smoke vent down the centre. One end was walled off to stop the through draught and the shed was quite warm in winter. It would only hold four tank engines, two on each road over an inspection pit, so the others were left outside. Each night at the end of their shifts the engines would be coaled from the stage and then placed on the shed roads in rostered turn, ready for the next day's working.

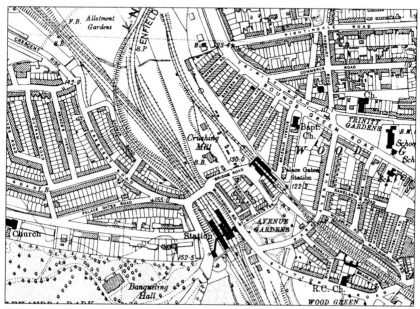

Palace Gates station, with the ex-GNR Wood Green station on the East Coast main line just to the left. *Reproduced from the 6", 1912 Ordnance Survey Map, revised 1938*

Chapter Six

Down to the Docks with 'Gobblers'

There was one engine stationed at Palace Gates that was a class of its own. It was an 'F7', a 2-4-2 tank with 4 ft 10 in. driving wheels. Built in 1910, it was the smallest engine I had worked on for main line work. Its only use was to operate the push-and-pull service between Palace Gates and Seven Sisters junction on the Enfield line.

It worked in conjunction with a two-coach set of suburban passenger stock. At the end of the rear coach was a driver's compartment, from which he would drive the train when travelling in the opposite direction. This accounted for the term 'push-and-pull'. It was a standard ruling in railway work that engines always pulled their load. The only time loads were pushed was in shunting movements over short distances in marshalling yards. At Palace Gates we pulled the train to Seven Sisters and pushed it back to the Gates. This saved the need to run round the train each time at Seven Sisters.

It was only a short trip, taking just nine minutes and that included stopping at the two stations on the branch line, Noel Park and West Green. The track was double, weaving round bends as well as up and down some steep hills; between houses and parkland, over roads and under bridges.

The train left Palace Gates engine first. When leaving Seven Sisters the driver would get into his compartment and test the brake and bell systems. The bell was on the engine and, according to the code ring, the fireman would drive the engine under the driver's instructions. This mainly covered 'open regulator' and 'shut regulator'. The unit was fitted with Westinghouse braking and the end compartment of the train had a Westinghouse brake similar to the one on the engine. All stopping and starting was done by the driver on the homeward push.*

The train ran in connection with Enfield trains to and from Liverpool Street and, apart from the rush hour connections, ran a half-hourly service. It was mainly patronised by housewives doing their shopping.

The main rostered jobs at Palace Gates were passenger trains to and from North Woolwich. A typical rostered working for one shift would be Palace Gates to North Woolwich, North Woolwich to Stratford Low Level, Stratford Low Level to North Woolwich, North Woolwich to Palace Gates. Sometimes we were relieved at Stratford and the engine would do a local shift between Stratford and North Woolwich only.

It was quite an interesting run and covered most aspects of London's sprawling suburbia and dockland. The bulk of the passengers were dock workers, or men and women working with the many industries that surrounded Stratford. The trip crossed many rail junctions and was a north-

---

* What the author describes here was against the rules, as the driver had direct control of the regulator from the leading carriage through the medium of compressed air. However, during the war and the consequent lack of maintenance engine crews found it easier to work in the manner described   , with the driver using the bell communication to tell the fireman when to open and close the regulator.

west to south-east movement across two home counties.

Starting from Palace Gates in the north of London, the eight-coach trains would cross the Enfield to Liverpool Street line at Seven Sisters Junction. The junction was on a high viaduct which allowed the Seven Sisters Road to pass under the many tracks without the need for level crossings. The platforms had timber decking. The main platforms for the Enfield line were straight but the Palace Gates' platforms were built on the curve.

As the Woolwich train left Seven Sisters it crossed the up and down Enfield lines and went down a curving embankment to join the LMS/LNER joint line to Gospel Oak. In the opposite direction it served Tilbury Docks. Needless to say it was a very busy line during the war and received much attention from the Germans by way of bombing.

The line taken by the Woolwich train went via South Tottenham Junction and connected with the main LNER Liverpool Street-Cambridge line. At this point the track curved right and joined a straight stretch of main line crossing the river flats that fed the River Lea, part of which was Walthamstow Marshes. It was the longest stretch between stations on the whole run, being about two miles.

The line on which the train ran went under the lengthy bridge which carried the Liverpool Street-Chingford suburban service. From the Chingford line came the connecting branch enabling the Liverpool Street-Cambridge expresses to link with the Cambridge main line at what was known as Copper Mills Junction box.

This connection was also used by the Hertford and Bishops Stortford trains. It was possible to get to Liverpool Street on the same line used by the North Woolwich trains, but this method was only used in emergencies as the line went through the major marshalling yard of Temple Mills and Stratford Junction.

After leaving Lea Bridge station the Woolwich train entered the Temple Mills area. Temple Mills was a major freight marshalling centre which handled traffic from the midlands of England, the London docks, the eastern region and various other companies railway. The up and down main ran through the heart of the yard and I always felt it was a dangerous situation although no major disasters happened in my time. About 20 shunting roads fanned out on each side of the main tracks, with the hump shunting yard being on the right-hand side when travelling towards Stratford.

The Temple Mills complex was about a mile in length, after which the train approached the vastness of the Stratford locomotive depot and workshops. A formidable gantry of semaphore signals straddled the many tracks and comprised of the up and down main to Stratford, up and down goods, up and down junction to Stratford Low level via Lea Junction and the up and down junction signals for the Liverpool Street to Epping line.

The North Woolwich train would veer to the right, under Temple Mills Lane bridge, clatter over the many crossovers, pass the many engine sheds, locomotive yards and workshops, carriage shops and repair sidings, and the dust covered grasses that somehow managed to survive on the banks of the sluggish River Lea.

At the junction with another LMS line the train turned east, ran beside the

Woolwich line carriage sidings and went under the main running lines of Stratford Junction by way of a tunnel over which ran at least 10 lines, being the major links between Liverpool Street and East Anglia. As soon as the train came out of the tunnel it stopped at Stratford Low Level station. This was a two platform station built in the middle of many brick buildings that housed the Permanent Way headquarters of the Eastern Region. Keeping on a low level, with brick lined walls encasing the embankment, the train went on to Stratford Market, about two minutes running time.

Stratford Market was quite a large area and had its own shunting engine, or 'mike' as we called them. A 24 hour shift worked the yard, placing incoming perishable foods, coal, timber and other freight for the London city. The yard was on the right-hand side of the station which once saw much traffic in the form of passengers but, with the coming of buses, dwindled to the faithful few.

The next station on the journey was Canning Town, after which, the train followed the various docks that went to make up the Royal Victoria and Albert Docks and the King George the Fifth Dock. Dockland was on the right hand side and houses were on the left. Stations served were Tidal Basin, Custom House, Silvertown and North Woolwich. The latter was also the end of the line and the station looked across Old Father Thames.

The track was four lines as far as Thames Wharf Junction, between Canning Town and Tidal Basin station, these being the up and down passenger and up and down goods roads. At times when passenger trains were less frequent, goods trains also ran on the passenger lines as they were more or less continuous. Most freight working on the Woolwich line was controlled by need rather than regular timetables and 'trip engines' from Temple Mills would feed the docks with empties and take back the loaded for marshalling. Sometimes there would be direct trains from other areas and these would be timetabled.

The journey from Canning Town to Custom House was uneventful. The track was flat and the main road through the area ran parallel with the railway on the other side of a fence. Once the residential side consisted of row upon row of late 19th century terraced houses along narrow roads. In 1942 it was like working in a battlefield. Bombing of the area during the Battle of Britain, and after, had left a scene of devastation.

Apart from the more modern buildings, which seemed to stand the blast more than the lath and plaster hovels believed to be owned by the Church of England, one saw nothing but row upon row of streets with just heaps of rubble between pavements. It was worse between Canning Town and Custom House than anywhere else. It was hard to believe that anyone once lived there. It was harder still to believe that all the bodies had been dug out.

After leaving Custom House the route divided. The railway either went over the River Thames or under it. The two tracks used by the passenger trains went through the Silvertown tunnel. The tracks that went over the top used a lift bridge and, if shipping was on the move, it took preference. Sometimes there was a long wait. Goods traffic nearly always took the top route and, from whichever side the bridge was approached, it, was a stiff haul, usually with a Little Goods or 'Buckjumper'.

Chapter Seven

Freight Trains with Passenger Engines

My first trip under the river to Silvertown was a nightmare. Nobody told me what to expect. The engine headed towards the black mouth down an incline of 1 in 50 and then roared into the abyss. Nothing but blackness was around me. Sparks rocketed from the invisible chimney and the angry glare from the firebox lit up the cab in sharp relief.

When the train reached the bottom level of the tunnel there was a sickening lurch. I thought we were off the road and waited for the crunch that never came. Another lurch, regulator opened fully and the engine was belching its way up an invisible incline. Suddenly a pinpoint of light came into view. The end of the tunnel! We were climbing a bank of 1 in 50 this time and it was getting lighter. Silvertown station was just at the top of the tunnel so it was a case of running in with full regulator and then shutting off half way along the platform accompanied by an application of the brakes.

I discovered afterwards that there was an S bend at the bottom of the tunnel. The line was constantly wet with water dripping from the tunnel walls so, due to the steep incline when leaving the tunnel, drivers dare not shut off steam as the engine would slip to a standstill.

Woolwich was an old time station built in solid brick with the usual Victorian ornamentations. Platforms had a curve to the right and it was always hard to pick up the guard's signal when departing for Stratford. We would run-round the train through a crossing loop and get water for the return run. With the old 'Gobbler' or the 'N7' it was rarely necessary to take coal as well. They had good sized bunkers. Coal could be loaded at North Woolwich or Stratford Carriage Sidings.

It was policy, by those who were conscientious, to top up the bunker when not pushed for time. This helped the coalman at Palace Gates at night when he would have up to seven engines to coal for the next day's shifts. There were always those who didn't care, or else Stratford crews who worked the middle shifts and didn't worry about Palace Gates crews. If you were unfortunate to strike any of these the final run home at night was worse than hard work.

The bunker would be very low in coal and, at stations where you stopped longer than others, the fireman would have to get into the bunker and pull coal down from the back shelf to keep the fire going. Another problem was that if the coal was very low in the bunker the wind would blow down the chute when the train was in motion, filling the cab with coal dust.

There were no regular goods trains worked from Palace Gates but, due to the depots link with the Great Northern system, there was often the unexpected freight train to work. If the night air raids had blown out a section of the northern suburban track, freight would be left in the nearby sidings that linked the eastern and northern systems and crews would be rostered from Palace Gates to take them through when the passenger services had stopped. This work was only done by the 'N7' as the 'Gobbler' had neither the pulling power nor braking ability to work freight which, in this case, was mainly coal.

The freight trains were always to Temple Mills for marshalling to other areas. There was nothing modern about the rolling stock used for freight by the private companies. Some looked good in their livery with company names painted on the wooden planked sides but their design had not changed since they went into service some 50 years before. The four wheel rigid wheelbase had no brakes except the handbrake. When working a train load of coal the only brake was on the engine, with another handbrake in the guard's van as emergency. This was why freight trains always seemed to travel slowly. Once movement reached more than 15 miles an hour it was difficult to stop in a short distance.

The golden rule when working freight trains at any time was to make sure the sanders were working properly. On the 'N7' the sand boxes were in the cab for the rear movement and next to the smokebox for the forward movement. The method was simple and not much changed since Stephenson's days. The cast-iron box carried the dry sand, which was poured in by the fireman using the lipped galvanised bucket to be found in all sand bins. A heavy iron lid sat in its grooved seating to keep the water out.

At the base of the sand box was a simple valve which covered the outlet through a metal pipe which went from the box in a diagonal line to a position just in front of the wheel. If the track was wet or greasy, and the driver needed sand on the rail to get adhesion, the fireman would work the lever in the cab in a backwards and forwards movement. This moved the valve rod in the sand box. The metal flap over the sand pipe would open and shut and sand would

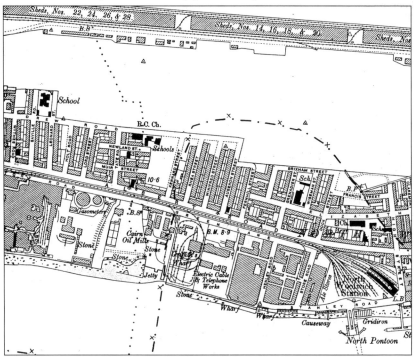

North Woolwich station.   *Reproduced from the 6", 1920 Ordnance Survey Map*

run down on to the rail to feed the wheels.

Sand was also vital for extra grip when starting with heavy loads or when braking with freight trains. If the rails were wet and no sand was available the application of the brake would simply mean that the brake blocks would lock onto the steel tyres of the wheels. The wheels would stop turning, becoming locked and just sliding on the rail surface, and the train would push with increasing momentum as the dropping gradient gave it impetus.

It was vital, when preparing engines for the road, that sand boxes be checked to see if they were working and that they had sufficient sand in them. Sand box controls could be all right but, if the engine had just come in from a day's work in the rain, the sand pipes could be clogged with wet sand that had been thrown up into the pipe as the engine slipped and tried to gain its footing. This was easily corrected by tapping the down pipe with the hammer.

When working coal trains from Palace Gates with 'N7' locomotives it was always a case of the crew keeping constant control over the train. Once it got away from you there was no holding it, and we crossed many junctions on the trip. Red lights don't stop trains! The 'N7' was designed for passenger work only and did not have the braking capacity found on engines designed purely for freight trains. Regular freight engines had steam brakes which worked on the boiler pressure and were instantaneous. When their boiler pressure was 180 psi, the brake really went on with a 'chonk'!

The 'N7', on the other hand, had the Westinghouse air brake system, in keeping with the Westinghouse braking system on the suburban carriage stock. The air brakes worked on 70 psi in the train pipe with 90 psi in the main cylinder so that they could be released rapidly. This system was foolproof on a train with every carriage having brakes applied to the wheels. With freight trains it was a very different matter. The full application could be applied and the train would still push you forward.

As I was the leading spare fireman at Palace Gates I was rostered regularly on the freight trains when they ran. Invariably I had Sam Phillips as my driver because he, in turn, was the senior fireman passed to act as driver. He was a likeable man, lived at Ilford and I had many happy times with him. He understood the engines of the day. He knew their weaknesses due to overwork and would coax them along. He was of a generation who knew what it was like to try and do the impossible. Those of the pre-war brigade never really understood what we new hands had to do in trying to keep the trains running. On the private railways of yesteryear there was no such thing as a faulty locomotive. In the war years a good engine was a luxury.

We would leave Palace Gates in the darkness of the blackout. Side curtains would be down and the heat would be stifling. Outside would be the distant barking of the Ack Ack guns as they tried to find the German bombers droning their way above the city on their nightly runs that were as constant as a bus service. One would drone over every 15 minutes, drop its bombs and return for the next load. In the winter this would start at four in the afternoon and still be going at five the next morning.

'Not too big a fire Rob', Sam would say, 'she'll push us to the Sisters'.

He would give her first port on the regulator. There would be a harsh hiss of steam through the cylinder cocks as I let the condensed water blow through. Slam the cocks lever shut and at the same time give a little sand. The old 'N7' would strain at the load of coal. Tightening three link steel couplings would jangle in the yard as the wheels slowly turned in their grease filled axleboxes.

'Choof, choof, choof, choof,' she would gently purr as we gradually moved ahead. The distant green light from the guard's oil handlamp would indicate that the train was together. We would acknowledge with a toot on the whistle of No. 2621. The safety valves would be just singing on top of the boiler as the steam gauge showed nearly 180 psi boiler pressure. The oil gauge lamp, hanging from the brass handle of the stop cocks on the gauge glass showed the water level dancing at about three-quarters full. Ahead, the home and distant signals winked their green aspect in the black sky.

Sam knew he was right to the next station and yanked the regulator to second port position. The engine jumped into action and a deep, clear cut bark from the exhaust bounced back from the station walls as we rumbled into the night. The heavy four-wheeled trucks, each holding ten tons of industrial coal, click-clacked over the rail joints. Sam shut off steam as we started to go down a 1 in 90 gradient. The superheater snifter valve behind the chimney made its peculiar 'phuff, phuff' sound and the hot fumes from the smokebox blew back into our faces as we looked into the blackness. There was a sudden surge as the trucks ran into us on the downhill slope.

Sam applied the air brake, gradually. If it went on too suddenly the trucks would run into us like a brick wall and the guard would be thrown from one end of the van to the other. Sam told me to put the handbrake on. This was a large steel wheel set in the back of the cab and was used to hold engines when they were stabled. I wound it on as hard as it would go. Steel brake blocks ground against the wheels and sparks flew. Sam released the air brake to recharge the cylinder. The hand brake was now holding the wheels at the same pressure as the air brake. Sam was working on the idea that, with the hand brake on at such a pressure, it would be sufficient to check the train down hill and enable him to maintain full pressure in the air cylinder.

We went nice and steady and the outer home semaphore signal's green light became bigger. Sam knew that, at that signal, the gradient changed to about 1 in 100 uphill. 'Take the brake off Rob!' he would shout above the noise of the train. He applied a little air on the brake so that I could start to unwind the wheel. When the hand brake was off he would release the air brake. The train pushed harder and we picked up speed. A sudden angry ball of fire lit up the invisible skyline about a mile ahead. A 500 lb. high explosive bomb had dropped round Islington way.

There was a sudden pull behind us as though some giant had grabbed the train. It was the action of the gradient change on the train. Our climb uphill was being countered by the gravitational pull of the down hill gradient we had just left. This was the sign that Sam had been waiting for and he yanked the regulator to first port. The clattering motions were taken up by the cushion of steam in the cylinder and a rhythmic 'choof, choof, choof, choof' urged us forward. There was another pull on the train and Sam knew that the couplings were now tightly stretched and would not jump off the drawbars. He gave the

'N7' second port and the engine barked its way up the hill. All this was done without seeing a thing. Pure instinct and feel that came from years of practice.

As we approached Seven Sisters Junction I started to build up a good fire as I knew it would be flat terrain to Temple Mills and we would be pulling all the way. Every engine had its own firing patterns and habits which you had to get to know. No good saying No. 2621 was one of a hundred off the production line. Every one of those locos had its own characteristics. No one knew why but that was a fact of life with all steam locomotives. This 'N7' steamed well as long as the fire was wedge shaped, deep under the firebox door and shallow under the brick arch. When firing up the coal had to be small as it went through a trap door in the main door which was only about eight inches deep. The coal had to be kept to the back of the long bladed shovel to sit deep in the cupped section near the handle.

The firebox was oblong in shape, about six feet long by four feet wide. Firing was worked on a pattern of four shovels down the sides, one under the brick arch at the front and three under the door. To get the shovel full to the front left corner, and firing on 'N7's' was left-handed, the fireman would throw the shovel forward to catch the bottom of the trap door on the right-hand side. This would throw the coal forward to the left-hand corner. Likewise, to get to the front right-hand corner the shovel blade had to hit the left-hand bottom edge of the trap door. To put the coal under the door the shovel blade had to go right into the firebox and then be turned over to place the coal where it was needed.

When an engine was in motion the draught of the exhaust would whip the coals into a golden inferno and, looking into the firebox, all one would see was a sheet of flame. To find out how the fire was burning, whether part of the grate was bare of coals and therefore letting cold air into the box and causing steam pressure to drop, the shovel blade was placed in the trap door on its edge. This would scoop air through the door and the flames would be temporarily parted to enable the fireman to see the firebox grate area. With experience it was soon possible to see how the fire was burning and feed to bare spots.

The 'N7' on the coal train liked the fire right up to the boiler lip at the firebox door and tapering to practically nothing at the front. So one built a wedge of hot coals and the motion of the engine, with the lift created by the exhaust, would take sufficient fire to the front without the fireman having to feed that position.

As the train rumbled towards the Cambridge main line we approached the gantry of semaphore signals operated from the South Tottenham box. The main LNER lines that passed the junction from Temple Mills were the up and down main and up and down goods roads. The whole area was marshy river flats with a large reservoir in the distance toward the Chingford line.

The gradient was nearly flat and the train had to be pulled along the straight section. There was no free rolling from the grease-filled axle boxes. Now and then an angry red blob would light up a cloud as anti-aircraft shells tried to find an enemy bomber. Searchlights would weave silently across the cloud base but sometimes, if the cloud were very low, they would not be used as their light reflected onto the ground below and helped the bomber crews more than the gunners.

At Lea Bridge station we were put into a reception road. This called for a sharper lookout. Signalmen would place freight trains into reception roads when they were waiting for access to marshalling yards. Main lines only had one train in the section at any time. Reception roads worked on the 'follow-my-leader' basis until the train reached the reception road outlet signal. Then they entered the marshalling yard one at a time. So it was a case of going at about five miles an hour in case there was another train in front of you.

We were lucky that night and had a straight run in. The small calling-on arm of the reception signal dropped and the green light beckoned us ahead. At the end of the siding road, where the track met a crossing line that linked about another 14 lines together for an outlet, a shunter's handlamp showed a flickering red light. A flick of the shunter's pole over the buffer sleeve and we heard the three link coupling drop off the drawbar hook. The red slide changed to green and the shunter sent us ahead to the engine road.

I placed the heavy old leather bag of the water crane in the tank of the 'N7' and turned the big steel wheel to let the water flow rapidly into our near-empty tanks. Tanks and tenders had a fascinating smell of their own. It was dank and cold, almost smelling of the sea. Tanks and tenders had big sieves sitting in the openings with holes about a quarter of an inch throughout to stop any foreign matter that could cause damage if it reached the injectors. The sieves would go down about four feet. The leather bag would slap-slap against the sides as the water rushed in under pressure from the large storage tanks which stood nearby on brick pillars or walls.

It did not pay to drink the water because one never knew what was in the tender. The water supply at Stratford was treated to help check the creation of boiler scale but, in country districts, it was just drawn from rivers or local supply lines. Sometimes when I had looked into tenders to see how much water was available I saw small fish. They must have come in when tiny and just grown in the tender with age.

Tank engines always had lids that screwed down to stop water slopping out when running into stations and stopping suddenly, such as with suburban train working. Tender engines had heavier lids. Some just flapped down over the hole; others had a hasp which dropped over a pin and stopped the lid from working open. Tender engines which had the water chute for picking up water on the run had lids with clamps for screwing down. Woe betide the fireman who failed to secure those lids! The force of the water entering the tender from the channel in the centre of the track at some 30 miles an hour would throw the unsecured lid back and the jet of water would shoot straight through the opening. Not only did the train get a wash but the tender stayed empty because none of the water scooped up stayed in it.

Having filled our tanks I would pull down the coal in the bunker and wash the cab floor down with the hose while Sam went round the engine with the oil can, just checking any needs and feeling to see that the axles were not running hot. The yard foreman told us that there was nothing to take back and so we were light engine to Palace Gates. I put the single white aspect oil headlamp in the middle of the front buffer beam and changed the rear lamp's aspect to red. This was the standard code for light engine and any signalman seeing us approach would know that we were the engined telegraphed from the previous signal box as light to Palace Gates.

Chapter Eight

Shunting at Temple Mills

By this time I had many firing turns to my credit and, under the terms of employment agreed to by management and union, a year's firing duties was recognised as 313 turns of duty as fireman. My move to Palace Gates had paid off, and I had reached first year's firing long before I would had I stayed at Stratford. Due to manpower shortages the company was constantly calling for firemen at Stratford and, as that station was nearer home for me, I decided it was time to return to the home depot. I applied for a fireman's position at Stratford and was duly appointed.

I started in the link system that I have described earlier, beginning with the depot shunting links. Coal Road, Disposal Pit, Loco. Shunter, Workshops Shunter . . . they all came in their turn but, luckily, I did not see much of them. There was always a vacancy to be filled in the next shunting link and, as fireman, I was first relief. The senior spare fireman took my place in the depot link.

By now I was receiving the set uniform for a fireman. Two pairs of bib and brace overalls, dark blue. Two overall jackets, dark blue. A peaked hat, waterproofed inside. A black serge jacket and an overcoat. Tin hat, gas mask and gas protective clothing. The protective clothing was a type of oilskin jacket and leggings with gloves that came up to the elbows. I don't think anyone could have fired in such clothing as it made you too hot. But it proved to us that air raid or gas raid, we still had to keep going.

I spent considerable time in the Temple Mills shunting link. It was not as boring as it first sounded. A lot was learned by just mixing with the train crews in the crib room, watching the make-up of trains, learning the meaning of different signals, whether fixed semaphore on posts, on the ground or just hand signals from signalmen and shunters. I learned the various yards, which trains went from where and which trains arrived from where. This was all valuable knowledge when going into the various goods links in later years; nothing like knowing your way around, especially in the dark.

The little old 'Buck Jumper' was the main work horse and the interior of those engines was kept immaculate by the regular crews. Copper pipes shone like mum's favourite jug, as did the brass ledge round the gauge glass and the brass cocks each end of the glass. The steel casing over the boiler shone like an army boot when rubbed with engine oil.

There were basically two kinds of shunting: the push and pull of trucks in and out of sidings or the hump method. In the level yards the shunter would take the engine to a train which had been left in a reception road for marshalling purposes. The three link coupling would jangle onto the drawbar as the shunter flicked it up with his shunting pole.

He would then face the driver and give a circular motion with his arm, going away from his body. This meant 'pull up' or go away from him. The driver would open the regulator slowly, letting the engine roll away from the train and so take up the slack in the couplings. It could be a 500 ton coal train and a sudden start could make the coupling jump off or even pull the drawbar out of the wagon.

When the driver felt the train moving he would open up the regulator and the 'Buck Jumper' would really start to bark her way up the yard. The tracks at Temple Mills saw little maintenance and they were anything but level like the main lines. Movement would be one of rock and roll as the engine went into a dipped joint and then lurched to the other side, at the same time being pushed by the following trucks. The bucking engine would reach about 15 miles an hour and then the driver would shut off and pull the blower on to stop fumes coming into the cab. The trucks would continue to push forward. The shunter, who had been riding on the side steps of the engine, would jump off and pick his spot from which to shunt the train. When he decided he had enough room he would face the driver and put both arms in the air. This meant stop.

To suddenly slam the steam brake on would be disastrous as the wagons would bunch into the engine and get locked buffers, with the possibility of derailments. The driver would ease the steam brake on, then release it. There would be the hiss of steam as it entered the cylinder, chonk as the metal brake blocks grabbed the steel tyres on the six solid wheels and another hiss as the brake was released and steam would escape under the floorboards.

The braking movement would cause the trucks to run into the engine and you would feel the surge. The release of the brake at the same time meant that the engine ran away from the surging tonnage and there was no bunching of the wagons. Another application of the brake, a little longer this time, and the trucks would push but be held. Brake released, brake applied and held longer still and the trucks would stop nicely. Although the engine had travelled another hundred yards since the shunter gave the stop signal it did not matter as the shunter had allowed for this margin. Such was the knowledge gained from experience in railway work. It was nothing to be found in a book. It was passed down from man to man, family to family.

The shunter worked out the various roads for certain trucks in his shunt. From a rake of 25 wagons there could be six different shunts. The line on which the main shunting took place was called the shunting spur. Off that line branched others that led to other lines on which new trains were being marshalled. There could be up to 14 lines running away from the shunting spur in one yard.

The head shunter would call out to his assistant shunters the number of the road into which he wanted the trucks placed. One shunter would be on the hand operated points and another would be further down the yard ready to work the hand brakes on the trucks if they came too fast. This meant that the normal shunting crew was a gang of three and one engine crew.

The head shunter would give the 'hit up' signal by having his back to the driver and bringing his arm, furthest from the wagon, upwards with vigour so that his hand travelled from thigh to over his head. This meant that he wanted the wagons to travel fast in the shortest space of time. The regulator would go to first port and the 'Buck Jumper' would surge into the trucks. As the engine started to bark, and there was no sign of wheels slipping or picking up water through the valves, the driver would give second port. 'Buck Jumpers' could accelerate rapidly due their small diameter, six coupled driving wheels.

Within a few beats of exhaust punching their way out of the tall chimney the trucks would be moving at about 20 mph. The shunter would then give the stop signal and the steam brake would slam on and off again. Couplings would become taut with the first check and, with the second application, the extended couplings would hold the train and the engine would dig its heels in. The trucks would stop in about 100 yards. The wagons uncoupled by the shunter would roll on into the road where they were wanted and, with good judgement, the trucks on the engine would be on the right side of the points for the next move forward. If the shunter had under-estimated the speed of the movement the points would be overrun and this would call for the engine to 'pull up' again before the next move.

Working with a good shunter, and also knowing the layout of the yard, made the work a joy to watch. Twenty trucks could be shunted singly into as many roads without the engine having to reverse once. Work was continuous in the shunting yards, 24 hours a day. The only break in the eight hour shifts was a 20 minute 'crib' break somewhere between the fourth and fifth hour.

The engines came from Stratford loco. depot every Sunday night and were dispatched either engine first or bunker first, depending on the yard in which they were to work. This was because all the shunting 'mikes' had the driver on the right hand side and the engine had to be in a position where the driver could see the shunter at all times, especially on shunting spurs. After arriving at the Mills on the Sunday night the engines would stay there until the Sunday morning of the next week when they would then be worked to the shed by the last shift.

A normal shift would start at 6.0 am and the shunting would go on till about 10.0 am. The 20 minute meal break would be worked in with 'requirements', as the period was known when shunters released an engine for specific locomotive work. Requirements for a 'Buck Jumper' was the recoaling of the bunker, getting water, cleaning the fire, smokebox and ashpan and oil up for the next eight hours' work. The crew was allowed 30 minutes for these tasks.

It depended on how conscientious the previous crew had been as to how much work you had to do. Some crews were more interested in a quick round of cards in the crib room with the shunters than making the engine fit for the next shift. So you could find yourself with a fire that had not been cleaned for eight hours and an ashpan full to the grate. On average the shunting crews were a good crowd to work with and, if you had worked your fire right with the shunting, you could clean it in ten minutes.

While the fireman was cleaning the fire the driver would be oiling the siderods, inside motions and topping up the axleboxes. The young fireman could be caught by having an old driver who saw his fireman as nothing but a slave. Such drivers would go and sit with the shunters and yarn about old times while the fireman did his work *and* the driver's. The best driver for the junior fireman to have was a spare driver, who was a fireman getting his first driving job. He would be working on the same principles as the spare fireman and there was a comradeship between the two learners. The acting driver would feel that he could teach the new lad a thing or two.

Like coaling the bunker. The solid shunting that took place at Temple Mills called for good fires and the 'Buck Jumper' only had a small bunker. After eight hours of punching trucks into sidings the coal would be well down and, if the bunker had only been filled to the guard rail on top, the fireman could be down to just dust in the final hour.

The idea was to shovel broken coal into the bunker until near the top and then stack big lumps all round the sides like castle embattlements. These lumps, and some could weigh over a hundredweight before being cracked with the coal hammer, would stand about three feet above the guard rail. More coal could then be shovelled in and the topped off bunker would have about a third again of normal content. The main thing was to ensure that the lumps were secure. If they were not they could fall off and injure anyone walking near the locomotive. This type of coaling was banned on passenger locomotives in case any fell off as the train ran into stations. Even so, I had seen 'N7' engines topped up in that manner, coaled at outstations. They never had the inspectorial staff snooping round as much as we did at Stratford.

Another thing that helped the coal supply was coaling the firebox while at the coal stage so that the fire would last about an hour before any more was needed. Large lumps would be put into the firebox and stacked under the door, right up to the lip of the firebox door. The fire would taper towards the front of the box and, by working the dampers and controlling the amount of fire up the front of the box, this type of fire would give substantial saving on the bunker's supply.

The 'Buck Jumper', or 'J67', had a character of its own. It was straight out of a children's story book with its stubby little body sitting over the 0-6-0 wheelbase, a small bunker behind a small cab with big porthole windows staring over the squat smokebox. The tall chimney, like some Georgian top hat, towered above the steam dome that was nearly as tall, and threw back the wet exhaust steam well clear of the driver's vision.

A businesslike tank sat each side of the boiler that never saw a cleaner's rag and cast-iron sand boxes stood at the base of the smokebox. In the cab was a simple boiler front with two gauge glasses, a long regulator arm that was usually bent towards the driver's side in a shallow semi-circle and a simple steam brake lever that worked on a to-and-fro application. The reversing lever was long, like a signalman's lever when operating semaphore signals, and went forward on an arced rack for forward movement; backwards for the backward movement.

On the fireman's side was the steam gauge against the cab front wall, the left-hand steam injector valve handle in solid brass, working in conjunction with the water valve handle near the entrance to the cab. There were no doors. Also near the entrance to the cab was the front sanding lever with the rear sanding lever against the bunker wall. Fixed to the bunker wall was a collapsible seat. A simple affair of a wooden seat on a bracket that bent at right angles when the seat was pulled from the wall. It had to be that way as there would be no room to fire up if the seat had been a fixture. As the old drivers were quick to tell us, we were lucky to have seats. In their days the fireman stood up all the time.

Some engines had automatic lubricators that fed oil to the pistons under steam pressure in the cab. The lever controlling the cylinder cocks could be found on either side. Hanging from the roof would be the whistle chain connected to the whistle stand on the boiler, just outside the cab and behind the safety valves. And that was about all you would find on the old workhorse that earned the Great Eastern Railway more than it ever cost.

The 'crib' break at Temple Mills, added to requirements time, would give the engine crews a 50 minute respite from the constant grind of shunting. During this time shunting would still be going on with spare locomotives known as relief 'mikes'. There was no forgetting the time. Dead on the dot the yard foreman would advise the signal box that it was time for the shunting engine to leave the engine road. The shunting stick, or dod, as we called the signals controlling movements in and out of the roads, would drop the short semaphore arm or spin its round enamel disc on the ground frame, and a shrill whistle from the company-issued whistle in the yard foreman's lips would accompany his upheld arm. It would mean right away to the shunting yard for another four hours of hit up, stop, back on, pull up, ease back steady, stop. Towards the end of the shift we would be looking for our relief crew who would have signed on at Stratford loco. depot and walked to Temple Mills by way of the railway track to start their eight hours' shunting.

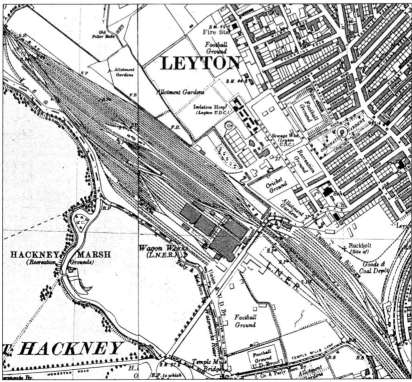

Temple Mills yard.   *Reproduced from the 6", 1912 Ordnance survey Map, revised 1938*

Chapter Nine

Secrets of Shunting

Temple Mills was just one maze of lines, crossovers, junctions and signal gantries. All traffic from the east coast region and heading for the north of England would come by local goods trains from Goodmayes, a marshalling yard on the main line from Liverpool Street to Norwich. It would enter Temple Mills from the southern end and use the same reception roads as traffic from the London docks area, Bishopsgate and Spitalfields marshalling yards. It would then be broken up into set trains departing from the northern end of the yard.

At the other end of the yard, entering from Lea Bridge station, would come freight from Cambridge and the Fen district, also coal from the northern coal mines via the big railway yard at March. There would also be the local goods trains from Hertfordshire and mid-Essex stations as well as transit freight from the LMS lines. That traffic would be remarshalled into trains for the central London depots, the docks or East Anglia.

Between the signal box controlling Temple Mills south and the junction that led to Leyton station on the Epping branch line were sidings predominantly used for storing rolling stock that was waiting for repair or destruction. On the Leyton side were the sidings that dealt mainly with the large amount of stores material used by the Stratford depot and its various workshops.

Although there was a very gradual incline through the marshalling yards from south to north, the yards were practically level and made shunting easy. All yards practised the loose shunting method. [Loose shunting was permitted by Rule 110 - with certain exceptions, against passenger stock, wagons of explosives etc.]

There were many factors to be taken into consideration when shunting wagons. They were the weight of the wagons being uncoupled, the distance they had to travel, whether that distance was on a straight piece of track or curves, whether it was a wet or dry rail and whether there was any variation in the gradient of the track over which the loose wagon was being worked. It was obvious, for instance, that three wagons of coal at 20 tons each, would gain more momentum when rolling loose than one wagon, or that one wagon of parcel freight would not gain the speed of one wagon of bricks. All this mental calculation had to be made by the shunter before he sent the wagon on its way, and the driver also had to study the contents of the trucks before he decided how much steam he would give the engine in the shunting movement.

The fireman was also vitally involved in this. When shunting was in progress a good head of steam was required as the steam brake was only as good as the boiler pressure. The 'Buck Jumper' worked at 180 psi and the ideal brake pressure was at that figure. If it dropped below about 150 the blocks did not grip with the tenacity required for rapid stops. If the steam pressure was more than 180 the excess steam would escape from the safety valves with a deafening roar. This not only killed any chance of conversation between driver and shunter but, if the boiler's water level was near the top of the gauge glass, the sudden stopping would cause the steam pressure to pick up the water and it would force its way through the safety valves in a fine mist, drenching everyone around for about a hundred yards. Shunters were not very fond of this treatment and the fireman was soon told what to do with his shovel.

Another requirement was that smoke should be kept to a minimum. This was one golden rule that a fireman had to carry out at all times during his career and starting on shunting engines was a good way to learn. It can be safely said that the more smoke that came from the chimney, the poorer was the fireman at his trade. The exception would be the condition of the locomotive and the grade of the coal supply.

When the days were damp or foggy, or when it was raining, smoke and steam would hang in the air and drift across the yards in swathes of grey mist. As the basis of all shunting was the estimation of distance and speed by visual approach, it was essential that smoke and steam emissions be kept to the minimum. Steam soon disappeared but smoke would hang round. The art was to have a good solid bed of fire that gave a silvery, golden glare. Having achieved this the fireman would fire up frequently with small amounts of coal so that, as soon as the new coal hit the fire, fumes were turned to incandescant gases rather than sulphurous, unburnt gases.

The use of the firebox door and blower would also control the density of smoke. On the 'Buck Jumper' the firebox door was simply a round steel plate over the boiler mouthpiece. It had a steel lever bolted to the centre, to which was attached a chain. The steel lever sat in a rack type bracket that was bolted to the boiler front and stood out at right angles but dropping in an arc of about 45 degrees over eight inches.

To get the maximum heat from the fire the door was shut tight. This was all right when on the run with a heavy load, when the beat of the engine would lift the fire and so burn the gases. As soon as the engine's supply of steam was cut off by the driver the smoke would billow out. The door would then have to be dropped back a notch or two or else the blower was pulled hard on. The ideal situation was working with the door two or three notches back from the boiler face. Sometimes, in the shunting yards, we would work with the door right down on the floor of the cab in an effort to keep steam pressure at the maximum and yet not blowing off at the safety valves. It was very nice in the English winter but hot in the summer.

Shunting went on in all weathers and emission control was important. It could mean someone's life. Even in fog we kept going. At times the shunters were invisible, cloaked by the pea soup fogs that used to roll in across the River Lea and from the docks. On those occasions it was all the more important that steam, smoke and noise be kept to the minimum. Shunting in fogs was done with a prescribed code of whistles, given by the shunter on whistles issued by the company. If you missed a whistled instruction because the engine was roaring at the safety valves it could mean a collision, derailment or even injury to someone in the yard.

Another vital part of the fireman's work was operating the sanders. Steam engines were precise pieces of engineering, not just the puffing billies that many people believed them to be. There was as much engineering prowess behind the locomotive as today's jumbo jets. The 'Buck Jumper' had six wheels of the best and was more steady on them than most. If the steel tyres began to wear and the engine did not go in for its normal overhaul, as was the case during the war, the tractive effort of the cylinders would overcome the adhesive or gripping powers of the wheels and the wheels would slip on the rails. No doubt many would remember the steam locomotive starting off with a heavy load with the steady, sonorous beat, slowly gaining momentum and then suddenly the roaring of the exhaust as the wheels lost their grip on the rails. Wheels would spin as the steam power drove the pistons at maximum power till the driver regained control.

When rails were dry the 'Buck Jumper' would grip like a bulldog and shunt the loads without a shudder. But on days when a mist blew in from the docks and frost was not far away, the little engines would slip and slide their way to the shunting spur. This was when the sand boxes had to be kept full and the outlet pipes clear from wet sand that had been thrown up by the skidding wheels. As the engine began to pull a rake of wagons from the yard to the shunting spur the fireman would get the sanders working. It was best to sand the rail as the wagons were being pulled out of the yard. This meant that the track was sanded for the forward movement once the engine reached the end of the shunting spur.

Sometimes after a loose shunt, when the driver applied the brake for the initial check, the wheels would pick up and the whole train would slide along the rails as though on ice. The golden rule was never to apply sand until the brake was off and the wheels were unlocked. If sand were applied as the engine was being pulled along by the wagons, which could be a combined weight of some 500 tons, the wheels could suddenly gain a grip and the power of the sudden grab would sometimes buckle siderods.

It was always 'release brake, apply sand, apply brake'. With good crews this came automatically. No words, just a full understanding of what the old girl needed. There were always three to a team.

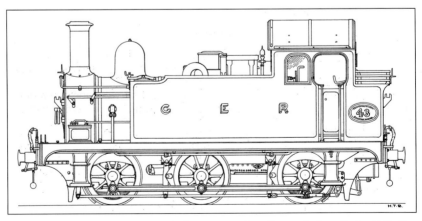

GER 'C72' 0-6-0T, reclassified 'J68' by the LNER.   *Great Eastern Railway Society Collection*

Chapter Ten

The Engine with the Hump

The hump yard at Temple Mills was at the northern end of the complex and, in its time, was the latest thing in shunting. It was nothing like the sophisticated hump yards that can now be found around the world with electronic controls and automatic braking systems.

Basically it was shunting by gravity. The shunting engine would pick up a train from the reception road, pull it over the hump and down the other side, which became the shunting spur of the orthodox yards. As the wagons slowly passed the head shunter, who stood at the top of the hump, he would read the wagon's destination card and decide on which road to place it in. He would then write the road number in chalk on the side of the wagon. By the time the engine had pulled the train over the hump, which was a man made gradient of about one in seventy, the train was marked up for marshalling .

There was a signal box on top of the hump which had a clear vision of the whole yard. The signalman controlled the key roads in the yard and he could see the road numbers on the wagons as they came up the hump. From the key roads that he controlled there would be other lines that were set manually by shunters who were in various positions in the yard. Their main task was to set the subsidiary roads from instructions received from a public address system used by the head shunter, and to slow the speed of the wagon as it entered the selected road.

The engine mainly used for this work was a sturdy tank engine known as the 'J50'. I don't remember it ever having a friendly name like the 'Gobbler' or 'Buck Jumper'. Maybe because it didn't have many friends. Brought to the Great Eastern area from the Great Northern, it was an 0-6-0 weighing about 58 tons. It had 4 ft 8 in. driving wheels and the cab was much more spacious than the 'Buck Jumper's'.

Its own characteristic was the unusual shape of the tanks on each side of the low boiler. They were a normal height next to the cab but, when about level with the steam dome, they began to taper off diagonally and finished near the front of the smokebox. This cut away portion was designed so that the engine could carry more water than a tank engine of comparative size, and yet not restrict the driver's view when backing onto a train, engine first.

The tanks also had a cutaway section underneath, between the steam dome and the start of the smokebox, so that the driver could oil the inside motions from the footplate without the need of a pit. It carried about two tons of coal and 1500 gallons of water. It was ideal for hump shunting because of its solid build and the specially designed tanks which helped the driver's view on the hump incline. One drawback was its steam pressure of 175 1b. This was only five pounds less than the 'Buck Jumper' but the difference was very noticeable if the maximum was not maintained.

Sometimes the 'J50' would be put on freight trains and that was bad news for engine crews. They would be regularly placed on a freight train from Temple

Mills to Goodmayes when being rostered to stay for work on the Goodmayes hump for a week. Being wet steamers they would soon pick up their water if the boiler were too full and the regulator was working at second port. The other problem was that although 175 1b. boiler pressure was easy to maintain when hump shunting, it was a very different task on the road.

A heavy train, a few tricky gradients and the 'J50' would soon start to hang its head. The needle on the steam gauge would flicker back to 150, 140 . . . the tractive effort would weaken and so would the driver's ability to stop, with the steam brake losing power. It was usually in such conditions that the water in the boiler gauge glass would be getting near the bottom brass cock, or 'in the nut' as we would say. The fireman would be praying for the next signal to be at danger, so that the driver would shut off steam and allow the spare steam to be used to operate the injector to fill the boiler.

The 'J50' really had to be nursed along with a train and many a time I have sat watching the steam gauge show about 100 lb., with water just in the gauge glass and the injector gurgling as it tried to lift water into the boiler. The driver had shut the regulator to use a drop in the gradient to push the train along, hoping the next signal would be off so we could roll a little further. The ideal situation with any train was to leave with a good fire, a full boiler of water and a full head of steam. With the 'J50' the best you could do was leave with a full head of steam and three-quarters of a boiler, so you were a quarter of a boiler down before the train was on the move.

By the time the junior fireman had spent a few months in the Temple Mills Shunting Link he knew the capabilities of the little tank freight engines, how to clean their fires in double quick time, how to fill lubricators, where to oil up the motions and the need to keep a tidy floor. He also knew the shunting hand signals for both day and night operations and could gauge the stopping power of the steam brake with a load on.

Some drivers never left their seats. Others would take it in turns about, with the fireman doing the driving. This was good and not only gave the fireman the feel of handling a live machine but also let him get used to shunter's instructions, judging distances and speeds necessary for good and safe shunting. He found out how hard it was to pick out a shunter's oil hand lamp on a wet night, with steam blowing down over the boiler. He learned how to inch the engine's way along a pitch black siding at night, closing the wagons up so that the shunters could couple them up. In fact he began to find out that the footplate man was a craftsman in his own right, in a world that nobody knew or understood, outside those men who were shackled to its confines.

There were about 26 weeks on the Temple Mills roster including the spare shifts. If one stayed in the gang for a year there was little chance of getting one set job for more than two weeks in the year. The senior fireman in the link was often called upon to man engines in other links, such as the local goods or suburban passenger. When the spare shift came up it was always a move to the local goods link and the senior spare fireman came off shed duties to staff the shunting engines.

The original idea of the spare shift was to supply relief for holidays but the war changed all that. Holidays were a forgotten luxury unless a doctor authorised a break because of the strain of continuous hours on the footplate. The government's ruling that railway work was an exempt occupation meant that all footplatemen were exempt from call-up for military duties. All enginemen were placed under government control. They were no longer employees of a private company and they lost all the rights that went with private employment. Railway locomotive crews had worse conditions than men in the armed forces during the war. This was especially true of those in the London area who lived, worked and died under combat conditions.

In the armed forces those who were directly involved with battle conditions were relieved after so many days and rested, ready to return refreshed. This was not so with the railways as they kept the strategic supplies moving day and night, regardless of weather, air raids, food supplies or any other thing that could go wrong on the home front.

The only right that an engineman could demand was nine hours off between shifts. The previous shift could have extended to 20 hours without a break. The driver and fireman then went home and, nine hours after signing off, would be signing on again for the next trip which could be anything from eight to eighteen hours, depending on available relief and the position of the train at the time of relief.

As if this were not enough, the crews could return home to find themselves bombed out with members of the family killed or missing. Regardless of those conditions it was report for work and make the best of it. Without belittling the carnage that the armed forces experienced during the war, I still believe that it is far easier to experience death and suffering on foreign soil instead of being blasted from one station to another in air raids that lasted up to 15 hours in the London area, and knowing that your family could be dead when you returned home at the end of the shift.

Living and working in war conditions on your own doorstep is by far the greatest traumatic experience that any man can suffer and yet the footplate men in Britain during the war, and after the war, were looked upon as the dregs of society. Without them the country would have collapsed and the forces overseas would have lost their main supply column.

Although the work was strenuous there was no allowance for it with the food rationing. The only extra food that footplate crews were given by the government was four ounces of cheese each week. It can be truly said that Britain's railways ran on bread and jam during the war. In country districts things were better with the possible chance of a rabbit of two, but in the cities there was nothing extra except the black market and railwaymen did not get that kind of money.

True, the pay packet was large at times with all the excessive hours but the government had all that worked out. One of Winston Churchill's great ideas was the Post War Credit Scheme. After a certain income, which was not large, incomes were taxed at about 17 shillings in the pound. The pound was 20 shillings. It was dubbed as a war effort by those lucky civilians earning big money, to help finance the war. This excessive tax was earmarked for repayment after the war. What was not said was when it would be paid after the war. Twenty years after the peace many were still waiting for the money and, when it was finally paid, it was just the sum that they had paid in the 1940s. What had been a worthwhile sum of money in 1945 had been whittled down to nothing by post-war inflation. The government did not pay any interest on the money forcibly taken from the wage earner during those years.

I was fortunate in living about 15 miles from Stratford in an easterly direction. Although the German bombers came in that way on their raids over London it was comparatively quiet, and the only time we had any bombs on Brentwood was when the anti-aircraft gunfire was so intense that the bombers were turned back or hit. Then they would jettison their load to make the plane lighter or less hazardous in attempting a forced landing. There were also times when they would pick Brentwood for attention as they knew it was a garrison town, headquarters of the Essex Regiment.

Many of my firemen mates and drivers lived in the Stratford area and I could see them gradually being worn down by the life under fire. I have seen men lose their reasoning after coming to work and being told that a bomb had hit their home. I'll never forget one man in the coal gang. He had just started the 10.0 pm shift and we were standing in front of the Jubilee Shed. Heinkels were droning overhead and we heard the swish of bombs coming down.

We all dived into an empty pit outside number one road and saw the skyline light up about half a mile away. The angry orange flare backed by the brilliant silver flash of the explosion lit up the entire area and we could see the jagged rooftops of houses either side of the explosion.

'My God!', he screamed, 'that's my house!'

We tried to tell him that it could have been further on but he was insistent.

'They've gone . . .' he mumbled and cried like a baby.

They took him to hospital for sedation. He was right, it was his house. His wife and four children died in the rubble. The last I knew he was still in a mental home.

Chapter Eleven

Local Goods and Diagrams

I was not in the Temple Mills link for long. As a qualified fireman, then on my second year rate of pay, I soon found myself promoted to the Local Goods Link. This roster was one of the largest at the Stratford shed and, from memory, it took crews 18 months to do one complete turn of the roster. This meant that you did not have the same job for more than one week in 78. The turns of duty covered as many geographic locations as they did in hours of starting. It would be no exaggeration to say that a local goods crew could be starting or finishing a shift at any time of the day or night, seven days a week.

Drivers in the Local Goods Link were among some of the best with which to work. They were mainly young men, as drivers went, in comparison with the old brigade in the shunting links and some of the suburban links. They were between 35 and 55 years of age, mostly family men with an understanding of youngsters and not too old to forget their firing days. They helped me shape my life more than any influence from home or local friends.

We had a common bond in that we, the young fireman, were trying to make the best of a job that was being done under adverse conditions and with poor tools. The drivers were men who had fired under the stringent conditions of private railway employment, with tyrants as drivers, and were now in a position to practice their driving ability with the same poor tools. Every shift was a challenge, every day was one more under the mantle of war and every day we'd say goodbye, wondering if we would meet for the next turn of duty.

They rarely expected the impossible from the young fireman, knowing full well that the engines of the forties were only a shadow of the engines they had known in pre-war years. This was a vital point overlooked by the old brigade. They had fired and driven on the cream of locomotives of private railways. Now, in their final years as drivers, they still remembered what the engines could do but did not allow for the fact that lack of proper maintenance had placed those engines more in line for the scrap heap than main line work.

Like most railway jobs with traffic, as train working was called, the shift either started with getting an engine ready and leaving Stratford for some marshalling yard, or travelling passenger to relieve a train somewhere in the metropolitan district or country areas. In the latter case the day could either finish by working the engine to the shed or being relieved on the track. To give a general idea of local goods working, I shall detail a shift starting at the shed and one where the crew is relieved on the road.

Three things had to be checked before crews even started work. The roster, indicating the hour for starting work and the job involved, the diagram showing the train working and the engine list which told the crew which locomotive had been allocated to them. The roster on this occasion tells us that we are starting at 3.30 am on Monday morning. The diagram is 354. All round the sign-on room are big black framed glass cases in which are the various diagrams worked from the Stratford depot. In one of these frames is diagram 354.

The diagram is a printed timetable of train running and covers the movement of the engine from the time it leaves the shed until its return, which could be days later. Diagram 354 covers the local goods service to Ponders End, a suburban town on the Liverpool Street to Cambridge line. Before leaving the sign-on room the crews check the supplementary roster for the next day. Individual shifts could change due to staff shortages. This means that the local goods firing job, although yours by right because you are the regular Local Goods Link fireman, could have gone to a spare fireman as you, being more experienced, were required to replace a fireman missing on a suburban passenger run. This was always a frustrating experience but one that had to be accepted. For instance, a fireman could have made arrangements to go out on the Sunday evening knowing that he was not on duty till early Monday morning, only to find that he was now wanted for duty at 8.0 pm on the Sunday night. This is a good indication of how a locomotive fireman's social life was non-existent. The old steam engine was his only guaranteed companion through life.

A check of the supplementary roster shows that Ponders End is still the job for Monday morning and, in the darkness of three o'clock, you walk the lonely streets of blacked-out Stratford towards the subway that snakes under the main line tracks and leads to the engine sheds. On nearing the depot more people are emerging from the murky shadows thrown by the austere yard lighting. Crews going home or others coming on duty; crews already at work on the various shunting jobs; boiler washers busy washing out boilers for the next day's work and fitters bashing away at some stubborn nut on a mechanically defective engine.

For some unknown reason there are no German bombers about and the limited lighting is allowed round the depot to assist in the important work of keeping the trains running. Solitary electric globes throw down their cold glare at regulated distances through the murky atmosphere. The Locomotive Running Department is in constant touch with air raid defence headquarters and works on a colour scheme for urgency of warnings. Green was all clear and normal lighting was allowed on night shifts. There was an intermediate warning known as Yellow. This meant that the enemy was across the coast and could be heading our way. Some lights were put out and everyone was on standby. When the Red alert came through all lights were extinguished and we had to fumble about the best we could.

Diagram 354 was on a piece of paper telling the driver his starting time, time from the Stratford loco. outlet into traffic, arrival time at Temple Mills North, departure time from Temple Mills and arrival time at Ponders End. It would then detail the working shift at Ponders End, such as relief in the yard at 9.30 am and return home 'passenger'. The middle shift would shunt the yard throughout the day and maybe go as light engine to another station or siding on the line to shunt there and bring back the empties ready for the train to the Mills that night.

The middle shift would be relieved in the yard and the late shift would work the train back to Temple Mills after the peak hour passenger traffic on the Liverpool Street-Hertford line had finished. On arriving at Temple Mills they

A line up of 'B12' locomotives cleaned and ready for action, outside the front of the Jubilee Shed. In the background is the building housing the sign-on offices with the dormitories for country crews on the first floor. The small hut just behind the cloud of steam was Joe's office, the engine cleaners' foreman.
British Railways

At the back of the Jubilee Shed showing all the tank locomotives stabled and ready for their next shift. A mixture of 'Gobblers', 'Buckjumpers' and 'N7s'.
British Railways

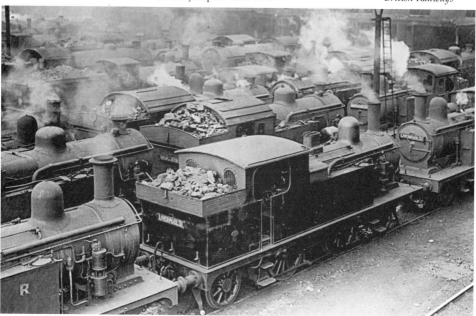

The front of the Jubilee Shed, Stratford Locomotive Depot, showing cleaners at work. The pipes on the left-hand side are the water supply for boiler washers. *British Railways*

'F4' class 2-4-2T No. 7111 is seen at Stratford on 12th March, 1938, with the massive coaler in the background, ready for North Woolwich line duties. The engine was withdrawn in April 1948 as No. 7161. *H.C. Casserley*

Stratford maintained an allocation of about two dozen 'Claud Hamilton' class engines during the 1930s but by Nationalisation this had declined to just 5. 'D16/2' 'Claud Hamilton' class 4-6-0 No. 8813, built in 1910, passes Stratford Western Junction with a fine head of steam on a down train in pre-war days with a GER suburban set, headed by a 6-wheel brake third.   *Photomatic*

The 'B17' 'Sandringham' class 4-6-0 was introduced late in 1928 to address the need for an engine to supplement the 'B12s' on the heavier trains on the GE Section. No. 2822 *Alnwick Castle*, delivered in 1931, is working the down 'Flushing Continental' train, passing Brentwood in the mid-1930s, before the completion of the widening preparatory to the Shenfield electrification. Note the three Pullman cars which were part of the train formation.   *Real Photographs*

Taken during 1936, just after the withdrawal of 4-wheel carriages on the North Woolwich line but before the removal from 'F5' class 2-4-2T No. 7790 of the condensing gear. The standard formation of 6 bogie carriages and a 6-wheel brake van waits at Custom House on its way to Albert Dock. It was still employed on the same service in the early 1950s and was withdrawn as No. 67219 in November 1956. *Lyn Brooks Collection*

'F5' class 2-4-2T No. 7100 stands at Ilford in the late 1930s, on the down suburban line, with a train for Woodford via the Fairlop Loop. The train consists of Gresley's 1935 non-articulated stock built for the GE Section suburban services. It was withdrawn as No. 67206 in September 1955. *Lyn Brooks Collection*

Several signal gantries spanned the approaches to Stratford from Liverpool Street, this shows the one close to Western Junction, with the signal box in the background. Although a late GER period print the gantry remained largely unchanged until the late 1930s. *Pamlin Prints*

The view is towards Liverpool Street from Western Junction signal box, taken in May 1922. The Western Junction signal gantry is in the centre, the poster hoardings front Thornton Fields, developed as carriage sidings in the 1920s but here still in use as the GER's sports ground. Beyond is the bulk of Bryant & May's Bow match factory. *BR/OPC Joint Venture*

Loop Junction signal box was situated on the double track loop line running between Loughton Junction and Fork Junction, separating the carriage department shops from the running shed. Behind the box is the Jubilee running shed, with offices and water tower on the right. Ahead are the carriage repair shops and to the left the end of Stratford Old Yard carriage sidings. On the skyline are the cooling towers of the GER's electric power station. *BR/OPC Joint Venture*

A view down the old Cambridge main line in May 1922 towards the Old Works and Stratford station. Behind Chobham Farm Box is the Carriage Department repair and lifting shops with the general offices on the skyline. Stratford Old Yard carriage sidings are in the centre background, with Loop Junction signal box at the right. *BR/OPC Joint Venture*

Channelsea Junction signal box is to the left of the running lines which diverge from the Colchester main line via Carpenters Road curve, bearing left past the box to Victoria Park. To the right the line passes High Meads junction to join the old Cambridge main line near Loughton Junction. In the foreground is Carpenters Road goods depot; opposite the box the running lines diverge to Stratford Low Level and the North Woolwich line. The carriages stand on Channelsea sidings, serving Woolwich line and Victoria Park services. *BR/OPC Joint Venture*

Colour light signals on Brentwood Bank. The telephone is in the box at the base.
British Railways

Allocated when new in 1929 to Stratford class 'J39/1' 0-6-0 No. 2729 was one of a batch of 20 equipped with the Westinghouse brake. With this equipment they were regularly employed on weekend excursions to Southend and Clacton, being able to utilise former GE Westinghouse braked stock. An 8-coach suburban set, probably strengthened at the end by a pair of 6-wheelers, makes its way past Brentwood station towards the seaside in the mid-1930s.

H. Gordon Tidey/Lens of Sutton

No. 7210 was the last of a class of 5 'Y4' 0-4-0Ts, being completed in 1921. It was always attached to Stratford as a service engine, working around the Old Works where it is seen in the late 1930s. It became Departmental 33 in 1952 and was withdrawn in December 1963, the last GER engine in BR service.

John Watling Collection

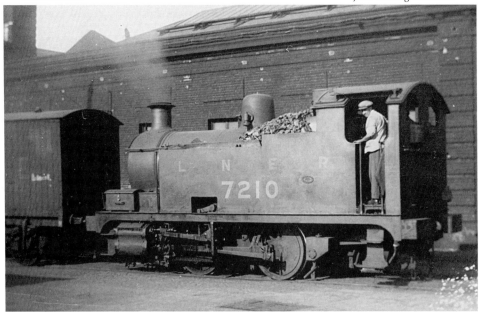

could take the engine to the shed for disposal or they might be called on by train control to work another train anywhere in the London area.

Thousands of these diagrams had to be worked out and train movements fitted into a pattern of operations somewhat like a jigsaw puzzle. It was a skilful task but we never met the men behind the organisation of train running. Not that it made much difference. The railway was rife with class distinction and, to them, we were just numbers in a book.

The next list to study was the engine list. This told us the engine allocated to diagram 354 and its position in the shed. Sometimes the list could bring forth a variety of statements such as 'not that old cow again!', or 'we're in luck mate, she hasn't been out of the shops for long . . .'. Sometimes the comments were made with great reverence. 'Old 1625 back on the road again eh? Didn't take them long to fix her up again. That's the one old Joe Beck had the night he and his mate Charlie were killed with that land mine. Good bloke Joe, one of the best . . .'

Diagram 354 had engine number 7512 against it. No surprise in being allocated a 'J15' or 'Little Goods'. They were the backbone of the suburban goods work during the war. It's only 3.20 am when we go out into the corridor that ran between the sign-on room and the cleaners' mess room. Overhead, above the timber lined ceiling, you know that crews from March and Ipswich are trying to get some sleep in the dormitories. Heavy boots echo on the bare boards as you make your way to the Jubilee Shed.

The knowledge of sleeping crews above you was a good insight into railway management's consideration for the well being of the footplate crews pre-war and during the war. After working some 10 to 15 hours in from the country districts they were rostered nine hours off in the company's dormitories before returning home with another train. Dormitories where grimed windows looked on to the main engine shed at Stratford, where constant clouds of smoke and steam wreathed their sooty particles against the bleak brick walls.

Fancy trying to sleep with all hell let loose just one hundred yards from the dormitory windows. Engines blowing off steam, firemen breaking coal, tank and tender lids clanging down on steel tanks as water bags were pulled out and various tones of whistles piercing the pungent air with sharp warnings that engines were about to move.

We are a bit before time but it is handy to have a few minutes up your sleeve. The allowance is 45 minutes in which to get the locomotive ready for work. This is known as preparation time. No allowance is made for the fact that the engine could be first in the shed on number one road, or three back on number ten. The difference would be another two hundred yards from the tool stores.

Our engine is behind two others on number seven road. The first engine has a crew busily cleaning the boiler front by the light of slush lamps. They will soon be off to the Stratford carriage sidings, ready to haul empty coaches to Liverpool Street with their 'D15', 'Claud Hamilton' class tender engine. If the rails are greasy they could have problems with her massive seven feet driving wheels trying to get a grip, tender first, with 10 main line coaches behind her.

The second engine, a sturdy 'K3' freight locomotive, has a March crew oiling up and waiting to go outside the shed for water when the 'D15' steams off.

They don't speak to us. Country crews rarely did. You'd never think we worked for the same company and relieved each other *en route*.

Our old girl stands patiently in the smoky gloom, a relic from the heady Victorian days of steam elegance but a bit of a museum piece in the days of World War II. They were first designed in 1883 and 289 entered the service of the Great Eastern Railway during the next 30 years. She didn't see a cleaner's rag during the war. Constantly on the run, seven days a week, she was lucky to get a boiler washout. Her wheel arrangement of 0-6-0 with 4 ft 11 in. driving wheels gave her a good pulling power even though she only weighed 37 tons.

We clamber up the steel steps to the cab and feel we're in luck. Usually on a Monday morning there is a good chance of getting an engine that has been lit up over the weekend with the consequent soot and grime all over the cab and boiler front. Our engine has been working during the weekend and the cab is reasonably respectable with just a film of grey dust in the cab, the result of cleaning the fire on the disposal pits.

Food bags are placed in the lockers which also form the seats on which we'll sit for the next eight hours. Most firemen carried their food in canvas bags similar to those that held the service gas masks during the war. Drivers were still with the old habits and many had the Gladstone bag or the tin box. Quite a few of the younger drivers went the firemen's way and carried the canvas type. Regardless of the bag, everyone had his tea billy.

Trains didn't stop for meals and if you didn't make your own hot drinks then you went without. With a good mate you could make the rations last longer by sharing brews. With others it was a case of making your own and make it last.

A quick glance at the boiler front shows that the firelighter has done a good job. By the light of my mate's cigarette lighter we can see the water in the gauge glass is near the three-quarters level, steam pressure is 100 lb. and the fire is nicely wedged under the door.

Chapter Twelve

Preparing the Locomotive

We hang our serge jackets on a hook on the cab wall and walk over to the tool store which is situated near the massive steel water tank that feeds the depot. It stands half way between the Jubilee Shed and the turntable at the disposal pits.

Inside the store is a long, low counter with a steel top, shining with the constant polish of oily cloths and the sliding of buckets across its surface. There is a characteristic smell about the place. It comes from the oil bottles, the napthalene that protects the cleaning cloths and worsted woollen skeins from the rats, and bars of good old golden soap, a regular issue to enginemen.

The two men behind the counter are ex-loco. staff who have seen better days. One is near retirement, the other has only one arm. He lost the other in a shunting accident. Both are quite content with their lot.

'Blimey! Look who's here!'

The old man winks at me and chides my mate.

'Have a heavy weekend Jack? Saw yer in the Crown on Saturday with that blonde piece . . .'

'That's all right Jimmy. You weren't doing so bad for your age in the corner neither. 7512 and we don't want any old rubbish.'

The number belonged to our engine and, in the tool store, all tools were stored in racks under the engine's number. The one-armed man brought the bucket and bundle of oil bottles. It was quite a strain for one hand but it was as big as a ham.

I check the bucket for contents. It's no good going back after leaving the store and saying you were short of some spanner. In the galvanised bucket should be a hand brush for sweeping the cab floor, gauge lamp, two slush lamps, hammer, open ended spanner of set widths for standard nuts on the locomotive, a monkey wrench, ring spanner, a tin cylinder containing 12 detonators and one red flag and a large and small oil can, or feeders as they were called.

The bundle of oil bottles, as the tin containers were called, should consist of four cans. The largest was for engine oil, second largest for lubricating oil, which was much thicker than engine oil, the third can was for paraffin and the fourth was for rape oil for the boiler gauge lamp.

We each received a couple of second-hand cloths for cleaning purposes and we could take as much cotton waste off the bench as was needed. While my mate exchanged more banter with the storemen, I chose a shovel and coal hammer from the stack near the door. It paid to check the coal hammer. If the wooden handle was a little worn round the head it was worth looking for one more solid as the hammer was a vital part of the fireman's equipment. A shift without one could be worse than hard work, remembering the size of some lumps that came from the Stratford coal stage chutes.

The shovel also needed careful choosing. The hand piece did not want to be loose as it could throw your aim out when swinging in that vital arc between tender and firebox door. A loose cross piece could also nip the skin off your palm and this was quite painful after eight hours before the heat of the fire. The blade needed to be worn, with the edge straight and firm. New shovels were as heavy as lead and the unworked edge, although only about three-sixteenths of an inch thick, seemed to jam against the coal rather than work under it. The ideal blade was about one-sixteenth thick.

The driver would take the oil bottles to get the supply for the shift while the fireman went back to the engine and started to prepare for the day's work. When going to the oil store, which was next to the tool store, one had to give the storeman the engine number and diagram number. This told the storeman the type of engine and how long the engine would be away from its home depot. In our case 7512 would be away for more than 24 hours so oil had to be supplied to allow relief crews to oil up during shifts.

By the time we were back in the shed the 'Claud Hamilton' had gone and the 'K3' was outside over the furthest pit. Each shed road had pits inside and outside. Outside there were two water cranes so that two engines could get water at the same time. This not only speeded things up but also saved making too much smoke in the shed, where fitters and boiler washers would be working as well as engine cleaners and firelighters.

My mate decides we'll go outside before we start preparations. I make sure we're not coupled to the engine behind and give him the all clear signal. I wait outside the shed because I know he will want me to set the engine for oiling up. By stopping the engine with the siderod couplings at a certain angle to the axle, the engineman can be sure that the connecting rods and big ends of the inside motion locomotive are in a position whereby he can oil them in one go by lying on the footplate round the boiler. This is all part of the knowledge that came from being interested in the job.

It was nothing that was taught in a training school or out of books. Learning to be an efficient fireman was a matter of constant attention to that which the driver would tell you if you asked.

Our 'Little Goods' engine has inside motions. The driver creeps forward with steam hissing through the open cylinder cocks. As she has been standing for some time the engine has a lot of water in the cylinders and it spurts out from the copper pipes which drain the cylinders as newly applied steam fills them. He sees me give the stop signal through the clouds of steam under the yard lights and stops with the steam brake.

The handbrake is wound on and then the steam brake is released. This is to make sure that the engine does not move while we are working round it. It could be run into from the rear by other locomotives being placed by shunters, or it could roll on its own. Steam engines are deceptive for their size. Rails only have to be on a slight gradient and, with the reversing wheel in the right position, one hundred tons of steel will quietly begin to roll without warning.

While the driver is oiling up, I get the bent dart from the tray on the tender to push the fire all over the box so that we can get steam up quickly and also have a working fire for the trip. At the same time I make a mental note that all fire irons are on the engine.

I pull the blower on to stop any blow-back. The golden light fills the cab as the fire comes to life and there is a discernible throbbing in the firebox as the air heats up rapidly. The firebox of the 'Little Goods' is not very large, being about four feet by seven. With the added glare and lack of fumes in the firebox I get on my knees and give the brick arch a check over as well as the plug in the firebox crown.

The brick arch is exactly what it is called, an arch of fire bricks which is placed against the boiler wall at the front of the firebox. It extends about a third of the length of the firebox from the front wall and stops flames from burning the tube ends by direct contact. In motion the flames lick the brick arch under surface, then curl back towards the firebox door until they find the edge of the brick arch. They then curl back towards the front of the firebox as the draught caused by the beat of the engine sucks the hot gases through the tubes and so heat the water before going out through the chimney.

Not all crews check the brick arch. Many argue that it is the job of the maintenance men in the sheds but the alert engine crew would always give it the once over. It only needed a brick to be missing or loose near the centre of the arch and the whole structure could fall down during a journey. This would completely kill the fire and make one hell of a mess to get out with the slice. Our brick arch is all right but has a fair amount of clinker on it, showing that it is getting near time for replacement.

The firebox plug is as dry as a bone, which shows that everything is all right with the firebox crown. The plug is a safety device and the section that is inside the boiler has a lead centre. If an engine's boiler water level gets too low the heat of the fire on the lead, without the water insulating it, causes the lead to melt. Steam in the boiler will escape into the firebox and put the fire out. This releases the pressure in the boiler and saves an explosion, so long as the crew is aware of what is happening.

If I had found the plug to be weeping I would have known that the previous crew had been in trouble with water running low in the boiler and nearly causing the engine to 'drop its plug' as we said in the sheds. Once again this was part of the work of the boiler washers when checking engines in the shed but not all jobs were done that should have been done, mainly due to manpower shortages. The best policy was to check for yourself.

While the fire was building up I would clean the boiler gauge glasses, trim the gauge lamp and hang it against the thick glass framework that protected the actual gauge glass. The lamp would hang with the light facing the fireman's side. This was so that the light, in the darkness of night work, did not impair the driver's vision when peering into the blackness for signals, trucks or any other items.

Making sure the steam supply was turned off I would then top up the lubricators that supplied the cylinders with oil. I would also check the steam brake for oil. The driver would be working on the footplate at the front, with a smoky slush lamp curling its flame around the underside of the dirty boiler. I would take the other slush lamp and place it on the highest point of the tender so that its flickering light gave an overall view of the untrimmed coal.

Luckily for me, when setting the engine for oiling, the water crane came into the right position for filling the tender. I struggle with the big, slippery leather bag that hangs from the tall steel column, fed with water from the tank near the tool store, and drop the end into the large round opening in the centre of the tender at the back. The heavy steel lid is placed on the bag to stop it from jumping out as the water flows. The steel arm of the water crane is fixed to the tender handrail with its cold chain. If this were not done, as soon as the water pressure surged through the bag the arm would swing out and the bag would jump out of the tender to swing in a wide arc, drowning anyone within reach! Not a very happy situation at four in the morning, especially if it happens to be your driver.

With the water pouring in nice and steadily, and knowing that the tender is only half full, I have time to break up the coal and draw it towards the front of the tender. I could also trim the tender by pulling in any overhanging lumps from the sides so that nothing could fall on men on the ground during train working, or fall off the engine as we went through stations.

When the tender is full I throw out the bag and close the heavy lid, making sure to drop the large hasp over the locking staple at the side. Some firemen did not trouble to do this, with disastrous results when the engine backed on to trains. The sudden surge of the water in the tender, as the engine pushed on to the stationary wagons, would cause it to cascade over the top of the tender and soak the person between engine and wagon when coupling up.

Climbing into the cab I find that my driver has finished oiling up and has checked the smokebox door to make sure the last person closed it properly. A loose smokebox door was a sure way to lose steam on the run, apart from the danger of it swinging open on running lines and fouling the opposite track. He had also checked the front sandboxes. I checked those in the cab and found that we needed a couple of buckets of sand in each.

The sand was kept in big steel bins between shed roads six and seven. It was fed by shed labourers from special sand trucks that had tarpaulin tops shaped like the roof of a house. The sand itself was dried in sand furnaces and was bone dry, running as freely as sand in an hour glass. Buckets of sand are no light weight and sometimes the fireman had to carry them 200 yards from bins to engine, stepping over rails and round inspection pits.

When checking the engine for equipment we find that the 'J15' has no lamps or destination boards. I go to the cleaners' mess room area to check for spare lamps while my driver goes to the stores to get a spare boiler gauge glass. Glasses have been known to blow during shifts and a boiler without a gauge glass was as good as a car without tyres.

I find three lamps but no boards so we go without. The burners are trimmed, tin reservoirs are filled with paraffin and glass slides are cleaned. The first part of our trip is engine only so I put one lighted lamp in the centre of the front buffer beam and one on the rear of the tender. The tender lamp had to have a red slide turned over the glass to give the red light required to be carried on the rear of any movement on running lines. It also acted as a rear light for anything coming behind us on roads where permissive working was allowed.

By the time my driver comes back from the stores I had tested both boiler injectors and found that they worked well in filling the boiler with water from the tender. At the same time I used the hose from the boiler feed pipes to wash down the floor, and stop coal dust from blowing round us by damping down the coal in the front of the tender. My driver pulls out his large pocket watch and studies the time. The watch is company issue with a plain face that measures two inches across and has Roman numerals. We wash in the hot water that I have put in the bucket, now as clean as a new pin after being wiped out with paraffin and cotton waste.

'Time to make a brew if you want,' he said. 'Kettle might be off the boil at the Mills when we get there.'

I take the blue enamelled billy can to the locomotive crews' mess room, just across the tracks from the tool stores. In the billy is an unsightly mixture of tea, sugar and condensed milk. It makes a good brew and the sweetness satisfies the needs of a stomach that might nag for food on a long shift. The huge kettle was singing on the gas burner and the glare of the electric lights hanging from the room's tall wooden ceiling are hard on the eyes after coming in from the poorly lit yard.

There are about seven or eight long wooden tables jutting out from the painted brick walls and each has wooden bench seats, scrubbed as clean as a washer woman's tub. There could be three or four crews sitting there. Some would be playing cards, others on the shove ha'penny board, while some would be dozing. They would be relief crews, disposal pit men or just crews who had finished their turn of duty and were waiting for the first train home.

'If it's not old Robbo,' someone sings out through the haze of cigarette smoke. 'Where are you off to son?'

It's the driver I had the previous week.

'Ponders End,' I tell him, filling up the billy and savouring the smell.

'Not a bad job if your relief's on time,' he said. 'Best to get on the station to meet them. Your train is usually on time and it's a long wait if you miss it!'

I nod and walk out into the darkness of the morning.

No. 7512 stands there with a golden glow filling the cab as the driver has opened the firebox door to give some light so that he can fill his timesheet. It also stops the old girl from blowing off excess steam. It will be nice and warm too as we start the journey. There is a small tray above the firebox door on which the billy can stand and keep warm. The driver rolls himself a cigarette and the end flares as the shag burns from the flame of the slush lamp.

'All ready?' he asks. I nod and hope we have remembered everything. He looks at the watch again.

'Might as well go. We're due at the outlet at 4.20.'

Chapter Thirteen

The Art of Firing

It was 4.10 am and the sky was still dark. He pulled on the whistle chain and its shrill sound echoed round the shed. He eased open the regulator and steam rushed to the cylinders, to roar out of the open cylinder cocks. The 'J15' was a wet steamer which meant that the steam collected in the high steam dome at the centre of the boiler went directly to the cylinders without being superheated, as in the more modern locomotive. A fine spray of water left the copper tubes that drained the cylinders. If the cylinder cocks were kept shut at this time, the build up of water could create such pressure that the cylinder end could blow off or the piston could buckle.

As the steam and water hissed from the open cocks the noise would soon change from a roar to a gentle hiss as pure steam replaced the water content. The front of the engine was enveloped in a cloud of steam, blotting our vision momentarily. I shut the cocks and the hiss is replaced with the gentle chuff, chuff, chuff, chuff from the tall Victorian chimney on the smokebox.

The twelve roads from the Jubilee Shed curved slowly left and, in turn, converged into four tracks, then two and eventually one which led to the outlet signal just beyond the disposal pits on the right-hand side. Every now and then a pool of light would slip by as we went under the yard lights sitting high on timber poles, lighting up areas where point handles would be for switching engines back on different roads into the shed.

The outlet hut was all on its own near the outlet signal which blinked its red light as we rolled towards it. This was a lonely job for a man but, once again, it gave a disabled footplate man a job. My driver applied the steam brake and I clambered down the steel steps between cab and tender and approached the little window.

'Driver Brown, fireman Robertson, engine 7512, diagram 354, light to North Box, Temple Mills,' I tell him.

He checks off the details on his list. 'OK son, drop down to the starter.'

We move towards the semaphore signal. The man in the hut rings the signalman whose box controls the shed exit and he fits us in as traffic allows. If everything was going right we would be away on time but it only needed a hold up with some train, maybe four hours previously, and everything would be delayed in a rolling pattern of lost minutes. The only golden rule on the road was that passenger trains took preference when time was involved. This did not always apply in wartime when essential goods were on the move and ships could be waiting at the docks.

A 'Claud Hamilton' class engine entered the disposal pit section, its huge driving wheels grinding on the curve as it leisurely puffed to the end of its shift. A bright shower of sparks light the air for a brief moment as a fireman throws out a slice of fire and red hot clinker from an engine already on the pit.

On the up goods road another 'Little Goods' was barking its way towards Stratford station, its cab windows shining like big golden eyes as the glare of the firelight in the cab throws its rays towards the black sky. The firebox door was down and the fireman was feeding the fierce fire in readiness for the stiff haul up to Bow Junction box. As she barked past us we could hear the clanking freight wagons. Mixed goods for Bishopsgate my mate said, as he stood with one leg up on the wooden seat, his hand resting on the warm regulator handle, the other holding his smouldering cigarette.

As the guard's van tail lights flickered by we heard the points slam over. The locking bar slid into place and the slack on the signal wire became taut as the outlet signal arm dropped to show the green aspect. A toot on the whistle, to let anyone around know that we were about to move and No. 7512 clattered over the points and on to the down goods road.

A little further on, under the road bridge, Leyton signal box switched us to the down main, as shown by the green light that appeared on the gantry of signals that stretched across six sets of railway lines. To come across a gantry of semaphore signals, day or night, is an awe inspiring sight.

Standing like regimented soldiers, the wooden columns support an array of arms and lights. There are the red signal arms with white bands, sometimes yellow arms with fishtail ends and a black vee, or small arms, only half the size of the main signals, known as calling-on signals. Amid this forest of signals could be arms pointing in the other direction, painted white with black bands. These were the signals controlling traffic from the other direction and indicating to the train crews facing them that they were looking at the back of the semaphore signal.

Temple Mills South had all 'sticks' off for us, our slang term for signals, and we quietly rolled towards the distant red light which indicated the North End home signal. On either side of us the yards were in a state of activity, either making up trains or dispatching them. Floodlights stood in groups and threw their glare down on the key sections of the tracks where rows of point handles followed lines as they branched off from the shunting spurs.

At the North End Yard we were directed to the road in which stood the made up freight train for Ponders End. We left the smooth running of the main line and felt the see-saw of the poorly maintained shunting yard tracks under our 0-6-0 wheels on the 'J15'. As we backed on tender first we could see the tender going up and down as we hit the slack joints on the 65 1b. track.

Shunting lines were allowed to deteriorate to an alarming degree. One reason was manpower, all gangs being required on the main lines, but it also went back to the false economy of the private companies who felt that shunting yards were set for a lifetime without maintenance, once laid. Considering the tonnage that moved over the mainly second-hand rail it's a wonder the wagons kept on the road as long as they did.

The main difference between the track in shunting yards and that on the main line was that the shunting yard track had its sleepers flush with ground level to make walking easier for shunters and train crews. On the main line, all tracks stood about 18 inches above ground level on a solid bed of ballast that not only locked the track securely but also gave the best possible drainage. It was in the shunting yards that much of the clinker and ash from the Stratford disposal pits was used as fill.

Dawn started to flush the sky and, against the eastern glow, my driver could see the outline of the leading wagon of our train. Constant application of the steam brake slowed the engine down to a walking pace until we heard the clang of steel as engine buffers met wagon buffers. The guard was standing in the shadows waiting to get the engine number and crew's names. I climbed down and went in between the engine and wagons to throw the solid three link steel coupling over the drawbar hook of the leading wagon, an old grey painted box wagon that had the smell of stale beer. Could be the town's supply.

I took the headlamp off the tender as we now had a train to pull and moved the front headlamp from the centre bracket to the one over the left buffer. This would let the signalman know, as we approached him, that we were a local goods train.

The guard had asked my driver to close the train together on to the guard's van so that he could couple up in a few places. He was working from my side and I watched for a signal from his paraffin burning handlamp. About one hundred yards away, in between the shadows of the wagons on the other line, I saw the small green light swinging slowly from side to side.

'Back on steady,' I relay to the driver.

He just about opens the regulator off the face of the valve and the old girl creeps backwards, as gently as a mare nudging her foal. The most gentle of beats leave the chimney and the wagons roll together with a musical collection of notes as different cast buffers meet others and give the ring of steel against steel.

The gentle movement comes to a halt as we find something more solid in the dark. The guard's lamp is still swinging slowly so we must have pushed into a bunch of wagons that was already together. The driver gives the 'J15' a little more steam and we surge. After about 50 yards the green light stops its sidewards swing and the green light changes to red as the guard moves the glass slide round inside the lamp case.

'Red light,' I tell my driver.

He shuts the regulator and waits for the surge as engine, train and guard's van run into the stops. When it comes he applies the brake to hold them together. The guard gives a green light to indicate that he has coupled all the train together and is ready to depart when we get permission. I acknowledge with a toot on the whistle and then drop the firebox door.

Using the blade of the shovel to direct air through the flames I can see that the fire is evenly spread but is a bit thin at the front. According to our timetable we have about 15 minutes to go but, with freight trains, they can give the 'right away' signal at any time. This is a problem for the fireman as he has to have a good fire on ready for the long haul and yet, if the start is delayed, he must not have the engine roaring off excess steam as it wastes coal and water.

My driver had gone round the locomotive to make sure that the axlebox lubricators were working, and that none of the corks had worked out of the siderod or big end oil cups. The corks were just ordinary household corks and screwed into the hole in the brass fittings through which the driver fed engine oil to lubricate the main moving parts. Although seemingly primitive the cork method was extremely effective and rarely did they come out, even on express engines that pounded the track for hours on end at high speeds. The main reason for their loss was that they had become old and the previous crew had failed to get new corks from the stores.

I drove the shovel into the tender to get some large lumps into the back of the shovel. The art was to keep the coal at the back of the shovel. From there you could direct it to any part of the box. It was not a good practice to try and get as much coal on the shovel as possible. It would never go where you wanted it and the fireman could end up with a heap of fire in the box where it was not wanted.

With a good size lump at the back of the shovel I put the blade in the firebox and twisted it to the left. The coal dropped into the left back corner. Then, with the shovel blade directly in the centre of the door, I turned it over so that the coal dropped directly under the door. Next the blade was directed to the right side of the box and twisted so that the coal fell in the right back corner.

With the back of the box fed with new coals I then directed the shovel to the right side, about one-third of the way down. The next goes two-thirds of the way down. The same procedure goes for the left-hand side. Finally three shovels of coal were directed against the front wall of the box, one in each corner and one in the middle, all under the brick arch.

On the average a fireman would go round the box with 10 half-shovels, in that pattern. Most engines liked a wedged shape fire, thick under the door and thin under the brick arch but, being the individuals they were, steam engines had traits of their own.

To get the coals down the left-hand side, when firing on a right-hand drive engine, the fireman had to bounce the shovel blade against the right-hand side of the firebox opening. Likewise, he went to the left-hand side to get coals down the right-hand side. And that was the main skill in firing to all locomotives. It was the way in which the fireman hit the firebox opening as to where the coals finished up.

There was not a lot of room in the cab of a locomotive for mighty swings, and the art was to use the deflection of the blow on the firebox plating to direct the coal with sufficient force to cover the distance. This was not too hard with fireboxes between five and six feet in length, although the problem was very real if the firebox door was the trapdoor type which left the fireman with an aperture about 10 inches deep at the centre in which to get the coal and the shovel blade.

On locomotives such as the 'B12s', the 4-6-0 passenger expresses, with fireboxes 10 ft long, the angle of deflection off the firebox mouth was vital to get the coal up the front. If you hit it too early, or too much on the cant, the coal would travel well but hit the centre of the brick arch and fall about 12 inches short of the front of the box. If you couldn't see what was happening and thought you were doing a good job, the steam gauge soon gave you the message. The needle would drop back steadily even though you had a good fire on.

Using the shovel blade to deflect the flames you would see that there was quite a mound of half dead fire under the brick arch, and the 12 inches between the heap and the firebox front was practically devoid of fire as the beat of the engine burned the remaining coals and only cold air from the ashpan was coming in.

This called for drastic action and the 14 feet long slice had to be dragged off the tender to push the fire forward from its position under the brick arch. The slice would have to go in, over the glaring inferno in the rest of the box. After placing the coals at the front to plug the gap the slice then had to be pulled out of the box. The protecting sweat cloth in the fireman's hand would be smouldering with the heat of the iron handle. All this had to be done with the engine swaying and bucking at 80 miles an hour.

So, although the local goods job seemed quite tame, it was a necessary training job for the bigger things to come. Getting the right deflections to coal a 'J15' firebox on the run was a good exercise for the larger engines on the main line goods and intermediate expresses. Due to the manpower problems in the war years young firemen found themselves on such trains long before their drivers had ever experienced such problems. Some sympathised with us - others gloried in the humiliation of our failures.

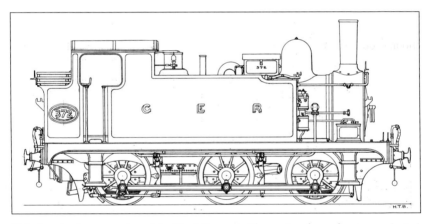

This drawing is one version of the 'Buck Jumper'. The engine shown here was adapted for passenger train working, as can be seen by the Westinghouse brake air pipe on the buffer beams, plus the screw type couplings. Those of the class used for shunting and freight train working had the three-link coupling and steam brake only.

Great Eastern Railway Society Collection

Chapter Fourteen

The Secret of Good Timekeeping

We heard a shrill whistle ahead and the shunter was standing with a green light held steady above his head. This meant we had the right of way out of the yard towards the starting signal. We acknowledge with the whistle. The old girl is whimpering at the safety valves and ready to go. It seemed easier to get maximum steam pressure on the 'J15' than the sturdy 'Buck Jumpers' but this was only because the 'J15's' maximum boiler pressure was 160 lb. compared with the 'J67's' 180 lb.

The driver eases open the regulator and she edges forward. We can feel the couplings stretching to their full extent as the train begins to roll forward. If the start is too sudden the three link couplings can jump the drawbar hook with the strain and we would then have the job of setting back to recouple.

It feels as though the 40 wagons are moving as one so the driver gives the engine first port on the regulator. The clear cut beat echoes from the tall chimney and the fire begins to change from its golden glow to a silvery glare as the coals burn to an incandescent gas. It pulsates like a human body. Choof, choof, choof, ch . . ch . . choof . . . The driver looks at me and winks. This is the first time the 'J15' has been under pressure since leaving the shed, and the exhaust beat tells us that her valves are out a little as the beat is slurred over one of the exhaust ports in the cylinders. Not as bad as some engines that have only three clear beats out of four.

No. 7512 grinds her way round the bend in the shunting yard and heads for the starting signal down the outlet road. The wagons lazily click, clack over the loose joints and I look back for a signal from the guard. There it is, against a sky which is getting quite bright now. I pick out the green light and acknowledge with the whistle. We know the train is intact and now on its way to Ponders End where most of the town is still asleep at five in the morning.

The starting signal which lets us on to the down main line drops to the 'off' position and pleases the driver who has the train moving nicely. Sometimes the signal stays at danger and the train has to stop which means that the crew has to get it rolling again. As it is we can go out on to the down main and settle down for a steady run.

We rumble under the bridge and through Lea Bridge station. The starting signal gives the all clear and the yellow fish tailed distant signal underneath it also hangs in the diagonal position. This means we have a clear run to the starting signal at the next station which is Tottenham. With the train well on the move the driver leaves the regulator at first port and winds the reversing wheel up from full forward to about 15 per cent off mid-gear. This is known as 15 per cent cut off. Our run is over a straight track with a very small rising gradient as far as Tottenham. Ideal running conditions and not one that calls for heavy use of steam.

The use of the reversing wheel in driving is the key to the perfect driver. Some forgot it was there and we called them 'bashers', for that was all they could be classed after seeing a proficient driver at work. The reversing wheel or lever not only changed the direction of travel but controlled the input of steam into the steam chest which, in turn, fed the cylinders. With the wheel full forward and the regulator at first port the cylinder was receiving maximum steam at first port working. This called for heavy use of steam supply, especially with wet steamers like the 'J15'. Once the train was on the run at the required speed, steam could be conserved by winding the reversing wheel towards mid-gear.

As it is with our train, my driver has left the regulator at first port and wound the gear wheel back to 15 per cent cut-off. This means that only 15 per cent of the first port supply of steam is being used to keep the train on the move. This gives the fireman 85 per cent of steam to play with for feeding the boiler with fresh water or for running a lighter fire as not so much steam is needed.

There is one great difference between driving a steam locomotive and a motor vehicle. Although the reversing wheel is known as the gear wheel, there are no gears on steam engines in the sense that cars have gears. The only thing the gear wheel or lever does on a steam engine is to place the steam inlet valves in the steam chest in such a position that, when steam is applied, the engine moves in the direction required. Having done that the wheel or lever is then used to control the amount of steam being supplied to the steam chest to keep the engine moving. The art of driving steam engines is the use of the supply of steam when required combined with the use of down gradients to 'roll' with speed or travel without any momentum being supplied by the engine. With both passenger and freight trains it is possible to run for miles without any steam being used when going down hill. It all depends on the gradient, the placement of signals, the make-up of the train and the driver's ability to use all three to his advantage.

One thing the raw recruit soon learns is to estimate speed and time. It was not until 1942 that the Stratford loco. depot saw its first engine with a speedometer. Through the war years trains ran on speeds judged by the driver as being the necessary speed to maintain timetables and it was surprising how proficient they were, especially on the 'Jazz' working where suburban trains were timetabled to stop and start at stations with only 30 second margins.

Crews attained an inbuilt sense of rhythm and the beat of the wheels over rail joints would often tell if section time was being maintained. For the stickler for detail there were always the mileage pegs alongside the track every quarter of a mile. With simple mathematics the driver could soon work out his speed over a given section with a combination of pocket watch and mileage pegs.

To the average passenger they meant nothing, the small white posts in the grass with two sides showing 1/4 then 1/2 then 3/4 and finally 5 or whatever mile it was from the London terminus. Supplementary to them were the other small white posts that had wooden arms each side, sometimes level, sometimes pointing upwards, at other times pointing down. They would have numbers on, in black paint against the white background, such as 200 on one arm and 90 on the other. These were gradient pegs and this example told the driver that he was leaving an incline of 1 in 200 to approach a climb of 1 in 90.

None of this worried us on the Ponders End local goods, now chuffing along at a steady 20 miles an hour. As we neared Tottenham station my driver shut the regulator and pulled the blower on to keep the smoke and fumes out of the cab. He had seen the station's advanced starter off but the distant signal was at caution. This meant that the Northumberland Park home signal was at danger and we might have to stop. No doubt an early morning freight train was leaving the marshalling yard at the Park and cutting across our track on its way to Cambridge.

We had a good fire on and steam was plentiful. The water in the gauge glass see-sawed at about half full so I put the feed on to build up the water supply in the boiler while the driver was not using the steam. The handle controlling the water supply from the tender was behind me on the seat. A simple lever that swung towards the boiler for on and towards the cab wall for off. I put it about halfway. When the water was running from the overflow pipe under the cab steps I opened the steam injector valve on the boiler front. The steam hit the flowing water, sending it in a spurting jet to about 20 feet from the train. This was one of the reasons why firemen had to pick the places where they put the boiler feed on. If it were done when passing a permanent way gang they would be soaked with water. Many a guard has had a bootful due to the lax working by inattentive firemen.

I have too much water so I work the water lever back and suddenly get that characteristic singing sound as water and steam combine in the right proportions to force fresh water into the boiler through the clack valve, usually just in front of the smokebox. The water flows into the boiler and the overflow pipe no longer runs onto the track.

The train is checked to about five miles an hour and we can feel the trucks pushing into us. The home signal drops to all clear and we can roll towards the starter, about a quarter of a mile away. The steam brake is released and the train pushes us forward again. The track is fairly level now so I do not need a big fire.

Apart from knowing the needs of the engine it is essential that the crews know the lines on which they are working. Such knowledge saves a lot of hard work and is invaluable in foggy weather, or at night time. 'Knowing the road' it is called and all drivers have to sign a work sheet at their depots to advise loco. foremen and other loco. running supervisory grades about the lines over which they have a good working knowledge and on which they could run a train without the need of a pilot.

The railway companies attached great importance to this and it was not infrequent that, if a driver had a spare shift and there was no great immediate demand for his time, he would be rostered for the week to travel on the footplate with other crews over lines that he did not know. This gave him greater scope for driving and also helped the locomotive depot to have staff that could be used anywhere at any time.

It proved to be invaluable during the war when many trains were worked over territories recognised as 'foreign' to many drivers in peace time. With such knowledge crews could relieve war equipment trains crossing from one company line to another, without the need for railway management to supply pilot drivers or relief crews.

Chapter Fifteen

Knowing the Road

Knowing the road not only covered the position of signals over some 200 miles of track. It meant knowing the gradients, the speed restrictions, road crossings protected by gates operated by signalmen and unattended road crossings in the country; the length of tunnels, the proximity of sidings and the length of platforms when running in with passenger trains.

Apart from the suburban sections being modernised before the war, most of the eastern region of the LNER, once the proud Great Eastern Railway, still relied on the old semaphore signalling system created a century before. The semaphore arm, with its red facing surface and white back surface and the red and green light given by the paraffin burner glowing through the coloured glass aspect at night, was the simple apparatus which controlled the iron horses of the steam era from Queen Victoria's time to the dark days of Hitler. Ironically, the tall old semaphore signal post of solid pine or latticed steel would still tower above the track after a 1,000 lb. high explosive bomb had blasted a hole in the track big enough to take an engine and two coaches.

The basic pattern of signalling with semaphore signals had the signal box as the heart of the operation from which the individual area was controlled by one man on a lonely eight or twelve hour shift. The box could be on a station, at a junction controlling a station, or on its own in the country controlling a rural siding and junction complex well away from any town.

Each box had up to five signals on each up and down line to control the acceptance and departure of traffic. This was apart from any subsidiary signals connected with station and yard working.

If a driver was approaching the section controlled by the signalman ahead and found the distant signal at the all clear position, this would indicate to him that the station was clear and that the outer and inner home, starter and advanced starter were also in the all clear position. In fact he had a clear run to the next distant signal. If the train were an express passenger or through goods this knowledge was worth vital minutes.

It saved checking the speed of the train because the driver knew that he had maybe five miles of clear track. The distant signal was a vital tool in the running of fast trains. Unfortunately a lot of signalmen would not use it to its full advantage and train crews would start checking the speed of the train because the distant signal was at caution, meaning the next signal was at danger.

However, when the next signal was picked up it would be seen as all clear and also all the others. So the distant could have been lowered giving the engine crew the chance to maintain speed. Checking a freight train in that manner meant lost minutes and the job of getting 50 or more wagons on the roll again.

The distant signal was the only signal that could be passed with the semaphore arm in the position normally indicating stop. Its yellow arm indicated caution and, at night, the oil lamp would reveal either a yellow or green light.

The main reason why some signalman failed to use the distant was because of its distance from the box and the physical effort needed to pull the wire controlling it over pulleys through grass and sometimes round bends for the best part of half a mile.

Any complaints by enginemen, recorded on their running sheets, could be covered up by stating that the section ahead was not clear in time to give the distant signal the all clear aspect. There was not a lot of love lost between signalmen and engine crews. It all stemmed from the class structure on the job. Signalmen thought their pay should be higher than a driver's because of the responsibility. Management thought otherwise and made the footplate grade the highest paid in the wages group.

During fog working it was a regulation that, if detained at a stop signal for more than five minutes, the fireman had to go to the signal box and remind the signalman that the train was standing there. His physical presence in the signal box was a reminder to the signalman of the situation, just in case he forgot that he had a train standing there and accepted another one from the signalman in rear.

Most signalmen became hostile at this action, seeing it as an affront to their efficiency. They never saw it as a safety regulation which, if not carried out and reported by the same signalmen to higher authorities, would result in severe disciplinary action being taken against the train crew involved. Many times in foggy weather I have stood in a signal box for 15 or more minutes and not a word has been spoken.

On the Ponders End train we see the Northumberland Park starter drop to the all clear position and, as we rumble through the old station, there are a few early morning passengers waiting for the workers' trains. In the distance we can see the guard's van of the train that checked us outside Tottenham so we know it will be a slow trip to Ponders End, about five miles away.

I went round the box a couple of times with the shovel as my driver opens the regulator. The old girl gives a friendly chuff, chuff and the smell of hot steam mixed with a little smoke and oil from the cylinders fills the cab. It is to be a pleasant part of my life for the next few years: a special smell that crews used to get from a locomotive that was performing well and everything was happening in the right sequence.

At Ponders End the starter was at danger but the subsidiary arm was off, indicating that we were to cross the main line and enter the sidings where we would be working until our relief arrived from Stratford. After clattering across points and frogs we entered the yard, and slowly made our way down a vacant road which led to the shunting spur for the yard. The guard gives us the stop signal from his van and then goes to see the station staff. I screw the hand brake on, which stands in its tall steel pillar on the tender. My driver has had the job before and tells me we can now have a bite to eat.

It seems the guard will have his with the morning shift at the station as they work out what is to be done in the yard. They never tell the engine crews what is happening but the news works down the line, through the various crews as they get the jobs. And so it becomes common knowledge that at Ponders End you can have breakfast when you get there as they never shunt the yard much before half past six.

My diet is fairly simple, partly due to the lack of variety at home with strict government food rationing and partly because there were no amenities on locomotives to keep food. It was different for drivers. They were the boss. They made time for that which they wanted to do and so brought food according to the shift they were working. Senior firemen were also in the same position, being accepted as equals. They had served their time with the old brigade. The wartime firemen were a different generation and had to prove their worth before they could enjoy the same mateship. I couldn't be bothered with the fickleness of drivers and so always took a basic food pack.

We drop the firebox door and the warmth makes the cab as cosy as the home kitchen. The driver goes to the station and finds the inevitable kettle of hot water on the stove and returns with a fresh billy of tea. It goes down well with my hot toast in front of the engine's fire and a block of cheddar cheese.

The driver gets the firing shovel and holds it in the tender. He puts the boiler feed on and, as the boiler is filling with water he turns on the hose which is used to keep the coal dust down on the cab floor and in the tender during the journey. It is called the pep pipe. He sends the jet of scalding water into the cup of the steel shovel blade where it joins the wooden handle and scours the metal as clean as a pewter jug.

The shovel is placed in the firebox to dry. A piece of dripping is placed in the cup shaped section and soon sizzles, giving off the mouth watering smell of roast beef. He breaks an egg and fries it as though using a frying pan and then puts in a rasher of bacon, to fry to perfection on the blade. Egg and bacon, with a billy of fresh tea and toast, and the early morning sun throwing its spring sunlight on the wet coal at the back of the tender . . . what better way to live?

At about 6.30 am we hear a whistle and find the guard calling us back. It's time to get the fire going so that steam can be maintained for shunting and the fireman can have time to watch the shunting staff for hand signals. The next hour or so will be spent in a fashion similar to shunting at Temple Mills, with the exception that this will be on a much smaller scale and will be mainly making up sidings to suit customer requirements instead of making up trains. The signals are the same, the shunting procedures are the same.

By half past nine things are shipshape and the shunter puts us in the engine road, as it is called at the various country sidings. It is a dead end of the yard, usually the furthest from the station so that the smoke and ash does not affect the passengers. There is a water tank but rarely is there a pit over which the engine can stand. Here we fill the tender with water, pull the coal down and clean the fire for the next shift. The driver checks round the engine to see we have no hot axle boxes and that all the oiling points are topped up. As I clean the fire on the 'J15' I have the tender water gauge turned on so that I can see the level of the water and turn the water crane off before we flood the yard.

The gauge is a simple affair, normally on the fireman's side and fitted to the tender wall. It is a steel column about one inch in diameter and as high as the tender's water storage area with an 'L' shaped handle bent at the top. The 'L' shape fits flush to the wall of the tender when not needed. To get a water reading the column is turned towards the cab, with the L-shaped handle at right angles to the tender wall. Water comes out of drilled holes in the steel column, regularly spaced up the column. When the water is running out of all the holes the fireman knows that the tender is nearly full and has time to turn the water off before it flows over into the tender tray. This simple gauge was on all locomotives, whether tank or tender.

Coal pulled down, footplate washed down and the boiler front wiped over with the old sweat cloth and 'Little Goods' is ready for its next shift. Unfortunately not all crews worked this way and, as a relief crew, you could get onto the footplate and find it covered in ash from the cleaning of the fire and nothing done to the coal or oiling.

The bucket is filled with hot water and we wash up, wipe out the bucket and hang it back on the hook on the tender, shining like a new pin. A slow walk to the station and it is time for the train from Stratford to steam in with our relief. The grimy 'V3' tank engine grinds to a halt with its five-coach set. The 2-6-2 wheel arrangement has not seen a cleaner's rag for many a day and the vacuum ejector throws out a jet of dirty water from the stumpy chimney as the driver blows off the brakes. We wait at the end of the platform to meet the crew as they cross the track after the 'V3' pulls out with the tango beat of a three cylinder engine. We tell them the situation.

'Fire's done, tender's full. You're going to Brimsdown for coal empties.'

Sometimes there is only a driver or fireman getting off the train with the gloomy message, 'Sorry matey, there s no relief for you . . . they say they'll send someone as soon as they can . . .'

It could be the fireman failed to sign on, or that he did turn up but a more important job was waiting for a fireman and the train running section authorised the use of your relief. Whatever it was, it was back to the 'J15' to work on until a fireman appeared. It could be on the next train. It could be four hours later.

Chapter Sixteen

Trip Work with a 'J39'

It was normal to keep the same shift for the week unless the train was not a daily event, in which case you would have another shift varying about two hours either side of the 3.0 am start. This meant that for the week you would be starting a shift any time between 1.0 am and 5.0 am.

The next week in the Local Goods Link was known as the middle shift and could vary from 10.0 am to 2.0 pm. Invariably it was a shift where you would sign on at Stratford depot and then travel to some point to relieve a crew already working a train. Our rostered turn was again a diagram number, this time 753. This covered trip engine working and all the timetable tells us is that the engine was prepared on Monday morning at Stratford, went light to Temple Mills and then worked as required by traffic control.

This was the basis of 'trip' working. It was something like a spare engine which the traffic section could use when the timetable became disrupted, or the backlog of traffic was too great to hold for the next scheduled train to a certain destination.

When we sign on we ask the roster clerk for the position of our train. He has already been advised by train control in the area and we are told to go the Bishopsgate to relieve it. Our sign-on time is 11.15 am, and we are allowed 15 minutes to read notices.

This covers the variety of matters pinned in the various notice cases around the wooden walls. They range from notices concerning the replacement of a semaphore signal at Ilford by a colour light signal, speed restrictions of eight miles per hour over a bridge partly destroyed by a bomb during an air raid, to men reporting for a medical check up during the week.

Many of the notices have vital information concerning train running, and it is no good claiming no knowledge if something goes wrong because the advice is there for all to see and every crew is allocated the time to read them. It would be no good saying that you didn't know the Manor Park outer home had been moved 400 yards after passing it at danger. The memo would be in the Signalling section notice case letting all crews not only know it had happened but when it had happened.

We made our way to Stratford station and asked the staff for the next train to Liverpool Street, stopping at Bethnal Green. It had to be one from the Woodford line as trains from Gidea Park were always non-stop to Liverpool Street from Stratford. The train steamed into platform five with an eight-car set of old suburban stock headed by an 'N7' which came to a grinding halt as the Westinghouse brake grabbed the steel wheels of the carriages. The Westinghouse pump on the side of the boiler panted away noisily as it recharged the air reservoir. We got into the first coach as it saved a walk at the Green.

A shrill whistle from the guard and the train was on its way to one of London's busiest termini four miles away. The 'N7' barked busily over the complicated junctions and crossovers on the up road as the line gradually turned right towards the Bow Junction signal box. Although a large box with many levers, it was dwarfed by the Bryant & May match factory behind it.

The carriage was one of the old gas type, still to be converted to electric lighting. As black out regulations practically cut the lighting to nothing the company had not seen any great need to complete the conversion programme. Fitted with straight- back bench seats each side, taking about seven passengers each side and about six standing in each compartment, the eight-coach train would disgorge about a thousand people as the train stopped at Liverpool Street in the rush hour.

It was only 11.45 am, and the train had a light passenger load. We had a compartment to ourselves. There was a familiar smell to those trains. A mixture of stale gas, smoke from the engine as it passed the air vents in the roof and smoke from cigarettes or pipes. If you wanted some air you could lower the carriage window in the door by pulling on the solid leather strap that held the window in a closed position. It was a simple device whereby the window sat on a wooden ledge when closed. A pull on the strap took the window from the ledge and it would slide down an opening in the door, between the inside and outside linings. When it was as low as you wanted it you placed the nearest hole in the leather belt on a brass stud on the door.

In the Stratford district an open window was worse than a closed one. Through the open window would come the foul stench from soap factories, fertilizer manufacturers and chemical plants. It was always recognised that even at night in a fog you would know you were approaching Stratford by the smell. In addition to that, being in the first carriage, small particles of ash would come in from the engine as the driver used second port and 45 per cent cut-off to get the train moving at the required timetable speed over the Stratford to Coborn Road section which was on a steady climb.

About nine minutes later we stopped at Bethnal Green. As we left the carriage the 'N7' blew off at the Ross safety valves and a fine spray of water drifted down on us. The fireman grinned and my mate put his head in the cab to remonstrate good-naturedly with the driver.

In front of them is the cavernous approach to Liverpool Street's 18 platforms. Six sets of shining steel ribbons wound down the gradient that disappeared into the smoke blackened viaducts, giving the impression that they were driving into the gates of hell itself. Daylight disappears as high walls encase the whole scene and no sun will shine again on the trains until they stop under the smoky glass canopy of the terminus nearly a mile ahead.

Bishopsgate Goods Yard ran over the top of the outlet from Liverpool Street and so the run to and from the terminus was practically like working underground. We crossed the up and down main lines after keeping a watchful eye on signals and trains. It was easy to get knocked over in that area. At any time of the day or night each track could be occupied by a train going in either direction.

When we crossed the lines we were in Spitalfields Yard, at the eastern end of Bishopsgate. Spitalfields handled most of the mineral freight for that part of London. Bishopsgate was a gigantic goods shed and yard which handled various goods as well as perishables for the London markets. Much of Scotland's whisky also came to Bishopsgate as it was also a Customs yard where Customs officers were on duty at all times to check the loads for Customs clearance before unloading. Due to this, Bishopsgate was also the main centre for intercontinental freight between Europe and England but that lucrative part of the Great Eastern's traffic ceased when the war started.

After walking the length of Spitalfields Yard we found our engine taking water on the road next to the viaduct wall over which, and about 50 ft below, were the tracks feeding Liverpool Street station. Our engine this time was quite modern, a 'J39' 0-6-0 mixed traffic locomotive with 5 ft 2 in. diameter driving wheels. The first 'J39' rolled off the production line in 1926 and the last one was built in 1941.

Altogether 289 were built and they proved to be a good engine for their task. Not too many ran on passenger trains, except at rush periods like public holidays, and also on troop trains. I had fired on them on evacuation trains from London to the country districts, taking children from the bombed areas.

Once again, this old work horse had not seen the cleaner's rag for many a long day. Just a drab black covering of paint, a smokebox showing rust for the want of some smokebox jelly and the numbers on the cab wall just about showing through the grime. 3090 was the engine number for the driver's sheets and guard's journal.

The crew told us they had filled up with water, oiled up and cleaned the fire. The fireman told me to watch the right-hand injector as the clack valve was sticking, otherwise 'she's not a bad old tub'. The driver told my mate that we were working a train of fish empties to Goodmayes. Often looked upon as a light load, empty wagons were sometimes worse to pull than loaded wagons, especially if there was a high wind, side on. The effect was very much like a brake dragging and instead of rolling down hill they had to be pulled every yard of the way.

The cab of the Standard, as we called the 'J39', was very different from the 'J15'. With bigger driving wheels the engine was higher above the track and the tender had sides that nearly equalled the height of the cab roof, whereas the tender of the 'J15' was low. On the 'J15' you could stand in the cab and look over the top of the tender. With the Standard the only way to see beyond the tender was to lean out of the cab window. Another restriction was the space between the tender and the boiler front. The two areas were much closer and called for greater firing skills in getting the force needed to propel the coal to a given spot in the box with less room to swing the arm.

Where the movement was mainly on a horizontal plane on the 'J15', from tender shovelling plate to firebox door, with the fireman working in that arc, the Standard called for a more upright stance. The fireman would push the blade into the coal in the tender then straighten slightly as he pulled it out. As he started the arc towards the firebox door he would have the shovel on a diagonal plane, with the top of the handle about level with his shoulder and the blade near the midriff. He would then turn to the boiler front and continue the downward arc until the blade entered the firebox door.

A problem for many fireman was that the 'J39' was left-handed firing through a trapdoor in the main firebox door. This was one of the improvements in loco. design over the course of time. Most engines, like the 'Little Goods', had the driver on the right-hand side. This meant that firing was also right-handed and, as most people were right-handed, this fell into the accepted pattern of things. It also meant that there were many times when the fireman would be occupied with his work at the same time as the driver needed him to be on the lookout for signals.

This especially applied on passenger trains where platforms were mainly on the left-hand side of the train. When standing at the station the fireman made the most of the opportunity to fill the boiler, judge his fire for the journey, damp down the coal in the bunker, sweep the floor and check the lubricators. This could not be done while he was waiting for the station staff to give him the right-away signal.

With the switch on later designed locomotives the driver was placed on the side where he could see the station staff at all times while the fireman could attend to his work without worrying about missing a hand signal. Such was the tightness of train running with passenger trains that lost time was religiously booked against those who caused the delay. If a train were allocated a one minute stop and it extended to two minutes the signalman would book it against the train crew.

The guard of the train in turn, would book it against the main cause which could be engine crew failing to acknowledge his right-away signal in time, or the station staff failing to have the train in a safe condition for departure in the given time. If the engine crew were logged then there would be a report required by the next shift, with appropriate disciplinary action if the happening occurred too often.

Contrary to the opinion of passengers, time was a controlling factor on the LNER when things were normal and even the loss of a minute in section time was frowned upon, unless it was made up by the end of the journey. During the war freight took preference and it was quite normal on the main line for trains to be running more than an hour late.

Chapter Seventeen

The Ups and Downs

The boiler of the 'J39' was much bigger than the 'J15' and had a pressure of 180 1b. It had Ross safety valves which gave most people a shock when they blew off. They only worked when pressure was in excess of 180 1b. and then released the surplus steam with a shattering roar. They stopped just as suddenly. This was much more noisy than the old Ramsbottom safety valves on the wet steamers. They would start to whimper as soon as maximum pressure was reached and grow in force as the pressure grew.

To the fireman this was a very comforting sound on the run. To hear the regular beat of the engine as it hauled its load of freight wagons at a steady 25 mph, interspersed with the white feather, as we called it, escaping from the Ramsbottom safety valves and the singing of the injector as water was forced into the boiler meant that you were on top of the world.

Due to the size of the boiler and standard engine dimensions the 'J39' had a stumpy chimney compared with the long neck of the 'Little Goods'. It was known as the flower pot chimney. The firebox was about the same size as the 'J15' but much deeper. The main door was a heavy, oval affair in solid steel. It clamped to the boiler front with a steel bar that dropped into a bracket at the base on the fireman's side. It was hinged on the driver's side and most of them had a protective metal shield that also swung from the driver's side and clipped to the fireman's side.

The only time the main door was open was when the fire was being made up at the start of the journey, or being cleaned. It was too hot to work with it open on the run. In the centre of the main door was a trap door through which the fireman had to fire-up on the run. The trap door was nearly the width of the main door and, at its deepest section, was about eight inches deep. It was something like a half oval. Through this aperture the fireman had to get the blade of the shovel with the coals on it for the fire. This meant that coal in the tender of the 'J39' always had to be broken to a set size or the fireman was in trouble.

It was not a comfortable engine on which to spend eight or more hours. The cab was not large enough for bench type seats. It had, instead, swivel seats on single leg stands and wooden arm rests on the window ledge. The forward view was restricted due to the boiler size. The best view was gained by leaning out of the window. This exposed the crew to hot ashes from the smokebox and the risk of being struck by objects near to the track.

The Bishopsgate Yard was restricted in size and traffic had outgrown all the ideas of the original planners. The road on which we stood ran on to the down outlet road, which was also the shunting spur for the North Side. To protect movement over those lines, in between the fixed section signals operated by the signal box that was perched high above the yards and halfway between Spitalfields Yard and Bishopsgate, there were little ground signals which we called 'dods'. Some railways called them 'dollies'.

The dod had the normal oil container that sat behind the signal on a semaphore post but, in this instance, it was bolted to the ground. In front of the lamp was a circular disc which had a hole at the top to allow for the coloured lenses that would give the red and green lights at night. For day work the disc usually had a white face with a red stripe painted horizontally across the face. Danger was indicated by the red line being horizontal and the all clear was shown by the line being diagonal.

A whistle came from the crossing man as he gave us the signal to leave the engine road. The dod was off and we eased the 'J39' down to the points. The Standard's inside motions clanked through their full circle and, as it was down hill to the starter, the engine soon answered the call of gravity. The shunter stopped us clear of the points. Rods slid over rusty guide wheels and the signal wire became taut in the stunted grass as the signalman set the road for us to reverse to the South Side for our train.

This was where the advantage of left-hand firing came in. My driver could see all that was going on as the shunters were his side. I could devote all my time to making up the fire which was fairly light because we never knew when the train would be ready. Being a trip engine we had no timetable and had to be fitted in with regular traffic.

I opened the big door and began placing large lumps under the door of the firebox. Golden flames soon began greedily to lick round the shiny lumps and it was appreciably warmer on the legs and arms as the heat intensified. My mate applied the steam brake in short bursts which meant that he was warming up the cylinder as well as getting ready for the final stop. Instinct told me that the leading wagon would be about 20 yards away.

Now for the old routine. One shovel to the right front, one to the left front, one under the brick arch, two up the sides. There was a musical clang as buffers met and the engine momentarily stopped. Coal rumbled down the tender towards the door as the nudge had dislodged it from the back. Someone called out for an 'ease up' and the driver gave the 'J39' a little more steam as we pushed the trucks together. I gave the blower a little more power as the smoke from the fresh coals was getting thicker. The added draught turned the dull orange, smoky flames to a bright gold and there was a faint haze round the stumpy chimney.

The needle on the steam pressure gauge was 30 pounds off the red line for full pressure. I shut the big door and pushed the trap door open with the shovel blade so that the semi-circular opening would let the air in. This helped eliminate the smoke from the chimney and turned the fumes into combustible gas. There was a ratchet type catch which came out from the top of the main door and its teeth enabled the fireman to regulate the angle of the trap door through to the 90 degrees as I had it. The catch on our 'J39' was well and truly worn and the only way to wedge it open was to find a suitable lump of coal and lodge it in the gap with the hammer.

By the time the guard had checked his train and told the driver that we were 'right away' to Goodmayes without intermediate shunts, the steam gauge needle was flickering near the 180. My driver gave the regulator a yank. They varied on Standards. Ours was something like butterfly wings in its angle to the boiler. Where it was bolted to the control rod in the centre of the boiler could be seen as the back of the butterfly. The steel handle was round and equal in length on both sides of the centre. This enabled the driver to operate the regulator from either side of the cab if required. We called them the butterfly regulator.

As he opened first port the snifter valve on the boiler, just behind the chimney, gave its characteristic 'phup' and closed to exclude the air that had been circulating round the superheater tubes. The 'J39' was superheated and so we had what we called dry steam, compared with the wet steam of the 'J15'. It was a system whereby steam already produced was run through smaller pipes placed in the smoke tubes of the boiler to receive extra heat and the finished product was more like a gas than steam, with greater expansion properties. Superheated engines were always more powerful than wet steamers and easier to work by way of maintaining steam pressure and water levels. This is not to say they didn't have their problems but one always seemed to cope better with a bad superheated engine than the bad wet steam engine.

We were now clanking slowly down the departure road at Spitalfields. The starter controlled by Bethnal Green was at danger as trains were coming to and from Liverpool Street on the six tracks to our left. To protect the up main, which we were approaching, there was a set of trap points. If we could not hold our load of 70 empties, and the weight of the train pushed us past the signal, the trap points would derail the engine and stop us from running across the path of the oncoming trains.

As we stood at the semaphore signal an East Anglian express glided round the corner from the eastern end of Bethnal Green station and, clattering over the points and crossings, rolled towards the terminus with its assorted 12 coaches, all packed with civilians and service personnel from the garrisons of the Home Counties. On the down Cambridge line a 'B1' barked its purposeful way up the 1 in 70 incline with an eight-coach train for Cambridge, its siderods clanging rhythmically as the 220 1b. of steam thrust the silver pistons in and out of the outside cylinders. They were a beautiful engine in action, their 6 ft 2 in. driving wheels rarely slipping when starting with full loads. With their sleek black bodies they were the latest thing and they literally ran like the South African antelopes after which they were named.

The 'up' and 'down' definitions on the LNER had nothing to do with the gradient of the tracks. All lines leading to London were up lines. All lines going away from London were down lines. We were on the Spitalfields down departure road, waiting to get on to the down main for Goodmayes, which was about nine miles away.

Why run a train of 70 wagons for only nine miles? It has to be remembered that thousands of wagons were moving every day and all major freight trains ran to and from major marshalling yards. Those yards were fed by smaller trains, such as the Local Goods Link. They could work in between the normal day trains that fed the main terminus with passenger traffic. This was full utilisation of track and equipment.

Goodmayes was the major marshalling yard on the line from London and was situated about two miles from Ilford, a town in which 45,000 of its 46,630 houses were damaged by German air raids during the war. Most of the bombs were meant for the railway and the goods yard. Ilford was also the junction for the Ilford to Woodford loop via Fairlop. It was a line predominantly involved with suburban passenger work although a local goods serviced the stations on the loop line. It linked the east coast line with the Epping and Ongar branch line.

Our starter was pulled to the 'off' position and we began to rumble forward over the brick arches of the viaduct on which we stood. It was a gradual downhill run to Stratford and so there was no great demand for steam. Regulator at first port and reversing wheel at 15 per cent cut-off kept us rolling nicely towards Coborn Road station. The train made a hollow rumble as we crossed the viaduct over the ground level shunting yards at Devonshire Street, which crossed under the main and suburban tracks. We could see the small 0-4-0 tank class 'Y4', bumping its way round the yard on tight curves.

The run from Spitalfields to Stratford is either over brick viaducts, road bridges or brick-flanked embankments with smoke-grimed terraced houses on either side. It is not until we reach Stratford that we really get to ground level. At Bow Junction we were switched to the down suburban line. Bow Junction gantry had to be seen to be believed. It was one mass of timber masts straddling all the running roads. The masts varied in height, carrying a multitude of semaphore arms that controlled the traffic over eight to ten tracks, into which came the Fenchurch Street branch line to our right. There were the up and down main, up and down suburban, up and down Epping lines, up and down goods lines and up and down carriage roads. The latter fed the major carriage siding at Stratford station with empty carriage stock from Liverpool Street to form all the main line trains.

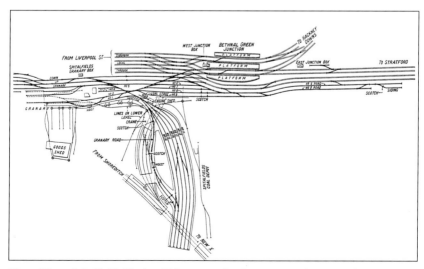

Plan of lines, Spitalfields Yard to Bishopsgate Goods station yard. *Railway Magazine*

Chapter Eighteen

The New Electric Signals

The trip to Goodmayes took us through a hotchpotch of signalling systems. Due to the war a signalling system that had been planned to improve the efficiency of the Liverpool Street to Shenfield suburban service had to be abandoned. It was the first thing to be restarted when the war ended. It was an electric signalling system which did away with the old semaphore arm and replaced it with a steel post on which was a signal similar to today's traffic lights. It was known as the four aspect colour light signalling system and proved to be the best system devised to keep a traffic intensive suburban service moving, even in the most adverse weather conditions.

The four-aspect signals installed by the LNER had four seperate lenses: from top to bottom they were green, yellow, red, yellow. With the exception of the two yellows there was only one light showing at any time. If no lights were showing when the train approached the signal it was accepted that the signal was at danger. All signals had telephones so that train crews could contact the signalman and check the situation. The colour light signals were placed at about cab height and no longer way up in the sky to be invisible on foggy days.

Red naturally meant stop. One yellow meant be prepared to stop at the next signal. Two yellows meant be prepared to stop at the second signal ahead, and green meant that the train had at least three clear sections ahead. This type of working would keep trains moving where, under the old system, they would stop and start many times. This lost time and momentum in speed.

The electric signals were spaced about 400 yards apart between stations. I have known trains to keep moving on two or one yellow through the thickest fog and lose no time. Before that we would creep up to a semaphore signal and, even knowing where it was, could not see what its position was because the arm could be some 25 feet in the air. The fireman would have to climb the ladder which was built with every signal post to find out if the arm was in the all clear position or at danger. He would then tell the driver.

The colour light system stopped all that and really speeded up the train service. We in the local goods appreciated the move as we could keep a train rolling for miles on one yellow whereas, under the old scheme of things, it was stop and start all the time. This was quite an effort with the old grease boxes on freight trains.

At Goodmayes we ran into the reception road at the bottom of the hump yard and were released by a shunter, to be placed on the down yard engine road. As I put the water bag into the tender and pulled the coal forward my driver went to make a billy of tea and find out about our next job. It was a return trip to Temple Mills with mixed freight and we were to leave about three that afternoon, before the rush hour started. My driver told Control that the 'J39' was very low in coal and we would be requiring coal at the Mills before we could go anywhere.

This trip was to be tender first which made things awkward from our point of view. You could not see over a 'J39' tender. It was a case of leaning out of the cab window all the time you were on the move. The coal dust blew back no matter how much you watered it down and, when firing up, the wind would rush through the tender opening and blow dust into your eyes. Also, when working tender first, the steel rubbing plates between tender and cab seemed to buck more than when running engine first. This meant that the fireman had to stand with legs apart, balanced for the swing of the shovel from left to right into the eight inch trap door. One leg would be riding up on the tender flap as the engine hit the rail joints, while the other leg would be moving with the different motion caused by the engine's driving wheels hitting the same joint seconds later. It felt like trying to fire up on a floor of jelly. The best way out was to push your backside tight against the swivel seat and just move the torso if possible.

The previous fireman had been right about the trouble with the right hand clack box. Clack box was the name given to the valve that sat on top of the intake pipe which fed the boiler with fresh water and was usually found on the side of the boiler near the smokebox. As the mixture of water and steam forced its way into the boiler through the injector so the clack would rise to let it in. When the injector was turned off the clack valve came down and sat on its seating under the pressure of the steam and water in the boiler.

Sometimes a piece of scale from the boiler would stick under the valve and, when the valve came down on its seating, there would be a slight gap through which water and steam from the boiler would escape and run out through the injector waste water pipe under the cab steps. As I turned the steam cock off on the Standard, instead of waste water flowing down the pipe there came the roar of high pressure steam forcing its way through the clack valve. This was not so bad when you were standing still as you could correct it but, on the run, it could be a major problem.

It sometimes meant walking along the footplate to hit the clack box with the hammer and so try to move the piece of scale that was causing all the trouble. Not always the best thing to do at 60 miles an hour. It was not expected of you under the rules but, if you stopped and lost time there was the inevitable inquiry and the engine was never at fault, according to the engineers.

The roaring steam, accompanied with water, soon emptied the boiler if not checked and, if the intake pipe became too hot, there was also a problem in getting cold water to flow up it. The best method was to turn the water control lever on from the tender then, when it checked the flow of the steam from the boiler, open the steam cock to work the injector as normal. When the injector took up the water we would let it work for a while then, instead of turning off the steam first as was the normal practice, we would shut off the water valve. This would cause the steam to roar through the open clack valve and, hopefully, blow out the offending piece of scale. The steam valve was then turned off sharply. With a bit of luck the problem was solved but, if the engine was in a desperate need for a washout, the shift could be a nightmare with the clack sticking every time the feed was used.

We crossed to the up yard and backed on to a mixed train of canned foods, gravel, steel and empty petrol tankers. The trip back to Temple Mills was on the up through till we reached the outer home for Manor Park. We were then switched to the up local so we could pick up the line that led us to the Channelsea curve from Stratford junction. It was a steady pull all the way and hard work as the coal in the tender was getting low and we were starting to get into the rubbish and dust that was found at the back of every tender after using the coal that would be used on a normal shift.

The train was pulling heavily as we had quite a few grease boxes on. These were wagons from the good old days of private company work. The axle boxes were packed solid with a kind of tallow for lubrication, compared with the more modern wagons of the time that had axle boxes lubricated with oil soaking a pad of worsted wool packing. Today the roller bearing replaces both of them. Grease boxes were known to stop in their tracks on a downhill shunt!

A look round the firebox showed that the fire was starting to cake with the dirt and dust. This was not good news as the last thing I wanted to do was use the pricker off the tender in the restricted area of the cab. My driver looked in and gave a knowing nod. He shut the trap door in the main firebox door and yanked the regulator open to second port. Then he let the reversing wheel out to full forward.

The old girl did a shudder in her tracks and then really barked out exhaust through the stumpy chimney. The smoke was as black as pitch but going up straight like a rocket. In between the cement walls of the cutting the exhaust barked with a deafening and dramatic impact. It sounded like the 'Flying Scotsman' punching its way out of Kings Cross with a 12-coach train.

The train gained in momentum and we went through Manor Park station at about 30 miles an hour, instead of the steady 20 miles an hour. Steam pressure had dropped back to 150 and the water swayed around the half way mark in the gauge glass. The Forest Gate distant was at caution. My driver pulled the blower on hard, shut off and let the train roll. I opened the trap door a fraction to clear the smoke and put the boiler feed on. A look at the fire showed that the tactic had worked. The fire was white hot and the steam pressure needle was creeping to the 180 mark even though I had the feed on. Siderods clanked on their revolutions as worn bushes allowed more than the necessary play. My driver stepped over.

'They're like women, lad. If they play up, treat 'em rough, then you'll get the best out of 'em!'

We coasted into Stratford station as the starter was at danger at the end of platform three. This was not unexpected because we had to cross six sets of tracks to get to the Channelsea curve which took us round the back of the Stratford complex of running sheds, repair shops, storage yards, carriage sheds and coal yards. The loop was also a vital connection with the LMS which went through north London and was the main link between the east coast and the major marshalling yard at Willesden Junction.

A 'B17' 'Football' class was slowly making its way up the carriage road with a set of cars for one of the evening country expresses. It, in turn, would work one down later that night. The nameplate over the central driving wheel glistened in the afternoon sun where cleaners had rubbed it with loving care. The brass replica of a soccer ball sat under the semi-circle of brass lettering which said *Manchester City* against a background of the club's colours.

A busy little 'Gobbler' clattered over the maze of crossovers and screeched to a stop on the down Epping platform with its eight-coach set. The starter dropped on the gantry and it was our turn. This would be the testing time. The wait at the station had given me time to whip a bit of dust and pieces of coal round the firebox to maintain the heat we had raised. There was no smoke now, just hot gases in a faint blue haze round the chimney.

Starting from the up local at Stratford was a problem any time. It was on a rising gradient and curved slowly to the left and right, depending where you were going. It criss-crossed over tracks that seemed to lead everywhere and it was on these rising curves that engines would lose their grip. We were tender-first which didn't help matters as most tenders dripped water from somewhere. It could be the catchment tray on the back or a leaking connecting pipe between engine and tender. It could even be a seam on the tender that had weakened and needed the welder's torch. Whatever the cause, that dripping water would turn dry rails into a slippery surface for us.

The couplings jerked to attention as the Standard answered the call of the open regulator. The driver felt that the whole train was stretched out and that all the couplings had taken the strain so he gave the cylinders full first port. We moved off nicely with a crisp, regulated beat. Then we began to cross the down suburban and the up Epping lines. The changing curves and dripping water on the rail surface was more than the 'J39' could take. The 5 ft 2 in. driving wheels began to slip madly on the greasy rails and the regulated beat from the flowerpot chimney became an uncontrolled roar. The engine rocked from side to side on one spot and the trucks ran into our rear buffer beam.

My driver immediately shut the regulator and, as the wheels came to a halt, I applied the rear sanders and hoped they were working. The regulator was eased open and we crept forward. I leaned out of the cab side and saw the sand running on to the rails. The 'J39' gladly gripped the rough surface and my driver gave her more steam. He told me to leave the sand running.

'If they like to give us a load like this, tender first, they can answer the consequences,' he said.

He was referring to the fact that, under the regulations, sand was not allowed to be used when working over points as it could damage the slide plates over which the point blades slipped into position. But we were in a predicament. Use no sand and slip and slide across six sets of running tracks, taking about ten minutes and holding up other traffic, or use the sand and get out of the way in section time. That was what my driver would tell them, if a report was needed following some ganger's complaint that we had used sand on his points.

There was no more trouble and we coasted round the Stratford works toward the Leyton signal box. As expected, the calling-on arm was off, letting us in to one of the Temple Mills reception roads. This was where goods trains lined up, waiting their turn to get into the marshalling yard. As we rumbled under the Temple Mill Lane bridge my mate gave a low whistle.

'We'll be here all night mate!,' he said.

In front of us was another goods train and the second reception road was also full. Things were 'on the block' as we would say. We rolled slowly toward the guard's van of the train in front and stopped. It was just a case of sitting it out and waiting for our relief.

This was quite a normal situation for crews on local goods trains and they had many ingenious ways of making the best use of their time in reception roads. The biggest hold up was usually at night, especially during the air raids. To save having to sit and keep a lookout all the time, to see if the train in front had moved up in the dark, the crew of the train behind the leading train would tie their front coupling to the rear coupling of the guard's van. As the train moved off, sometimes so quietly you'd never hear it, the string would break and the coupling would clatter on to the steel buffer beam of the engine. This allowed the crew of the rear train to stretch out on the bench seats and have a doze while they waited. If the shift had been about 10 hours on the shovel you were glad of the snooze.

This wouldn't work if you were on the leading train, standing at the outlet signal. The practice in this situation was to stop the train just level with the signal post. The fireman would then climb up the ladder on the post and hang an empty bucket on the semaphore arm. As the arm dropped to the all clear position the bucket would slide off, landing with a loud clatter that would wake any sleeping crew. These little tricks were very helpful on long shifts but they were not a lot of use with an engine such as ours. You couldn't get very comfortable on the swivel seat of the 'J39'.

About an hour after we had entered the reception road the train in front moved up and we followed as far as the outlet signal which was now at danger. By this time the sun was well below the horizon, not that you could see the skyline from the Temple Mills yard. Nothing but railway wagons all around you on the left hand side of the goods road. Over towards Leyton the yards disappeared into houses and buildings that climbed the hill leading towards the town itself.

I climbed down and went to the front of the engine and lit the oil headlamp. It was on the bracket over the front left-hand buffer, indicating that we were a slow goods. Slow was the operative word that day! Three hours since we left Goodmayes, some nine miles away, and still had to get into the yard. Not that this was so unusual during the war. So much traffic was on the move with so few crews to move it that things were stretched to the limit. Our eight hours were nearly up and we hoped that relief was on the way. We would find out when we got to the yard.

Back in the cab I lit the other lamps in case we needed them and also hung the gauge lamp on the boiler, its mellow rape oil light glowing through the thick glass shield which protected the gauge glass itself. The fire was kept going to the minimum degree. We had to have enough steam available to pull the train into the yard but not that much that the safety valves would keep popping and wasting water.

Twilight had turned to darkness when the reception road signal gave us the green light for the South Yard. At the same time the air raid sirens gave the wail of the first alert for the night. I rolled down the blackout sheet from the cab roof which clipped or tied to the front of the tender. We left the side curtains for a while as we would not be making much light. The fire was sufficient to get us

'N7/1' class 0-6-2T No. 971, one of 20 built by Robert Stephenson & Co. in 1925/26, seen at Stratford on 21st March, 1936. It still retains its condensing gear and carries an Ilford headboard. No. 993, a 1924 Stratford built example stands behind. *F.M. Gates*

Class 'F4' and 'F5' engines at Grouping were largely employed on London suburban trains, until displaced by 'N7s'. 'F4' class No. 7219, built in 1907, is one of those sent to the country districts and is seen at Colchester shed during the late 1930s. It was withdrawn as No. 67163 in December 1951. *Lyn Brooks Collection*

This photograph of class 'J17' 0-6-0 No. 8153 was taken at Stratford to show the arrangement of the anti-glare screens for tender engines, made out of old wagon tarpaulins, March 1939.

British Railways

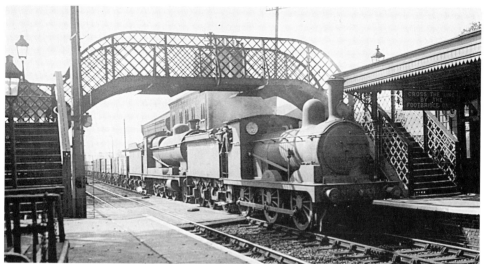

A down train of coal empties from Temple Mills passes through Stansted on its way to Whitemoor during the 1930s, headed by ex-GER 'J15' 0-6-0 No. 7851 and ex-GCR 'O4' class 2-8-0 No. 6251. Class '04s' were allowed to work along the Cambridge main line to Temple Mills from 1930 onwards. No. 6251 was sold to the War Department in October 1941 but the 'J15' was withdrawn at the relatively early date of October 1936. *N. Shepherd*

Stratford station, looking east towards Forest Gate. From left the lines are down suburban, up suburban, down main, up main. The other lines are associated with the goods road coming from Stratford Low Level and the goods yard. The signal gantry covers up and down main line working. The signals with the black bars on a white background show that we are looking at the rear side. The signal being cleaned by porters is the down main starter with the Maryland Point distant below it. From the left hand side, the up main signals read: up main to Channelsea Curve, up main to up suburban, up main with Bow Junction distant, up main to No. 1 platform, Stratford, up main to Stratford Low Level. The lone signal on the right is from goods road to Stratford Low Level. Although this photograph was taken in 1936 the scene never changed during the war, except for the loss of some buildings due to air raids. *British Railways*

The start of clearing up, following a direct hit on the front portion of the Jubilee running shed on 30th September, 1940. *British Railways*

A view of Stratford railway workshops from the Low Level line near the Fork Junction box, February 1941. The buildings in the background are the paint shops. 'N7' No. 2640 is in the foreground with a slice just visible on top of the tank. The wagon in front of the engine is a typical 10-ton capacity open wagon. *BR/OPC Joint Venture*

The main erecting shop was in the Old Works, accessible through the arch in the Locomotive Department offices. It had bays on either side; one dealt with side and tender tanks and was provided with a 2 ton gantry crane. This view is taken from the store which was located above part of the bay. The damage seen here in this April 1941 view has been cause by a gantry crane from the adjoining boiler shop dropping through the roof. *British Railways*

A view taken on 9th October, 1940 from outside the carriage department lavatories situated at the end of the carriage lifting shops, looking towards High Meads carriage paint shops, which can be seen in the background. The signal gantry spans the old Cambridge main line. The carriage remains are those of M&GN 6-wheel luggage brake, No. 84998, built at Melton Constable in 1924. *British Railways*

The boiler shop was within the Old Works, close to Angel Lane and adjoining the main erecting shop. In April 1941 it received a direct hit, the roof being completely destroyed. Here complete chaos reigns, the force of the explosion damaged eight adjoining shops but these were brought quickly back into production. *British Railways*

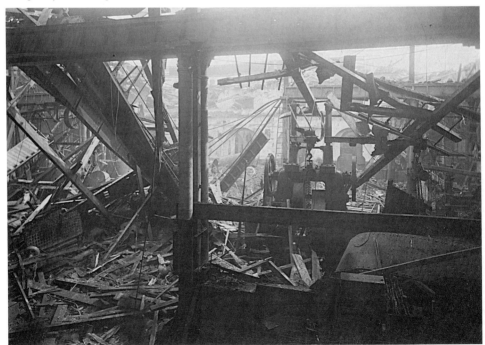

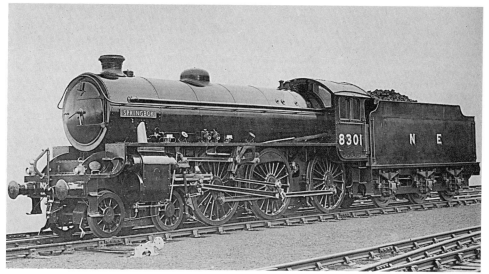

A posed official view of 'B1' class 4-6-0 No. 8301 *Springbok* of the 'Antelope' class as completed by the LNER at Doncaster at the end of 1942, in wartime livery with the abbreviated lettering 'NE'. In all 410 'B1s' were built, the last appearing in 1950. Eight of the first 10 were allocated to the GE Section, another 20 came in 1946 after production had got under way, handling all the principal express trains between Liverpool Street and Norwich.   *British Railways*

The day after the accident described in Chapter 33. 'B12' No. 8580 lies in the crater with the train on top, about 1 mile north east of Shenfield on the Ipswich main line . The crater was more than ten feet deep, 4th March, 1943.   *BR/OPC Joint Venture*

The wrecked cab of No. 8580 showing silent witness to the driver's attempt to stop. The regulator is shut and the Westinghouse brake has full application. The fireman's shovel still has the store's number chalked on its blade, 4th March 1943.

BR/OPC Joint Venture

into the yard. As my driver had told traffic control that the engine needed attention before we went anywhere we knew that we would not be placed on a train straight away.

After leaving the train in the siding we went to the outlet road. The yard foreman told us that we were 'light engine' to Stratford as there was no relief. Searchlights were scanning the sky and, as we stood waiting for the signal to the up main, we could hear the drone of a Heinkel III. When your life depended on quick decisions you soon became familiar with sounds that spelt death, and the steady throb of the Heinkel was easy to pick out against the sounds of British aircraft.

Anti-aircraft guns on the Hackney Marshes behind us opened up and the immediate surroundings were lit for a fraction of a second by the explosive charges. Seconds later the muffled 'whumpf . . . whumpf' of the exploding shells would be heard thousands of feet above as angry red blobs stabbed the sky. Down toward the docks the skyline would give a bright white glare as incendiaries found their mark and the magnesium ignited on impact. The whiteness would die as a deeper golden glow would take over. The nightly battle between air raid defence forces and the Luftwaffe had begun.

Neither of us said anything but each wondered who was working in the docks area that night and whether a mate would quietly disappear from the roster sheets in the sign-on room. Our signal gave the green light. I had changed the headlamp code to one white in the middle of the front buffer, indicating to the signalman that we were engine only. My driver studied his departmental watch. We had been on duty for ten hours so it was a case of leaving the 'J39' on the disposal pits for one of the shed crews to do the necessary.

We rumbled on to the pits ten minutes later and became the fourth engine waiting attention. It wasn't only the shunting yards that had problems that night. Handbrake hard on, cocks open, reversing wheel in mid-gear, boiler nearly full. She was all right for at least an hour. Now we had to get home through the raids.

Chapter Nineteen

Working with a 'B17'

After a week of middle shifts on the trip engine we studied the roster and found that we had managed to get a Sunday off. This was because our Saturday shift didn't finish till one o'clock on the Sunday morning. Our next turn of duty was the night shift and that could start any time from eight o'clock to midnight. In the Local Goods Link we had reached the spare shift section. The supplementary list showed us on together at 11.00 pm as shed duties. Strange to say we had not been split but, as my driver said, there was a method in their madness.

By that time I was being recognised by the roster clerks as a regular fireman. They knew I had been on many lines and the experience I had gained was to their advantage. My mate was one of those young drivers who had also been through the mill and knew most roads to most places so, together, we were a good combination to have from a running shed foreman's point of view. Disposal pit duty, relief on the road, preparing suburban engines for early morning jobs and working the first shift if the regulars didn't make it . . . even to taking a 'K3' to March with coal empties if needed.

Eleven o'clock on Monday night saw us at the signing-on book. A study of the notices, a bit of a joke with the others who were coming and going and we then made our way to the crib room. The bright lights hurt our eyes at first, entering from the blacked out yard. There was no air raid warning at the moment but it could come at any time. Two or three crews sat at the plain wooden tables that were scrubbed down every day by Dan the cleaner. The room was spotlessly clean and woe betide any man who made it dirty, not only from the cleaner who was an ex-loco. man, but from any who used the room. There were not many jobs where we could sit and eat in conditions that came somewhere near those of home and we respected them. Normally it was a sandwich in a hand, a swig of tea from an enamel mug as the engine swayed and bucked over the running roads.

Talk immediately centred round the trains and the men who worked them. Had we seen old 2834 lately? How she kept on the track was anyone's guess. What d'you think of those Yankee jobs on the lease-lend scheme? Yeh, good steamers but how long are they going to last . . . I mean to say, steel stays in the boiler!

The door opened and the night foreman walked in. Another bit of light banter as he gave out the engines on the pit for disposal. He didn't give us a job as he knew there were many shifts starting in the next hour or two and we could be a handy standby for vacancies or relief. Midnight came and we were thinking of taking a walk to the canteen for a cup of tea when our job arrived. One of the major passenger trains was running three hours late. This had thrown out the engine working for early morning paper trains to the east coast, as well as crew rostering.

We were to go to the disposal pits and dispose of 2847, then get it ready for a certain diagram working from Stratford. It was working a set of main line coaching stock to Liverpool Street and then semi-express to Ipswich. We should get relieved before then by the regular shift coming on at four that morning. At least we knew we would not be sent on another job at that time of the morning. By the time we got back to Stratford it would be nearly six o clock. If the foreman was in a good mood he could allow us to knock off. It would make a welcome change to have a seven hour shift.

The engine was one of the 'B17' class that held together the Great Eastern fast passenger traffic. They looked, and were, powerful machines with their three cylinders and 6 ft 8 in. driving wheels. The 4-6-0 wheel arrangement had hauled many an express in and out of Liverpool Street and, when in tiptop condition, could easily make up lost time if things went their way. They bucked and rolled quite a bit and a pair of wheels under the cab would have made all the difference, but Gresley thought otherwise when he put the 'B17' on the drawing board. No. 2847 was one of those named after the stately homes of England. Her name was *Helmingham Hall* and it was displayed very proudly in brass on the middle driving wheel splasher.

The main difference between the 'B17' and other express passenger engines was the cylinder arrangement. There were the normal two cylinders, although they were outside the main frame and not under the smokebox like the inside motion express engines. However, under the smokebox was a third cylinder, giving the engine that extra power as well as the characteristic tango beat of the exhaust. Instead of the stately choof-choof-choof-choof of the two cylinders with the Stephenson's Link inside motions, there was the choof-choof-choof . . . choof-choof-choof of the Walschaerts gear as impressive outside combinations of connecting rods, siderods and silver pistons combined to give a graphic display of unleashed power.

But 2847 was doing none of those things. She was just standing quietly on the pit road after a good day's work and needing some attention. The gauge lamp still shone against the boiler as we climbed into the cab. A deeper tint of red came from the trap door to the firebox. The 'B17' had firebox doors similar to the 'J39', in that there was a trap door through which to fire and set into the main door. The engine was also left-hand firing, had a boiler pressure of 180lb., Ross type safety valves and the flower pot chimney which really suited her sleek lines.

An unusual feature of the engines was that they only had a vacuum brake for train working. Most passenger locomotives had the vacuum brake and the Westinghouse air brake. As the 'B17' was designed for express work only, and all main line carriages were vacuum braked, there really was no need for the Westinghouse pump. The engine had a steam brake for use when working engine only.

I lit the slush lamp and took the shovel and handbrush round to the smokebox. Usually, to get to the smokebox, one had to climb up two steel steps riveted to the main frame just in front of the buffer beam. On this occasion I could step from the cab and walk along the top of the bank of ash and clinker and step straight onto the footplate in front of the smokebox door. With the engine having 6 ft 8 in. driving wheels, this gives a good indication of the amount of ash and clinker lying around the disposal pits, thrown out by various crews during the weekend.

The whole area was supposed to be kept at ground level but, with the lack of manpower, ash just heaped up until the situation called for drastic action. It wasn't until a piece of clinker, maybe with a section of broken brick arch welded by the heat into its surface, had derailed an engine as it came on to the pit roads that four or five 10 ton wagons would be placed on the disposal road and a gang of engine cleaners would be rostered to load them up with the good old No. 8 shovel.

My driver had partly put the blower on so that when I opened the smokebox door the fumes from the firebox did not blow back into the cab. I pushed the door back and was thankful that there was no great wind that night which could blow the door back on me. I would not be the first fireman to have been knocked over by a closing smokebox door. Going by the level of ash, up to the level of the first hinge on the door, 2847 had done a lot of work since the smokebox was last cleaned.

Balancing the slush lamp on the steel crossbar into which the door locked, I dug the shovel into the fine black ash and threw it onto the pile of clinker beside the engine. As I cleaned the box I had a good look at the formation of the ash for any evidence of faulty exhaust. If the bolts holding the exhaust stack were working loose there would be telltale channels cut through the ash by escaping steam. Such a defect needed immediate attention otherwise there could be big problems on the run.

I also checked the boiler plates for any leaks and made sure the firebricks in the bottom of the smokebox were correct. Everything seemed in working order so I shut the door, making sure the locking handle was in the vertical position before winding the other handle to get the tight lock.

Back in the cab my mate had been busy. As I have said, it depended on the generation of drivers that you were rostered with as to whether the job was easy or hard. The disposal of a locomotive was purely fireman's work and if you had a mate from the old breed that was how it was on the disposal pits at Stratford.

They would seat themselves in the driver's seat, suck on the old pipe or shag cigarette while the fireman sweated it out on the fire, smokebox and ashpan. When it was all over they would say 'Right mate?' A nod from the weary fireman and they would make the first move for some 40 minutes by opening the regulator to drive the engine to the coal stage. Imagine that on an eight hour shift of shed duties on the disposal pits! An average of four engines and the fireman would go home like a wet rag. The old driver would sit with his peers, shaking the greying hair and say, 'Not like in our day mate, they don't even give the boiler a wipe over.'

My driver had pulled the coal down in the tender, cracking it with the coal hammer so that we had handy sized pieces in the tender doorway. This meant that I would have good size coals to put on the fire after cleaning it. We would also be saved the problem of large lumps of coal falling into the doorway when going to the coal stage for coal.

No. 2847 had a steel shield in front of the firebox door, partly designed to protect the crew from the heat and also to cut down the glare from the trapdoor in the event of air raids at night. The shield could be clipped back on the driver's side so that it did not impede work in the firebox area. I clipped it back and opened the main door. The fire was nice and even. It did not take long to rake the good fire to one side and break up the clinker on the bars with the pricker. The firebox was about eight feet in length.

During the constant updating of locomotives some tender engines were fitted with drop grates in the firebox, and we were lucky to find that No. 2847 had the drop grate. It was the answer to a fireman's prayer. The front section of firebars in the box was fitted to a framework which could be wound down from the cab. The grating dropped to the bottom of the ashpan and clinker would go straight into the pit. No heaving long slices in and out of fireboxes and trying to work the clinker-laden blade through the narrow doorway without dropping it on the cab floor. It was just a matter of pushing the clinker down towards the front of the box, lowering the grate and pushing it out.

After cleaning one side of the firebox I placed the live fire back on to the clean grate. Moving live fire around soon reduced it in content. If it was about 12 inches deep all over the box there was no problem, but if it was thinner it became necessary to put fresh coal on the embers to maintain the body of the fire before cleaning the rest. This made the job harder because, having added fresh coal on the embers to maintain the body of the fire, you also created more heat and smoke. This made it harder to see the clinker still to be removed. To clear the air you would put the blower on but this, in turn, livened up the fresh fire and so it would get hotter. Quite a vicious circle and one which we always tried to avoid.

With the fire done I went into the pit to rake out the long ashpan. The ashpan rake was a hefty piece of equipment, made in the railway workshops. About 10 feet long, it had a semi-circular blade at one end. The top of the semi-circle was joined to the solid iron handle, all in the one piece and belted out by the blacksmiths. The blade was at right angles to the handle. It was pushed into the ashpan and then dragged forward, bringing the ash with it.

After scrambling along the mountain of ash and clinker beside the pit I found one, dragged it back to the engine and dropped it into the pit. It was not my night. The pit's drain was blocked and someone had left the damping hose turned on. Water was about six inches deep in places. The wind was blustery, and coming from under the tender which meant that as I pulled the ash out of the pan it would blow all over me in a fine grey dust. There was no hose where the engine stood so I could not spray the ash before I pulled it out. We could not set back to where there was a hose as two other engines had come in since we started work.

It was a case of making the most of a bad job. I took the clean sweat cloth out of my overall pocket, tied it round my face in bandit fashion and started to rake. The hot ash spat and spluttered as it fell into the water. It stifled the heat of the fresh clinker in front of me which had come from our firebox through the dropped grate.

Between the two elements I was enveloped in an area of choking sulphurous fumes and powdery ash. It stung my eyes, made me catch my breath and created one hell of a problem. I scraped blindly at the ashpan, working more by instinct than sight. The empty sound made by the rake on the steel base of the ashpan told me that it was as good as empty.

Looking up through the smoke and haze, with the aid of the slush lamp that burned fitfully beside the rail on the edge of the pit, I could see a clear ashpan with the new fire burning brightly on the bars above. Dragging the rake with me and crawling along the pit I found the opening above the front buffers of No. 2847. The engine had been clean when we found her but now, with the ash blown all over the place, she had several patches of grey. Not the best way to send an engine into traffic without the cleaners' attention but then, it was a dirty engine or none at all.

It would never have happened before the war. Something else for the old boys to shake their heads about. As far as we were concerned we had been brought up in the austere manner of wartime operations. As long as the engine had all its bits and pieces, that was good enough.

My driver thought the ghost of Stratford had climbed aboard.

'Have trouble lad?' he grinned, knowing full well what it was like. I brushed myself down as best as possible and held wet boots before the fire. Not too long though as they would shrink and clothing was rationed. The company did not supply boots and many of us used to buy our footwear from the stores that sold surplus army equipment. They were second-hand boots but at least they saved the coupons.

We moved towards the turntable at the end of the pit roads. The golden rule was to stop before reaching the turntable and check its position as well as the position of engines on the other lines. Three tracks converged on to the table and it could be that some engines had been left foul of the other lines. This would result in a collision with the other engine. To get off the disposal pits the turntable had to be set for that road. This meant that the other two roads led to nowhere . . . except the turntable pit.

It had been known for crews to be talking as they made their way to the turntable and misjudge the distance. By the time they looked out to see if the road was clear, and the table was set, it was too late. They either ran into the other engine or, worse still, went into the turntable pit. This called for severe disciplinary action but it always gave other crews a laugh during crib room yarns.

Chapter Twenty

To the Street and Back

We rumbled on to the table and balanced more than 100 tons over the centrepin. We had to turn No. 2847 as she had come into Stratford depot engine first. She would leave Liverpool Street engine first with her train so we would have to be tender first going up with carriage stock from Stratford Carriage Sidings. These were things that engine crews had to remember on the various shifts. An error in judgement when leaving the shed could cause chaos at Liverpool Street. There was a turntable there but the problem was getting to it if the job did not roster its use. Everything worked to split timing with trains in and out of the 18 platforms throughout the day and night. An engine unexpectedly wanting the turntable road was the last problem signalmen wanted.

The Stratford table was power operated and this made life more pleasant. In country areas most turntables were manually operated. Sheer physical strength was used to push the locomotive round and woe betide the crew who could not set the engine right to get the point of balance. When balanced they went well but, just off the mark, and it was a case of getting into the turntable pit and easing the engine round with the pinchbar under the big steel wheels at the end of the table as they followed the curved rail round in a half circle.

As No. 2847 nearly completed her turn, power was switched off so that she would roll the last few inches. The locking lever snapped home and the table shuddered as it came to a standstill. We steamed to the tool shed and my driver left to get a fresh supply of oil. We kept the tools as she was going out again. He told me to take her up to the coal stage while he found out which road we could have in front of the Jubilee Shed for preparation work. The road to the coal stage went between the dormitories, cleaners' mess room and the Jubilee Shed. Just two silver lines cutting through the surface of oiled coal dust and ashes, with joints pumping up a black, oozing jelly when it rained. Maintenance was nil.

I stopped under the first available chute, wound the handbrake on and left the cab. Only fools stopped in the cab as the coal cascaded down into the tender, turning everything black and making any human being a black and white minstrel. As the coal stopped I climbed back, released the brake and steamed back towards the shed. For a fleeting moment I lived the dream of all young firemen, sitting in the driver's seat on an express engine, easing the regulator open and hearing the snifter valve take up as steam hissed into those powerful cylinders that forced the huge driving wheels into motion. So effortless and yet so powerful, slinking along the rails like a panther unleashed and sensing the excitement of the run ahead.

The fire was throwing its golden glow on the blackness of the cab roof and the boiler began to give off that characteristic smell of oiled plate warming up with the boiler's increasing heat as the steam gauge needle crept toward the magic figure of 180.

My driver met me at the end of the shed and we had been allocated number six road, under floodlights still free from the air raid alert. It was a good road to get as the sand bins were quite near containing sand that was as fine as that in an eggtimer. As my driver put the oil feeder into the many oil cups on rods and valves, screwing back the corks with meticulous care, I trimmed the headlamps, tidied up the tender with its latest batch of coal and filled up with water. The injectors sang sweetly as the boiler filled and the dampness of the wooden cab floor rose in steam laced with the smell of fresh coal dust as I washed the footplate down for action. They were the smells that no locoman would forget as long as he lived.

Liverpool Street station, with the North London Railway terminus, Broad Street, alongside and the GER Bishopsgate goods station to the north east.

Reproduced from the 6′, 1920 Ordnance Survey Map

With the inevitable billy of fresh tea on the boiler front over the firebox door we gave a short blast on the whistle and moved off to the outlet box. The regulator on the 2800s was different from most in that it was flush to the boiler face, standing vertical from the horizontal bar that linked it to the lever connecting it to the steam dome. The handle was duplicated on the fireman's side so that the engine could be controlled from either side of the cab. To open the regulator the vertical handle was pulled towards the driver from the boiler face. Some were so stiff that the driver had to put his foot on the boiler front for leverage as he pulled the regulator open.

It was a good design and could be adjusted with precision and kept open, which was more than could be said for some regulators. The type which pulled up from the centre, like the 'J15' and 'J39', would often work back to the closed position with the engine's movement. It was either a case of the driver sitting there all the time with his hand on the regulator or wedge it open with a piece of coal.

2847 gave her tango hiss as we rolled toward the outlet box with cylinder cocks open. 'Wiss . . . wiss . . . wiss, wiss . . . wiss . . . wiss . . .' This was where the advantage of left-hand driving came in. My driver had full vision of the road ahead and he could tell the outlet man all the details because the box was his side. I could make up the fire for the trip ahead. I had the main door open as the fire was low and I could place pieces of coal that were too large to go through the trapdoor. I built up under the door to about the boiler lip and then directed coal down both side of the eight feet box, leaving odd pieces to roll into the centre. It was a nice wedge shape when I had finished and burning brightly with little smoke. The main door clanged shut and we left the steel shield clipped back as the night was not that warm and the extra light helped in the cab.

The outlet signal gave the all clear on to the main line and then a shunting dod gave us the right of way on the up carriage road to Stratford Carriage Sidings. The sidings covered many tracks between the loco depot and the main station and carried only main line carriage stock. There were corridor and restaurant cars in the famous varnished teak style from Gresley's drawing board, mixed with large parcel vans and guards' vans that ran with the main line expresses.

A shunter set the road and we backed on to our set of carriages which would form the first train to Norwich via Cambridge that morning. It was not the normal type passenger train but one we called the milk train. It could be a ramshackle collection of passenger carriages, parcel vans and milk tanks going back to the Fen country to be filled for the London dairies that night. All would be built for high speed work, and fitted with vacuum brake so that the complete train would be braked from the engine. Very different from the loose couplings of the freight trains that we had been working.

As the smooth buffers of 2847 met the oval buffers of the first coach, the driver gave a little more steam so that we eased on to the stationary train and gained that little extra room for coupling space. I hung the coach screw coupling up as we would not be using it and placed our screw coupling over the drawbar hook. It was not that easy. The couplings were of solid steel and weighed about 50lb. On top of that, the corridor extension of the coach was above the top of the drawbar hook, giving limited clearance in which to place the engine's coupling. It sometimes meant getting skinned knuckles if you were clumsy and skinned knuckles were very painful in front of the locomotive's firebox.

After getting the coupling on and screwed up tight it was a case of clipping the vacuum pipes together and then linking up the steam heater pipes, as it was an early morning train. Steam from the engine would travel the length of the train, heating a steel cylinder under each seat and giving the comfort of central heating throughout the journey. That was the theory anyway. In practice there were many problems.

The main problem was the steaming capacity of the engine. Steam heating took a lot of water and steam on a 12-coach train and, if the trip was going badly with a poor steaming engine, the first valve to be turned off was the steam heating cock. Then there were poor fittings, where steam would leak profusely from the joints in the faulty pipes along the length of the train. Rolling stock fitters would remedy this at terminus stations by blocking off the offending coach. The result was that no steam would go past the fault. If it was on the third coach from the engine then, with a 12-coach train, the remaining nine would have no steam heating. If the temporary repair was not logged by the fitters, that set of coaches could be in that condition until some observant guard noticed the defect. This usually happened when the guard's van was the last coach and he had no heat.

After coupling up I put the headlamps on the tender in the set code pattern for number nine platform, Liverpool Street. I had just left the tender when the lights went out. Air raid alert. Shortly afterwards the sirens wailed their mournful message. For us it meant rolling down the blackout blind on the back of the cab roof and fixing it to the tender, plus rolling down the side curtains. It didn't worry us as we were going tender first and the curtains would help keep some of the coal dust out of our eyes as it blew back.

We snaked our way out of the sidings on first port and entered the up carriage road which would, in turn, put us on the up local at Bow Junction. The tender bucked awkwardly in protest as it led the procession over many points and crossovers. A tender with six solid wheels never negotiated curves and crossings with the ease of an engine that led with a four wheeled bogie under the smokebox. The engineers knew this and covered themselves in case of accidents by shaping the rules to read that no engine working tender first should exceed 75 per cent of its recognised speed in the forward direction.

As we rumbled through the deserted platforms of Coborn Road station, and the ring of the outside motions echoed against the walls of the terraced houses that backed so closely to the railway embankment, we saw searchlights weaving ahead. The angry stars of ack-ack shells burst against the dark morning sky and London shuddered in her sleep under the crump of high explosive bombs.

We steamed through Bethnal Green and down the cutting between blocks of flats and goods yards. Under the towering goods complex of Bishopsgate, signals were blinking their reds and greens through the haze of smoke made by two trains barking their way up the bank, one on the down main and the other on the down Enfield line. The early morning suburban service was on its way while thousands turned over for another two hours' sleep.

It had been a good run and within section time. We rolled into platform nine with two minutes to spare. The station was in darkness due to the blackout and air raid in progress but our eyes were accustomed to this mole like existence. We could see the barrows lined up, piled with newspapers, mailbags and parcels. Within a few hours people in the country would know the latest about the battles against Hitler, new conditions concerning food rationing, receive letters from loved ones on some foreign battlefield . . . It made you feel important.

A porter's handlamp called my driver forward slowly as he set the coaches in the loading positions. We came to a gentle stop about 50 yards from the blinking oil lamp that marked the hydraulic sleeved buffer stop. I walked to the front of No. 2847 to uncouple the train. She was warm, almost human as I passed her sleek shape in the darkness. A friendly heat radiated from the smooth pistons as they stood halted in their thrust into the cylinders. This was the language of a contented locomotive to its crew.

Coupling off, vacuum pipes broken and placed on their respective steel plugs so that the next crew could get brake pressure, and steam heater pipes unlocked, to be hung, up on their supporting chains with cocks tightly shut so that steam did not escape when the engine backed on to take the train to its destination. All these little points did not seem very vital but, if not carried out, could cause problems for others and were easy ways to lose five minutes on the timetable.

Now it was a case of waiting for relief. I put some coal on the fire, mainly under the door, to keep the steam up for the coming crew. We didn't want the old girl to go 'off the boil' but I had left the glass showing half full in the boiler. It was handy to have room for water in case the steam pressure built up to excess. It was taboo to blow off steam at stations, especially Liverpool Street which also had a hotel as part of the building. It startled passengers who were not aware of the habits of the iron horse. Train spotters and little boys didn't mind, in fact the latter used to encourage us to make the noise.

Fifteen minutes before the train which we had pulled in left the station two locomen stepped into the cab of 2847. At least we knew one problem was solved. We would not have to work the train down. They told us that we had to pick up an engine now over the disposal pits at Liverpool Street and take it to Stratford loco. depot. It seemed the engine had broken down and could only travel light. We exchanged the usual advice such as, 'get water before you go all lubricators are full and working, the sanders are OK, don't get her too full or she'll prime . . .'

We found our new charge on a short road that led to a coaling stage from the maze of lines that twisted their way through and out of England's biggest steam terminus. It was a 'D15', better known to engine crews as the 'Claud'. This was because the prototype had been named *Claud Hamilton*. They were a great engine in their day but railway operations had left them behind. Their main advantage, and also their liability, was the huge seven feet diameter driving wheel.

Housed under wheel splashers on the footplate that curved at the top to accommodate their size, the four great wheels would give the engine the speed of a greyhound on the level. The 'Clauds' ran well in the Fen country with five- or seven-coach trains but when brought into the hilly terrain of the home counties and put on 10- and 12-coach trains they hung their heads and gave crews all sorts of problems. Such was the locomotive problem during the war that the 'Claud' was a standby for most work although they never had the capability. Once I had a 'Claud' on a freight train, and anything worse than a seven feet driving wheel for starting a freight train has yet to be imagined.

My mate was told by the chargeman that No. 8887 had valve trouble and was for the workshops. A quick look at the old timer told us she was overdue for a major overhaul. Normally a very spick and span engine, in their black paint with red line livery on boiler bands, splashers, cab sides and tenders, No. 8887 had none of this. Half the red lines were worn away. The footplate over the wheels was rusty and the smokebox was like an old boot after being left out in the winter rains. Even the hand rails to the cab were rusty, a sure sign that she had been standing unused in some siding because of mechanical trouble. She had worked a train up to Liverpool Street but had lost so much time that they couldn't risk her again, not even with empty cars to Stratford.

When the dod gave us the green light out of the siding and let us on to the down main we soon found out why No. 8887 had no friends. Although the cylinder cocks were shut she still blew straight through on the fireman's side. As the huge driving wheels moved her forward the siderods clanked on worn bushes and the exhaust from the stumpy chimney sounded like an asthmatic old man. No clear cut beat of four exhausts from the two cylinders that sat under the smokebox. One beat, two beats, a long drawn out gasp of steam and then a stuttering fourth beat. How they ever worked a train with her was beyond us as we laboriously made our way up the 1 in 70 gradient from the terminus.

The all clear sounded as we went over Devonshire Street Goods Yard and dawn was beginning to flush the eastern sky. The night was beginning to tell on us and slow yawns creased our blackened faces. At least we were travelling engine first to Stratford. Various clocks in the city struck seven as we made our way on to the disposal pits with No. 8887's wheels grinding in protest as she bit into the ashy surface of the worn rails.

Reversing wheel in mid-gear, handbrake on, cocks open, boiler full . . . all ready for someone to drop the fire and give her a well earned rest in the workshops. We told the foreman where she was and made for home. The front of the Jubilee Shed was crowded with engines in various stages of preparation. A 'K3' throwing a mantle of thick smoke over the area as the crew tried to get steam in a hurry. A 'B1' standing proudly with shining boiler and nameplate, nearly ready to depart for a mid-morning express run and a cheeky 'Buck Jumper', or 'J69', standing in front of her with a fitter flat out on the footplate trying to do a last minute repair job on the eccentrics.

Chapter Twenty One

'Gobblers' to Woodford

My time in the Local Goods Link was short lived. I didn't get half way round before I found myself elevated to the suburban passenger links. There were many rosters and crews at Stratford to work the network of suburban passenger trains that fed the capital with workers from the outer city areas and dormitory towns, spreading in a 25 mile radius from the city's centre.

Once again rostering was done by degrees of responsibility and experience. Whatever people may have thought of the Great Eastern suburban service, it held pride of place with officialdom and it could be truly said that it was the best suburban service at the time in London. It was based on split second timing, rapid acceleration and high speeds in sections. The fact that bomb damaged track, signal failure and locomotive wear and tear blemished this reputation during the war in no way destroys the record that the Great Eastern suburban service was something of which the crews were proud.

Of course they never showed this prowess and they were, in fact, the services' greatest critics. Let any Chingford line man say his service was more reliable than the Epping line and there could be a punch-up in the mess room. The links that called for the greatest expertise by driver and fireman were those serving the Liverpool Street-Chelmsford line and the Liverpool Street-Hertford line. To get the required skills, the new entrants to the world of the suburban passenger services started in links which mainly worked carriage stock to and from Stratford, mixed with runs on the Stratford to North Woolwich line.

The next step was the Stratford to Woodford, Woodford to Liverpool Street, Liverpool Street to Ilford and Ilford to Woodford via the Fairlop loop line. After that there was upgrading to relief shifts on the Enfield line, the Chingford line and the Epping and Ongar line. The pinnacle of achievement came with the promotion to the Hertford and Chelmsford lines. By the time you had survived all this and had a few corners knocked off your ego you were ready for the semi-fast express passenger links.

Whether it was because I had already proven myself on the Palace Gates to North Woolwich line before becoming a fireman at Stratford I don't know but I didn't start in the carriage train working and went straight to the Woodford Link. I had only seen the line twice, when working with the local goods. I had never been over the Fairlop loop line that crossed the countryside between Woodford and Ilford.

This was a double first for me. It would be the first time that I had been on the suburban services worked from Stratford, and the first time that I had a regular driver in that he would be with me for all time, and vice versa. In the Local Goods Link it was often the case that you lost your mate for a higher grade job or he lost you for the same reason. To maintain the efficiency in the suburban service links crews were only split when all other ideas failed. The philosophy was that two men would get to know each other's ways and the end result was an efficient crew where time was essential.

This was good planning because, as engines differed so did drivers. Once the fireman had mastered the way in which his driver managed a locomotive he adapted his firing to that driver's style and the characteristics of the engine. In the higher grade links the regular crews had regular engines. This was an unknown luxury for those of us who had battled through the goods links with any old engine that was available, whether it suited the work or not.

The main engines rostered on the Woodford link were the old 'Gobblers' or 'F5' as they were officially classified. Occasionally we would get an 'N7' and think we were in paradise. Then again we sometimes had an old 'Buck Jumper' and thought we were going back to Stephenson's days. If we put it that way we were soon told by the old drivers that the 'Buck Jumper' had proved that it could run the Liverpool Street to Enfield trains faster than any electric traction. We were then told the saga of the 'Jazz' service and how it came about. An interesting piece of Great Eastern history but a bit boring after the fiftieth version.

The 'F5' was another locomotive that owed the GER nothing. In its own right it was a beautiful little tank and one that you could get to love. It rode well, much better than the 'N7', because of its 2-4-2 wheel arrangement. The whole suburban service was based on tank engine working. This saved time in turning engines and being able to use short recess roads at stations when waiting for the next train. As much work was done bunker first as was done engine first. Whichever way the 'Gobbler' travelled it had a pony truck to guide the engine into crossings and curves. It made the engine's passage much smoother and the 5 ft 4 in. driving wheels would negotiate the track much better.

The only pony truck under the 'N7' was at the bunker end and the best ride was bunker first. When travelling engine first all curves were met head on with the solid 0-6-2 wheel arrangement of the 4 ft 10 in. driving wheels. The 'N7' always lurched into a curve or crossing, compared with the 'F5' which glided over frogs and points with effortless ease.

The 'F5' was a wet steamer with the tall chimney of Victorian times. The boiler was low with the big steam dome and Ross pop safety valves. Some of their boilers were old enough to still have the Ramsbottom safety valves in the characteristic steel housing and the adjustment lever that fed itself into the cab's front wall.

The cabs were roomy and it was easy to get the fire irons off the top of the side tank, through the front window of the cab, when cleaning the fire. There was plenty of room to hang your jacket and bag, and the fold-down wooden seats against the back of the cab made life quite comfortable. Some had steel doors at the side that clipped together with a metal clip that dropped over the top of the two doors when placed together. Others had no doors.

The cab front was simplicity itself. Just a short regulator that pushed over from the driver's side in an arc of some 30 degrees to 90° for first port and the same span for second port. Two gauge glasses were placed one each side of the boiler in their usual three-sided frames of thick protective glass. There were brass cocks top and bottom of the glass for use when changing glasses or, in the case of testing the boiler water level, the bottom cock only. The steam gauge registered the 180 1b. working pressure. Then there were the Westinghouse air pressure gauge, vacuum brake gauge, the chain connected to the whistle stand on the boiler and steam cocks which controlled the steam to the water injectors.

The 'F5' was a right-hand drive engine and had the reversing wheel on that side, with the wheel held in the chosen position by a steel clip on a chain. Cylinder cock levers, sand levers, front and back damper levers and a round steel plate as the firebox door, like the 'J15', and that was the sum total of the fittings in the cab of the 'Gobbler'.

Fire irons were on top of the tank, fireman's side and, in the cab against the back wall, were the rear sand boxes. The front sand boxes were beside the smokebox and the Westinghouse pump was against the front of the water tank, driver's side. The back wall cab windows had iron bars running vertically across them to stop coal from breaking the glass when coaling. The door to the bunker was simply a sheet of steel that slid up and down in steel groves and was held at the required height by a steel pin which fitted in a series of holes drilled in the framework of the cab. Usually when running engine first the flap was up about a third of the way all the time but, when working bunker first, it was shut between firing spells because the dust would blow back into the cab.

In its own right the 'Gobbler' was a wonderful engine but, 40 years after it was built, many of them were being called upon to do work never designed for their wheel structure. Give an 'F5' a five-coach set of suburban stock, pre-war, and a level track and she would keep time with the best of them. But in wartime England with lack of proper maintenance and already worn out, the eight-coach sets of London suburban passenger trains crowded with up to a thousand people and working on one minute stops at stations, with 60 mph section times, the gallant 'Gobblers' sometimes gave up the ghost.

The main problem with the 'F5' was slipping when leaving the stations or climbing gradients. It was all due to the weight of the train being greater than the tractive adhesion of the driving wheels on the rails. Simply a matter of the trains being too heavy for the engines, but that argument didn't carry with management. Whether you had five, eight or ten coaches, the timetable had to be maintained.

When I found my name on the Woodford Passenger Link I felt partly afraid, partly elated. Afraid because I had not worked any passenger trains except the North Woolwich line and elated because I felt that I must have made my mark in a trade that had been restricted to railwaymen's sons for so long. It seemed to prove that you could do anything if you put your mind to it. It wasn't the money that made it appealing because the rate of pay was the same. The firing rate, like the driver's rate, went by years of service, from one to about five in the grade. After that you stayed at that rate until you were promoted from fireman to driver. So although I was entering the hallowed ranks of the suburban passenger crews, my rate of pay would be the same as when I was firing on the scruffy local goods engines with stinking fish wagons behind me.

A couple of firemen, about three years my senior, were with me when I traced the roster along with my finger and found that my driver's name was W. Cole.

'One of the old brigade, Rob. He'll make your life a misery, mate.'

I first met him when I signed on at 4.0 am that Monday morning. I had found the engine number and shed road and went to hang my gear up before getting the tools. Lunch bag, tin hat, gas mask, gloves and leggings took a bit of carrying around without a bucket of tools. He was already on the 'Gobbler'.

'Hullo sonny, what d'you want?'

'I'm on this engine', I said. 'Diagram 625 to Woodford.'

I thought he was an old firelighter or somebody on the shed staff.

'Are you now. Then you must be this Robertson fellow I've been rostered with.'

I seemed lost for words. He was not as I had pictured him. That was how I first met Bill Cole, the man who gave me my first real coaching in what it meant to be a fireman. A short nuggety man in his late fifties, Bill was about three inches shorter than my 5 ft 8 in. He looked like a typical fisherman who sailed in the one man boats round British shores, only he was a railwayman born and bred. He had sparkling blue eyes beneath the shining peak of his cap. A walrus type moustache framed his lips which often puckered into a boyish grin. He had a ruddy complexion and full face, with thick grey hair that jutted from under his cap as though there was too much of it. Bill Cole, the last of the railway greats . . . that's how I came to see and respect him.

His knowledge, readily given when he found that I was prepared to listen, formed the foundation of my understanding of locomotives. We also formed a comradeship that was hard to let go when I eventually moved on to higher links.

The work on the roster concentrated us in one area so I soon picked up the lay of the land, where signals were, where old Bill would shut off and roll, where I could pick up a bit of steam on a bad run and other things that made the job much easier and enjoyable.

We worked from Liverpool Street to Ilford, round the Fairlop loop to Woodford. Other times we went from Stratford to Woodford and then round to Ilford. We would stop there to make a connecting run back to Woodford, or we would go on to Liverpool Street. In the rush hours we also operated to and from Fenchurch Street, working over LMS lines and joining up with the LNER at Bow Junction. Sometimes we started from the carriage sidings at Leytonstone but, in general, it was in that circle from Liverpool Street and Woodford that the old 'F5s' earned their keep.

Bill understood the little tanks more than most. To him they were human. He taught me to understand that no two machines were the same.

'Now old '65, it don't matter how you start off with her, she must have her little slip. It's a case of first port, full cut-off and away she'll go with that little slip. Shut the regulator and open up again, fast like, and she'll bite the rail as though her life depended on it. No sand mind, just that double start.'

'Don't know why but a lot of the young 'uns will never use second port on the "Gobbler". Silly you know. They use a lot of water and steam with just first port. What do they think the bloody valve is there for if they don't use it? I remember when I was a lad my regular mate always used second port and we had eight or nine coaches in those days . . .'

What old Bill didn't say was that their eight or nine coaches were the old six-wheel, rigid wheelbase carriages of Victorian times. Not the eight-wheeled

Austerity freight locomotive class 'O7' No. 7300, taking water, 30th March, 1943.
BR/OPC Joint Venture

An example of the US freight locomotive sent under the Lease-Lend Agreement, 15th November, 1943.
BR/OPC Joint Venture

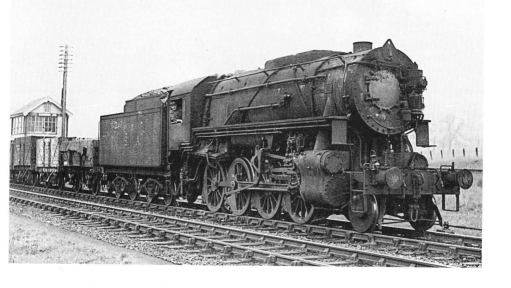

Work on the bridge at Coborn Road on the morning after the 'V1' destroyed the tracks into Liverpool Street, 14th June, 1944.   *BR/OPC Joint Venture*

A 'B12' with the first train to cross the repaired bridge at Coburn Road only 36 hours after the 'V1' fell, 14th June, 1944.   *BR/OPC Joint Venture*

On 17th November, 1944 class 'J17' 0-6-0 No. 8200 suffered extensive damage from a 'V2' rocket at Channelsea. All the boiler and firebox cladding was stripped off, the cab twisted almost beyond recognition and the smokebox door nearly wrenched off. The boiler and firebox were liberally peppered with holes. It was clearly beyond economic repair even in wartime and was taken out of traffic, some 10 years before normal withdrawals started.   *BR/OPC Joint Venture*

The crater beside No. 8200 made by the 'V2' on 17th November, 1944.   *BR/OPC Joint Venture*

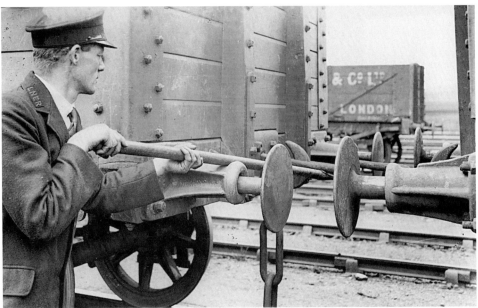

A shunter using the shunting pole to couple up freight wagons with three-link couplings.
British Railways

View from South Tottenham West Junction, looking towards London, on 16th June, 1948. The GER Hackney Downs to Enfield line passes over the Tottenham & Hampstead Joint line and the gradients necessary to pass beneath the bridge can plainly be seen. The spur to the right is the connection to Seven Sisters, used by Palace Gates to North Woolwich trains. The up starting signals are, from left to right: South Tottenham branch starter, with St Anns Road distant distant beneath, South Tottenham branch starter, with Seven Sisters down branch distant beneath, and Seven Sisters down main distant.
BR/OPC Joint Venture

'J67/1' class 0-6-0T No. 7399, later 68511, stands at Stratford in June 1945, carrying a wartime stovepipe chimney. Built in 1890, it was unfitted throughout its working life and thus confined to local shunting duties.   *British Railways*

Most class 'F6' 2-4-2T engines remained in the London area until the end of 1947. Here No. 7238, built in 1912, heads a train of empty carriage stock through a dismal looking Coborn Road on 2nd December, 1946, a mere 6 days before its closure, towards Stratford. It was withdrawn at the end of 1955.   *H.C. Casserley*

'B12' class 4-6-0 No. 1547 at Bethnal Green on 2nd December, 1946 awaiting entry to Liverpool Street. The West Junction signal is behind the engine and in the background are the Spitalfields sidings, the shed for the shunters is beyond the end of the tender. Rebuilt to 'B12/3' in 1937, by the post war years many of the class were based at Stratford for the Southend Victoria services.

H.C. Casserley

Class 'F3' 2-4-2T engines were latterly employed on empty carriage stock work in the London area and the North Woolwich branch. No. 7137 stands at Stratford in 1947, probably condemned as it was withdrawn in November. Note the wartime stovepipe chimney. *L&GRP*

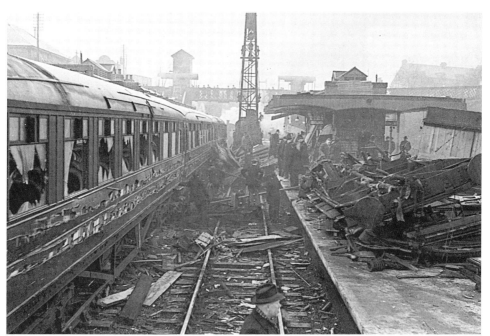

The scene at Gidea Park station on the morning of 3rd January, 1947, after the Ipswich express ran into the back of a Southend-on-Sea train standing at the down main platform the night before.   *BR/OPC Joint Venture*

'B17' class 4-6-0 No. 1602 standing in a siding at Gidea Park after being removed from the wreckage. It was the locomotive heading the Ipswich train when it ran into the Southend-on-Sea train at the platform.   *BR/OPC Joint Venture*

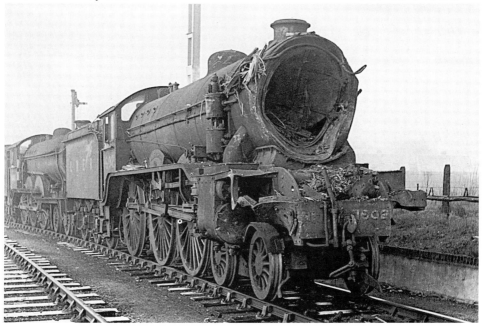

The first 'L1' class 2-6-4T No. 9000, was completed in May 1945 and allocated to Stratford. Following extensive trials in various areas of the LNER system it returned to the GE Section where it remained for the rest of its service. It is seen here at Chelmsford on 26th April, 1947, in green livery and bearing the full LNER lettering applied in June 1946.   *Ken Nunn*

'L1' class 2-6-4T No. 9000 stands at the head of the 1.10 pm Liverpool Street to Chelmsford train, formed from a GE 8-coach suburban set, on 26th April, 1947.   *Ken Nunn*

bogie type that we were pulling around the suburbs and carrying three times the passengers that fitted into his six-wheelers. As long as you didn't remind him of those facts life was quite pleasant. He would tell me these tales as we stood in sidings, waiting for the signal to draw down to the station platform to start the journey. He would sit on his wooden seat with his feet up on the reversing wheel, boots as shiny as ebony, sucking on his old briar pipe and reliving the past.

Very early in our partnership Bill asked me if I smoked. I told him no whereupon he said I was very wise. I found out later that he smoked herbal tobacco. It was foul smelling stuff. Thick yellow smoke wafted towards the cab roof when he lit up and I would hang out the side for fresh air.

'Won't hurt you, lad,' he'd say. 'Pure as the air itself! Not like that baccy I used to smoke . . . I tell you, that nearly killed me!'

The greatest advice I ever received, when working on wet steamers, came from Bill. We stood in a bay at Liverpool Street shortly after I went into the link. It was to be my first trip out of the terminus with a heavy passenger train and I was worried. I knew that if I did the wrong thing and we lost time it would reflect right through the suburban service with all trains losing minutes, that's how tight the timing was. It was not just the case of the train behind us. It was time lost at signals by other trains because we were late in section running time at the junctions. Old Bill could sense my anxiety.

'Stop worrying Rob, you'll send me silly!' he said.

We had 15 minutes to go before we backed on and were right away. I went to make up the fire from the bunker and felt his hand on my arm.

'You get on the coal stage and find me some decent lumps, Rob. It'll save our bunker,' he said.

The coal on the stage was some of the good hard stuff from the collieries in the Midlands. We didn't see much good coal in those days and had to make the best of a bad lot. I carried the lumps that would more than fill the shovel in one go and Bill placed them in the firebox. By the time he had finished the fire was up to the lip of the firebox door. Flames were licking hungrily through the blackness and smoke was thickening from the tall chimney.

Bill had only put the coal under the door and it sloped like a thick wedge to the front of the box under the brick arch where there was a thin bright layer of coals.

'Keep it that way lad and we won't have too much smoke. Don't worry about the front of the box with this old girl. She helps herself from the back when we get going.'

A train rattled by, entering the station platform at about 30 miles an hour with some 300 yards to go. That would be our train to work back to Woodford via Ilford.

Chapter Twenty Two

Rush Hour with Edwardian Engines

The dod clattered to the 'off' position and my moment of truth had arrived. Bill eased the 'F5' out of the dock with cocks open and blower slightly on. The flames round the door were now like liquid gold, lazily licking the mouthpiece and curling towards the brick arch. The needle on the steam gauge quivered with life and the Westinghouse pump panted away with urgency, eager to be on its way.

Hundreds of people were milling around the eight-coach train along the platform, taking it for granted that Bill and I would do the right thing and get them home on time, before the air raid sirens caught them on some strange street. It was surprising how many people felt safer in their own area.

The engine nudged the big circles of the coach buffers and Bill gave a little more steam to push the buffers into the sleeve so that I could couple up without having to unscrew the coupling. I locked the Westinghouse train pipes into position over the coupling, between bunker and carriage, and the pump immediately began replacing air from the reservoir which was flowing through the train pipe. We both hoped that the incoming crew had kept the train's air pressure at the required level.

Sometimes drivers did not watch this and would run with a train with higher pressure in the pipe than was necessary. When the other engine backed on, if its pump was not capable of reaching the abnormal pressure it meant that the brakes stayed on. The only remedy was to walk along the train and pull the release wires so that the pressure returning to the brake cylinders was that of the engine about to haul the load. This took time and was not a job that we needed in the rush hour.

As I climbed back into the cab I saw Bill having a look at the fire, then studying his departmental watch. Five minutes to go.

'Give her a little bit up the front, Rob. Not too much, just three or four each side.'

The steam gauge needle crept from 175 to 178 and the blower kept the smoke to a very faint haze. Old Bill sucked contentedly on his pipe.

'Don't get more than three-quarters of a glass,' he said. 'I know, they all say you need a full boiler with a 'Gobbler' when you start from Liverpool Street or you're in trouble by the time you reach Bethnal Green.'

He looked out of his side of the cab to see how things were on the platform. 'It's nonsense lad. What happens when a 'Gobbler's' got a full glass? Why, she primes, that's what happens. Then what? Open cocks, blow the water out - and your lubrication - wait for her to settle down, shut cocks, have another go, off she primes again, open cocks . . . and so it goes on. By the time the train is on its way you've lost half a glass of water and about five minutes in the section.'

I knew what he said was true. I had seen it and experienced it with lesser men than Victorian driver Bill Cole. Two minutes to go. The old girl was about to blow off at the safety valves, a crime in the terminus. I put the boiler feed on and it sang sweetly as water rushed through the clack valve just in front of the tank. The water level in the glass reached three-quarters full. I shut off the feed and the waste water gurgled down the waste pipe under the cab steps and on to the ballast. The steam needle wavered below the 180 mark.

Whistles shrieked through the summer air under the tall ironwork that supported the roof above the lengthy platforms. In the distance the guard's green flag waved. Porters relayed the signal above the heads of those still opening carriage doors. Bill yanked the whistle chain and our 'F5' knew that she was on her way. Stratford, Ilford and all stations to Woodford via the Fairlop loop. On the front of the smokebox, hanging in brackets made especially for them, swung a black enamelled destination sign with yellow lettering which told passengers on the platform that we were Woodford via Ilford. It was not always possible to find destination boards and it was not in the regulations that you must have them, but it looked very professional if you did. Old Bill insisted that we had them. Our run was quite a mighty task for an engine built in the Edwardian era and hauling a train twice the size intended by its designer.

'Little bit more round the box and then shut the door tight,' Bill said. The heavy steel door banged on to the floor of the cab. The fire was as bright as Dante's inferno and the heat drew smoke from my scorched overalls.

'What about sand, Bill?'

'Blow the sand, lad. Only novices use sand!'

My shovel clanged against the firebox mouthpiece and the steel had that special acid-like smell as it heated rapidly against the flames. The coal sprayed around the mass of flame and the door was shut on the last notch before the boiler. This usually caused the fire to belch black smoke as the combustion was not perfect. Too much gas and not enough air but old Bill knew what he was doing.

The front damper was wide open and the 'Gobbler' was beginning to bark like a 'B12' as Bill left the gear wheel full forward with the regulator at first port. It was a perfect start as the 5 ft 4 in. driving wheels gripped the rails and drew the train over the crossings towards the right hand curve that went under the busy commercial streets of Bishopsgate. When we left the crossovers and frogs behind Bill gave her second port. It was something I had never seen before. The old girl seemed to get her second breath and, as the exhaust bounced back from the baffle plates under the bridges, you would have thought we were the 'Flying Scotsman' itself.

Bill wound the wheel back. The power of the beat on the fire built up a heat which absorbed all the gases and there was no sign of smoke from the tall chimney as it led towards the bank. What was more amazing was the steam needle creeping over the 180 mark and the sudden roar from the safety valves.

'Put your feed on, Rob!' shouted Bill, over the noise in the cab as exhaust beats, banging firebox door and roaring safety valves made normal conversation impossible.

The feed was on and the boiler held its own level as we approached the steep incline with Bethnal Green at the top like a mirage in the smoky atmosphere of the brick lined cutting. Wait till I told the boys about this! Climbing out of

Liverpool Street with an old 'Gobbler' and the feed on. They wouldn't believe me. I felt a nudge at my side. Bill's cheeky face was next to mine, his pipe stuck to one side like Barnacle Bill.

'What'd you think now, eh? Who said they were no good?' She took the 1 in 70 in her stride.

'Don't touch the fire till we get over the top at the Green,' Bill shouted. I nodded and shut off the feed. We had the road through Bethnal Green and the distant for Coborn Road gave us the all clear through that station. We were on the level now and approaching the steady downhill drop to Stratford. Bill shut off, then opened to first port. The wheel was now at 15 per cent cut-off and the 'F5' was clipping along at a steady 60 miles an hour with the eight-coach train. I dropped the firebox door and looked round with the shovel blade. We had lifted a fair bit from under the door and it had levelled to the front. I built up under the door but not to the extent that we did at the coal stage. A couple down each side of the box and the door was up on the second notch from the boiler front.

Once again the safety valves were giving the first signs of a whimper. The water see-sawed with the motion of the engine at about half a glass. I put the feed on again! Due to the regular beat of the engine I couldn't hear the feed working but a look at the waste water pipe told me that it was picking up all right as it was as dry as a bone. The rhythmic clatter of 64 steel wheels behind us echoed as we sped past Coborn Road station and came up to Bow Junction.

The distant was on and Bill shut off steam, at the same time pulling on the blower to keep the fire out of the cab. We were moving now purely under the momentum gained during the journey. About 50 tons of engine and eight coaches rolling along at 60 miles an hour on steel ribbons. This was the joy and the secret of the steam engine's power. There were no gears to check the movement and, as long as there was room to move, the expert application of steam to moving parts at the right times plus the judging of downhill runs would enable crews to gain speeds that were only governed by the speed limits on the track, not the engine's limitations. This was where the joy of steam train driving could never be equalled. It was predominantly an understanding between man and machine. It was also a battle between the two for mastering the situation.

Bill hung on to the whistle and shrieked his protest to the signalman for checking the train's progress. He began to apply the air brake when the home signal dropped with an air of reluctance. Bill acknowledged with a 'toot' and we rolled on. He never gave the 'Gobbler' any more steam. She was rolling with the ease of tumbleweed. He checked his watch. Right on time in the section.

Stratford's down home was off but the starter was at danger. This didn't worry us as we were stopping there. We snaked over the junctions and the leading end of the platform was met before Bill attempted to apply the brake. Then there was the characteristic hiss of the Westinghouse as he made a 25 per cent application of the brake. We could feel the steel brake blocks starting to grab on to the solid wheels of the bogies. We were still doing 30 miles an hour and only 100 yards to go.

He made a 50 per cent application and the brake blocks really began to bite on the wheel flanges. Just before we stopped he released the brakes. By the time the release had applied throughout the trainpipe the train had stopped without a jerk. A perfect stop with the engine at the end of the long platform and people already getting in and out. The busy little pump recharged the cylinders and we were ready to go again. It all seemed so simple, but in that stop was years of practice and understanding of the tools in Bill's experienced hands.

Many drivers of many years experience could not handle the Westinghouse brake satisfactorily and, again, not all brakes worked the same. Some would apply the brake too hard initially and the train would jolt to a near stop. There would be the frantic blowing off of brakes and sometimes steam would be applied to get the train to the end of the platform as the brakes still dragged on. Then another application because the train was going too fast. Standing passengers would fall into the laps of those about to rise and the driver was cursed loudly.

The brake had two gauges by which the driver could see the air pressure in the train pipe and the reserve cylinder which released the brake, once applied. But the expert driver never watched the gauges as he stopped the train. He would only look after the stop to check that the air pump was recharging and that the reservoir was back to normal. The actual art of the stop was in the 'feel' of the brake. Some trains had brakes that went on faster, depending on the thickness of the brake blocks and the state of maintenance of the mechanism under the coaches.

With Bill, his initial 25 per cent application gave him the feel of checking the train's momentum. He knew that it was uniform throughout and not dragging in a jerky fashion. If the grab had been sudden, due to mechanical faults on the carriages, he would have released the brakes and then made a greater application later. As it was, everything went well and so he held the 25 per cent application and built up with the next. End result, perfection and happy passengers.

By the time the guard's whistle came and porters gave the right away, the starter semaphore signal was up in the all clear position and we were off again. Next stop Ilford. We pulled away in fine style and I had built the fire up as Bill had taught me. What I had thought was going to be a nightmare trip was turning out to be an unforgettable experience. Maryland Point, Forest Gate, Manor Park were all taken in the 'Gobbler's' stride and a steady 60 miles an hour was reached in no time.

As we roared under the bridge at Manor Park Bill shut off and we rolled to Ilford, giving me ample time to build up water in the boiler. After leaving Ilford we went round to the left at the junction before the Seven Kings signal box, going behind the large factory of Plessey's and the Ilford carriage sidings. It was then all stations on the Fairlop Loop. Newbury Park, Barkingside, Fairlop, Hainault, Grange Hill, Chigwell, Roding Valley and then Woodford as we joined the up main of the Epping to Liverpool Street line. By this time we were facing in the direction of Liverpool Street, having turned a complete semi-circle since leaving London.

There had been plans to electrify the Fairlop line before the war but Hitler put a stop to that and the steam suburban service kept the line going for many more years. It was one of my favourite lines as the setting was very rural. The cramped streets and barrack-like buildings of suburbia were left behind and one entered the world of the child's story book where rabbits sat on grassy embankments and chewed the dandelions while watching with wondrous eyes. The line itself was like something out of fairyland. It went up and down hill in rapid undulations, never being level for long.

Through cuttings and along embankments the line would weave, fields gracing the skyline and the smell of new mown hay filling the cab on early summer mornings. Children would sit on the five-bar gates and wave to us. They knew the timetable better than we did. The stations had flowers in tubs and even the signals seemed to gleam brighter along that line.

The worst train to work on the Fairlop loop was the local goods. Not because of the tonnage or work but because of the ever-changing gradients and the need to check breakaways or bunching. It was a flat out pull to the top of some banks with the rapid application of the hand brake as you topped the rise, before the train began to give the engine an uncontrollable push. All in all, the Fairlop line was looked upon as a convalescent area and most crews enjoyed a spell round the loop. Some station staff would offer vegetables for sale and, on the odd occasion, a rabbit would help out the meat ration. It never seemed as though the war really reached that rural haven and yet it stood in the middle of some of the worst bombed parts of Essex.

Chapter Twenty Three

The Teachings of Old Bill Cole

During my months with Bill I got to know the Liverpool Street to Epping, Liverpool Street to Woodford and Liverpool Street to Gidea Park lines quite well. I also mastered the 'Gobbler' in most situations. The only time I ran into trouble was when Bill and I were split on spare shifts and I would get drivers who never really understood the old 2-4-2 and her Victorian ways. They would want sand at every start and, even then, make a hash of it. Instead of letting the loco. get a grip before giving her more steam they would have the sand running and give the 'F5' the lot. She would slip herself to a standstill because she had not moved sufficiently forward enough to get the sand under the driving wheels for such power.

It was not for a lad like myself to tell drivers with years of experience where they were going wrong but Bill's tuition had shown me all the flaws in driving a 'Gobbler'. With these amateurs we sometimes lost three or four minutes in a section purely because of slipping. This in turn ruined the fire and lost at least half a boiler of water. Once on the run, this loss was never made up and the whole trip became a nightmare.

There were times when we did get away from 'Gobblers'. Some shifts began by relieving Epping crews at Stratford station and working a couple of rounds on the Epping to Liverpool Street suburban service. Most of the engines at Epping were 'N7s' and, being a country depot, were in excellent condition. It was like entering into another world to get on one of those for a day's work.

Specifically designed for suburban work to give rapid acceleration and speed on short sections, the 0-6-2 tank locomotives had 4 ft 10 in. driving wheels and a compact body well balanced over the engine framework so that the wheels enjoyed the best possible traction. It was very rare to hear an 'N7' slip. If it did it was more the driver's fault than the engine.

The 'N7' locomotives on the Epping line were some of the earlier versions with Belpaire boilers that had the square build over the firebox. They also had a slightly higher chimney and differed from the regular flowerpot version. This chimney design gave them a characteristic difference in the beat of the engine under steam when compared with the softer bark of the flowerpot chimney. It was more crisp and clear cut.

Other changes in engine power were sometimes unexpected due to breakdowns or shortage of engine power at Stratford Depot. I remember once Bill and I were rostered to relieve at Liverpool Street and work on the Gidea Park service. He must have heard my jaw drop when we walked to the engine dock and saw a 'Buck Jumper' standing there.

'Not a "Buck Jumper" on the suburban!' I muttered. I'd had them shunting, on the local goods, but never on a passenger train. Old Bill stuck his pipe to one side of his mouth.

'What's wrong with that Rob? Can't you handle 'em?'

He rolled like an old salt with his tin box in one hand and his rolled up overall jacket under his other arm.

We climbed aboard and the other crew seemed eager to get off. Everything was done in the way of requirements. We were due out in 30 minutes with an all stations to Gidea Park. It was midday and part of the off-peak service. As we gave the boiler a rub over, checked the water and began to make up the fire in the little firebox old Bill told me the story of the 'Buck Jumper'.

It seemed that in the pre-war years there had been a battle between the Metropolitan Railway in London and the Great Eastern over the running of trains on the Enfield line. Electrification was in the air and it was felt that a better service could be given if the line were electrified. The Great Eastern argued otherwise and said they could match anything electrification could do and not increase costs.

The challenge was on. The electrification lobby brought out a timetable which they said they could run on the line. The main advantage of electrification over steam was the rapid rate of acceleration. The speed in the section was not as great as that of the steam engine but the rapid getaway made up for that. The Great Eastern engineers converted some of the 'Buck Jumpers' for passenger work. The main conversion was the addition of vacuum and Westinghouse brake systems. They put them on the Enfield section and the 0-6-0, 4 ft driving wheels revelled in the conditions.

The eight-coach trains were chicken feed for the sturdy little engines that usually battled with 200 tons of freight. Running like terriers, they would bound up the bank out of Liverpool Street in record time and even knock minutes off the proposed electric traction timetable. That was the end of the challenge for a while and then the war stopped all thoughts of changes to the service.

It was not a regular practice to run 'J69s' on passenger trains but, when the running staff were up against it, it was a handy standby. Once again, under Bill Cole's coaching, the sturdy little old locomotive came through with flying colours. It was amusing to see the faces of passengers as we ran into the stations. They would expect the normal 'N7' at the head of the train and eyes would open wide when the 'Buck Jumper' rattled round the corner with its squat little body and tall chimney. Some would have a good old laugh and shake their heads in disbelief.

Trainspotters would make a special note of the event. We proudly bustled on our way, the tall chimney barking in defiance at the bridges and station awnings as we kept time in every section. In fact we were two minutes before time into Romford. It was a long section from Chadwell Heath and we were on top of the world. Bill winked at me and gave her the lot. We rattled along at more than 60 miles an hour and the Romford gasworks came up on our right before he shut off. Two minutes off the section running time and steaming like the kitchen kettle!

Old Bill taught me a lot. He showed me how to change a broken gauge glass and how to make the woollen dollies that fed the oil from the oil boxes in the cab to the axle rubbing plates below the floor. He showed me how to pack the gland on a blowing steam valve with asbestos wool. All this knowledge was on a practical scale and easier to follow than the stilted phraseology in the textbooks.

It's funny how, out of a million experiences through life, certain happenings stay clear in the mind while others drift on to the world of forgetfulness. One of the most vivid memories I still have of my time with Bill Cole concerns an early morning shift from Stratford to Woodford, and then round the loop to Fenchurch Street. By the time we did the Woodford to Fenchurch Street section the train had entered the rush hour run.

It was a wet winter's morning and my overalls were quite damp from the rain as we prepared the old Gobbler for her day's efforts. When we backed on to the empty carriage stock in the Stratford yard, to pull it to number seven platform at Stratford station, I jumped down to couple up. Usual procedure, screw coupling of the coach to be hung up, our screw coupling placed over the goose neck of the carriage drawbar, Westinghouse brake pipes coupled up and taps turned on . . . and that's when it happened.

All Westinghouse hosepipes had metal tags on the pipe where it joined the train pipe. The tag carried the date of when tested and put on the engine. I did not notice until too late that the tag on the pipe on the bunker was sticking out towards the valve handle and, as I pulled the valve handle down, the tag cut into my index finger like a razor blade.

A clean, painless cut, down to the bone of the first finger joint. It did not take long to bleed and I was stunned to see blood running down my finger, through the grease and coal dust, to drip off the end with the rain.

'That's nasty, Rob,' Bill said, 'wants a couple of stitches, like. Go up to the control box and see if you can get relief. We've got 10 minutes.'

I went up the wooden stairs to the control box that stood on the London end of the four and five island platform and they phoned through to the loco. foreman. There was a black haired girl up there, quite attractive and only about 18 years of age. All the boys would give her a whistle if they saw her. She was a rarity in a man's world and must have felt flattered with all the male interest. She gave me an understanding smile.

'He said sorry but no relief available. Keep going and they will bear you in mind.'

I thanked her but knew what that meant, out of sight out of mind.

Back on the 'Gobbler' I told Bill the sad tale. He had been busy making up the fire in good old Bill Cole fashion. He wiped his hands with the sweat cloth and grinned. 'Well, we'll just have to grin and bear it, eh me boy?'

By this time I had the finger wrapped in my handkerchief, the only clean piece of cloth to be found. No first aid boxes on locomotives in those days. We tied it there with a bit of string off the oil bottles. The guard's whistle blew and we were away. When I fired up the heat really played on the open cut and every time I knocked the water lever on to work the boiler feed my hand would jar with agony.

I saw the shift through and, nine hours later, was on the way home. The finger healed of its own accord during the week but I still have the scar to remind me of that wet and dreary day on the Woodford locals. I think that might be why I never enjoyed a trip on the Fenchurch Street branch.

Chapter Twenty Four

Into the World of the 'N7'

It was about 1944 when I had my next move through the rosters at the Stratford Loco. Department. I went into the 'N7' links, the cream of the suburban service. It was a service that was doing its best to get London's multitude of workers to their jobs on time and home again, between air raids, shortages of spare parts, lack of food and a general depression in morale.

I found my name next to Driver J. Tant. Another stickler for doing the right thing. No messing around with Jimmy Tant. My mates warned me that he was trying to be the next loco. inspector, to them a good indication of what he would be like as a mate.

Locomen in general were great ones to try and make mountains out of molehills and thoroughly upset a bloke's well being. It was all done in fun but they had a funny sense of humour at times. Monday morning came and we were rostered to work a train to Hertford from Liverpool Street, leaving about 6.0 am. Then one back from Hertford in the rush hour. An eight hour fifteen minute job if everything went to time.

Four o'clock on a spring morning and everything seemed right with the world. We even had a night without an air raid. When I signed on I found that Jim had already booked on. Not that I was late. How could I be when the train I had to get from Brentwood got me to Stratford 45 minutes before my rostered time.

Our engine number was 2633. She was one of the few 'N7s' with a Belpaire firebox and flowerpot chimney. I found Jim in the cab when I climbed aboard on number six road, outside the main shed. He would have been six feet tall if he had stood straight but he seemed to have a permanent bend at the shoulders. I found this to be a characteristic of the men who did their firing during the depression years. Due to lack of promotion they were firemen for much longer than the standard period. It was the constant bending as they fired. Some also kept that stance as they stood at the side of the cab or sat between firing spells. The outcome was a perpetual stoop, the trademark of their long apprenticeship with the shovel.

He was thin but strong and wiry. He had the high cheek bones that one associated with the Asiatic and his cheeks were slightly sunken. But his blue eyes were full of vitality. He also had the characteristic of pre-war footplate men who kept the top button of their overall jackets buttoned right up to the neck. We youngsters wore the jackets like single breasted coats with the button stopping at the chest. The older men had the top button done up and looked like Chinese peasants.

He was wiping his hands with cotton waste. After the normal introductions he told me he had oiled up, pushed the fire over and filled the Westinghouse pump lubricator. In fact he had not left me much to do. We were ready to leave the shed at least 30 minutes before time. He pulled out the departmental watch and studied the Roman numerals.

'Time for a cuppa I think Robbie. Let's go over to the canteen.'
This came as quite a surprise to me but a welcome one as it was two hours since I had breakfast, if you could call it that at three in the morning. Under the fluorescent lights in the green and cream painted canteen we sat at one of the long tables and sipped the sweet mixture. It was nothing to recommend but helped out the rations and gave us something to work on.

'There's one advantage from being in this link,' Jim was saying. 'We have regular engines. Each turn of duty is roughly on three shifts as you know, early middle and late. Well, those three shifts are allocated a regular engine and it's up to us to look after it so that we can get the best out of it. Know what I mean?'

I nodded. I knew what he meant all right. One thing that was wrong with the locomotive section at Stratford was that engines had no regular crews, with the exception of the express passenger links. Even then, things could get out of running and it could take a week to get the engine back to rostered requirements.

As everybody had any old engine, no pride was taken in its performance or appearance. If it had a mechanical defect no one could be bothered to report it in the fitter's book. So a minor defect became a major breakdown in the end and everyone suffered indirectly.

With each set of crews getting its own locomotive, it would look after it, do minor repairs, keep it clean and, what's more, get to know its own peculiar ways.

'2633 has to be coaxed,' Jim told me. 'I only got her because no one else wanted her.'

We had finished our tea and were walking back to the main shed. 'She'll only steam on a light fire, Robbie. Give her the normal fire for an 'N7' and she'll go off the boil. Keep the fire about six inches deep all over the box and she'll never let you down, you mark my words.'

I was beginning to see problems already because a fire only six inches thick did not seem feasible on a passenger train from Liverpool Street, going up the bank to Bethnal Green. What I didn't know was the way in which Jim drove her and the state of mechanical prowess he had achieved with her working parts.

We left Stratford with empty carriage stock for Liverpool Street and ran into platform seven. We had run up bunker first and Jim had been nearly mid-gear most of the way. With that amount of cut-off the fire had barely lifted and yet we had kept section time with ease. There were no piston glands blowing, no cylinder cocks only partially shut, no clacks dribbling or blowing and no knocking big ends.

It was like working on a prize locomotive straight from the shops. But it was to be complete team work. Jim could only drive that way if I kept the fire that way. This meant that I had to fire up more frequently in between sections, broke coal smaller than usual and, in all, nursed her like a pedigree through the trip as though it were a race. I enjoyed this because the engine practically talked to us. It was a loving combination of men and a machine. Something that might sound trite but proved to be very correct in future months.

Our remaining rostered work was down to Hertford and back, getting relieved at Liverpool Street. It was a six-coach train of corridor stock, as usually run on that line, and vacuum braked. Hackney Downs first stop and then all stations to Hertford. The run was no stranger to me after my time at Hertford as a depot. In fact I quite enjoyed the rural simplicity of the Hertford run. After Ponders End suburban blocks gave way to countryside with fields, rivers and farmland in between small towns.

With 'right away' from Liverpool Street Jim gave 2633 first port and, as soon as it was obvious she was not going to slip, straight into second port. The rapid acceleration had the train moving well and he would bring the reversing wheel up to about 60 per cent cut-off. Her valves were in perfect setting and the exhaust really chopped itself into four distinct beats through the stumpy chimney. Crisp and clear they were, a delight to any engineman's ear.

Under the arches and up the centre of the incline we barked. The fire was as bright as silver and the Ross safety valves were ready to roar with excess steam. I put the injector on and fed water into the boiler. It hardly seemed to move the needle on the steam gauge which quivered on the 180. It was a joy to work on that engine. By the time we had reached the top of the bank I went round the box with half shovels of small, cracked coal, firing through the oval trap door.

It was good to have a trap door that really worked on its steel ratchet, and then I found out why. The previous ratchet had worn teeth like the rest of them. Jim had taken ours off and had a friend in the boiler shop make him a new one. The result was a firebox door that worked as planned by the designer and needed no lump of coal hammered in the gap to keep it open.

The trip was the forerunner of many more where driver and fireman worked as one and the engine was an intimate part of them. We were before time at stations more than we were running late. Smoke was kept to a minimum and cleanliness was the password in the cab. Fire up, break up the next lot of coal, sweep up, wash down with the hose and be ready for the next firing. That was how it went for the whole trip. And 2633 purred like a contented cat.

Some shifts involved an hour in a carriage siding where we would clean the fire and generally prepare for the next run. On these occasions the cab would get extra attention. The copper steam pipes were rubbed over and gleamed like Aladdin's lamp. It was surprising what could be achieved with an old rag, greasy from oiling up, and covered with dry sand from the sand boxes.

The boiler casing was cleaned till you could see your face in its blackness. Sand handles and cylinder cock levers were rubbed down with emery paper, then wiped with oily cotton waste to stop rusting. They finished up looking like prize pewter. We even had the roof as clean as the floor. Normally the roof of an engine was the least to be cared for by crews. It would be caked with soot, ash and rust. On No. 2633 the roof was spotless and the riveted joints stood out like organ stops.

Jim was also striving for mechanical perfection and there was plenty of room for that. The shortage of fitters at Stratford meant that only the major jobs were done. You could book a faulty Westinghouse pump lubricator for attention but it would not be done until the pump seized up. So we did most of the minor jobs on No. 2633 in conjunction with the other crews. It could be said that we had hidden motives. We knew that if the engine was put off the road due to mechanical faults we could lose her for at least a month. We would get some old crock that had a beat like a winded horse and wouldn't steam in a month of Sundays.

The 'N7' was designed with a dual braking system for passenger train working. Most of the suburban service carriage stock was fitted with the Westinghouse air brake but there were times when vacuum braked rolling stock was used, such as on the Hertford line. The brake on the engine was Westinghouse and, if the train being worked was fitted with Westinghouse, this meant that there was a continuous brake throughout the train and engine. The stop was fully controlled by one application and there was no 'pull out' or 'run in' as experienced when the train had one braking system and the engine another.

That problem always existed when the 'N7' worked a vacuum braked train. The 'N7' was fitted with the vacuum brake ejector but it did not apply as a brake to the engine. To get a perfect stop the driver had to apply the vacuum brake to check the train and the Westinghouse brake to stop the engine. This was very difficult and rarely operated efficiently due to the great variance between the two braking systems. The vacuum brake was not as rapid in its actions as the Westinghouse.

Realising this, the company had perfected a system whereby, if the 'N7' was working a vacuum fitted train, the Westinghouse and vacuum brakes could be operated together by using a special valve which linked the two systems through the train pipe. As the driver pulled down the vacuum brake lever the Westinghouse valve would response with equal pressure on the engine's air brake system. In theory it gave the perfect stop. In practice it caused more rough stops than enough and made crews lose time in sections by checking trains too soon or too late.

Rather than face all the problems that the system incurred the majority of crews worked on the separate applications of the two brakes. The main reason for the failure of the two systems to work in harmony was dirt and dust that would collect in the controlling valve's diaphragm. The parts never received the servicing they needed and, with the constant background of dirt and ash on locomotives, it was quite easy for the delicate mechanism to get clogged with foreign matter.

Jimmy Tant was a perfectionist. Everything on No. 2633 had to be in working order. He spent many hours cleaning the valves of the vacuum and Westinghouse brakes and it was through his teaching that I gained a lot of knowledge never taught in other ways. Our combination brake worked as one on the Hertford line.

Chapter Twenty Five

Old Crocks on the Hertford Run

Life on No. 2633 was heaven. We adjusted sand pipes so that the sand went on the rail in front of the wheel and not half on the rail and half on the ground. Jim showed me how to clean the boiler's tubes by having a good, hot fire and, with the blower hard on, force sand through the tubes off the shovel by getting it over the brick arch. The sand would scour the tubes and take all the rubbish with it. No wonder the old girl steamed on a matchstick, so to speak. But it was a team effort.

I remember times when Jim was off sick and I would get a relief driver. He would not take any notice of me, just a young fireman with fluff still on his face. He would drive the 'N7' like the standard engine, first port and full wheel most of the time. 2633 would not take it and it was no good giving her a bigger fire. It would just lay dead in the firebox. Those trips were nightmares. Water in the bottom of the glass, a fire that wouldn't come to life, a driver who thought he knew best and a steam gauge that struggled to stay on 100 lb. most of the time.

Jim was a master with locomotives. I remember when we had an 'N7' that was the curse of the Stratford depot. She was overdue for the shops and nobody could do a thing with her. Valves blew, clacks leaked, lubricants failed to get to the right places . . . even the dampers wouldn't stay open on the run.

We had her on the Hertford run, relieving the crew at Stratford on the way down. You could see the look of relief on their faces as we stepped into the cab.

'Good luck mate, you'll need it,' said the grimy faced driver.

I noticed they had half a glass in the boiler and the steam gauge was on 125 1b. The full working pressure was 180 lb. Things were not the best. The blower was hard on and the firebox door was shut tight. Smoke was rolling out like a factory chimney and the boiler feed was not picking up too cleanly. Jim gave a big grin.

'What are you looking so happy about, Rob? Lost a fiver and found a tanner or something?'

I had to admit the next eight hours did not hold a great deal of encouragement for me.

'Never let it be said that an engine got the better of us,' Jim said as the guard blew his whistle and we were right away.

Still half a glass but the steam had crept up to 140. I shut the feed off, pushed open the firebox trap door and had a look round. The fire was bright enough but only sections seemed bright. Other sections just lay there as though clinker was on the bars. The fireman had assured me that they had cleaned the fire before leaving Liverpool Street. It was soon evident why the fire was only partially working. Jim gave her second port and the beat was pathetic. None of the four clear cut exhausts of No. 2633. Choof! Choof! Choooof . . . Choof! was the sound from the stumpy chimney.

The valves were out to some order and we were only working on about one and a half cylinders. I cracked up some coal and tried the little and often trick.

It did help. Going through Temple Mills Jim had her notched up to nearly mid-gear with second port and we were maintaining section time. He shut off before the usual spot when approaching Lea Bridge station and we rolled for about half a mile. I had the feed on and the needle on the steam gauge flickered on 130.

The main problem on the Hertford run was that the trains were all vacuum braked and once the steam pressure dropped below 100 lb. it was hard to maintain the vacuum pressure level of 20 inches in the train pipe. This meant that if you had been running with 20 inches on the vacuum gauge and the lack of steam pressure caused the vacuum to drop back to 18 inches, then you had a two inch deficit in the train pipe and the brakes would start to drag on. It was quite a vicious circle. Lack of steam caused the brakes to go on so the driver would give the engine more power to try and drag the coaches along while trying to blow off the brakes with the large ejector. This in turn used more steam, which we didn't have, and more water, which would be getting low.

We got to Hertford but only just. The one feather in our cap was that we did not lose time. We were bunker first back to Liverpool Street and wondered if it would make much difference. Some tanks worked better the other way round. I cleaned the fire but it was not that bad. Before I made it up Jim said he would like to look in the smokebox. After a while he called me round.

'What can you see that is unusual, Rob?' he asked.

I couldn't see much out of place. The exhaust stack seem to be of a different design, some firebricks were missing at the base and the blower ring was on the tilt.

'Look at the top of the box near the chimney,' he said.

I looked at the black expanse of steel and noticed that part of the smokebox side near the chimney fitting was cleaner than the other side. Jim pointed to that area.

'That shows the exhaust stack is not bolted in its true position,' he said. 'It should be dead centre, under the chimney so that when the exhaust blast comes from the cylinders it goes straight out, without any obstruction. Because the stack is slightly off line the exhaust is being baffled against the ledge where you can see the effect of the baffled blast. That stops the full effect of the blast beat on the fire and, coupled with the faulty valves only giving us three and a bit beats, the combined effect is a fire that does not burn correctly. He closed the smokebox door. 'Here endeth the first lesson,' he winked. 'Should never be on the road.'

On the way back to the cab he showed me the right side piston. It was dull and as dry as a bone. Not the glistening silver rod that I was so used to seeing in No. 2633 as I stood filling the tank.

'Lubricator's failing to get the oil through. Wonder she hasn't seized up.'

He felt the axles in the centre of the driving wheels and told me to do likewise. They were warm on the centre and leading wheels.

'Axle boxes not feeding oil too well,' he muttered. 'No wonder she doesn't roll that well. Have you noticed?'

Although it was a serious situation it gave me much comfort to know that it was not my firing that was letting us down. We backed on to the train in

Hertford station for the return journey. Jim sat on the fireman's side.

'She's all yours, Rob. I'll have a go with the shovel.'

Jim was like that. Once we got to know each other, and he knew that I was willing to learn, he taught me everything in a practical manner. I nearly had a fit when he first told me to drive.

'Don't be stupid boy!' he said. 'You can't learn to drive out of a book. Got to get the feel of things.'

Quite often, towards the end of our time together, we would take turns about on rostered jobs. It was a wonderful experience and he would never jump on you if you did something wrong. He just used it as an example for next time. Neither did he pick or choose the jobs. Whether it was an easy trip or a rough one, whether the engine was good or bad, it was always turns about.

He made the fire up while I coupled up to the train. Back in the cab I tried to blow off the brakes but the vacuum gauge would not go above 12 inches. The steam pressure was nearly 180 lb., the highest it had been on the shift, so it was not lack of steam.

'What d'you reckon, Rob?' Jim asked me, testing me in his own way.

'Pipe's not on the rear plug properly,' I suggested. Jim thought I was not far out so I took a walk to the rear of the train. Sure enough, whoever had uncoupled as the train ran in, they had not placed the pipe on the steel plug or dolly as we called it. Consequently the vacuum ejector would be trying to create vacuum in the train pipe but, as the train pipe was not blanked off, the air would rush in as fast as it was sucked out. With the pipe on the plug the gauge soon reached 20 inches.

The maximum vacuum measure was 21 inches but most crews worked with 20 inches in the train pipe. This gave the driver an extra inch up his sleeve if anything went wrong. The greatest problem was backing on to a train brought in by another crew who had a good ejector and had been using 21 inches throughout the trip.

You could back on with an old tub like the one we had that struggled to maintain 20 inches. The result was a train with an extra inch of vacuum through the train pipe that could not be released by the engine working it. Sometimes this was not realised until it was time to leave. The engine would surge forward to find the coaches staying stubbornly in the platform. It was then a case of walking the length of the train to release the brake cylinders manually by pulling the release wires on each coach. Five minutes later the train would be ready to leave and that was five minutes that would be hard to make up.

Our broken down 'N7' was now roaring at the safety valves with a minute to go before departure. Jim intended to get her hot! The station staff gave the 'right away' and I took it easy out of Hertford station. The going was level. In fact there were no great inclines on the Hertford run so I planned to get the five coach train along as easily as possible. The track was flat till it reached the market town of Ware. There were always rivers near the line, among the lush greenery of the fields. I remembered the winter when they were in flood and Jim and I worked the last passenger train from Hertford as the floodwaters began to cross the track. It was a weird experience, running along on two bands of silver rails that traced their way through the eddies of river water as it swept through the fences. Nothing could be seen of the track until we reached Ware. It put the line out of action for about a week.

Jim was doing a good job up to Ware and there was the usual banter about nothing wrong with the engine that a good fireman couldn't put right. By the time we reached the junction with the main Cambridge line things were looking differently. She was hanging her head and steam pressure was down to 120. The starter was against us so I let her roll towards the semaphore signal that stood high and proud against the sky. A quarter of a mile away a 'B12' suddenly came into sight doing a steady 80 miles an hour across the junction points and snaking her way towards London with a 12-coach train, the steam from the chimney wreathing down across the boiler and disappearing in the willows that lined the River Lea. The tranquil Lea where, in that area, you could go down to the water's edge and pick yourself some watercress to go with the cheese sandwiches. Hard to realise that it was the same River Lea that stagnated behind the Stratford railway workshops.

The express soon cleared the section and the starter dropped to all clear. Jim had been round the box a couple of times and then shut the trap door, which was unusual for him. I got the train on the move and yanked the regulator to second port. His hand was on my shoulder.

'Don't touch the wheel for a while,' he shouted above the bark of the exhaust. 'Give her the lot!'

We went round the junction bend and on to the main line with the roar of an express train. Thick smoke rocketed out of the chimney and it all looked very impressive. We reached about 70 miles an hour in no time but the water in the boiler was going down fast. I could see Broxbourne home signal against us and so pulled on the blower and shut off.

Jim opened the trap door to reduce the smoke and the needle started to climb. The shock treatment was slightly successful but it was not something we could do for the whole trip. The home signal went to the all clear and I just let the train roll. We had a minute or two up our sleeve and instead of using extra steam to get us to the station I put my boiler feed on.

'Good thinking Rob!' shouted Jim, who had his feed on. He was beginning to look grimy.

We left Broxbourne and reverted to the normal driving style. No more shake ups. The old girl couldn't take it. Jim took his cap off and hung it over the steam gauge.

'We won't bother about that any more,' he said. 'Out of sight, out of mind.'

The hat stayed on the gauge till we reached London. We lost two minutes on the whole trip and that was mainly signal checks. When Jim took his cap off the gauge it showed 100 lb. We often wondered if it went any lower during the trip. If it did we could safely say the engine had a good vacuum ejector as there was no brake trouble.

Chapter Twenty Six

Disaster at Hackney Downs

Time welded us into a great partnership. We were more than workmates. We were friends of a close nature. Jim did not enjoy the best of health and living in air raid shelters at Leyton didn't help. He was a family man and had his share of problems during the war. If I was early for a turn of duty, which was quite usual on the early morning shifts when lack of passenger trains saw me at work some two hours before I was due to sign on, I would get the engine ready. When Jim arrived all work would be done and we would sit in the cab, with the firebox door open and the flames throwing their friendly glow around the blackness of the cab walls. We would make a can of tea and talk over the happenings of the day, what we thought of the war, would we see the end of it, the latest air raid damage in his part of the world, what it was like at Brentwood. As I said, we were more than workmates.

At other times, when my train reached Stratford giving me limited time in which to sign on, Jim would have a lot of the work done. It was obvious why he was in line for higher things. He was not a bosses' man. He loved engines and they were part of him. He was not afraid to report their failings, whether it was because of ill design, mechanical defects or just laziness by crews.

One day we were both agreeably surprised. Although the war called on the raw resources of the country very heavily there was still the need to build new locomotives to replace the old ones, those destroyed by enemy action or those sent overseas. A new suburban passenger engine had just been built at the LNER's Doncaster Works, and we were rostered on it when it went into traffic.

It was known as class 'L1', an outside motion tank engine, with a 2-6-4 wheel arrangement and its number was No. 9000. What made it more exciting was the livery. It was at the end of the war and the locomotive had left the paintshop in the bright green colouring of the LNER.

We were assigned to No. 9000 so that Jim could give a report on its mechanical performance. It was like a trip to an enginemen's heaven. Everything worked in perfect order. No joints blew, all lubricators worked and damper rods stayed where you put them. No closing up on the run so that you didn't know until the fire started to die. What was extra special was the supply of electric headlights and a speedometer. There was also a light in the cab!

We had her on the Liverpool Street to Shenfield run in the rush hour. These were rostered turns of duty that became a nightmare for crews trying to maintain times with engines that would not steam. With No. 9000 they became paradise. She would purr out of Liverpool Street with the least fuss, quietly but very precisely barking out her crisp beat from the flowerpot chimney. Like a miniature express she would tackle the bank with the confidence of a 'B1', silver rods tracing their arcs as pistons thrust in and out of the cylinder chambers. The 250 1b. boiler pressure gave her the added punch and many a time we would climb towards Bethnal Green with boiler feeds on and steam wisping from the safety valves.

You didn't do that too often during the war. On the Shenfield run things were not too bad with a good engine as far as Romford. If you were on top of things at Romford, the rest of the trip looked good. If not, then there was a battle ahead. After Romford the track began to climb, slowly but surely. It went from about 1 in 115 to 1 in 100 at Gidea Park. By the time you reached Harold Wood station the bottom of Brentwood Bank had begun. Four to five miles of 1 in 100 to 1 in 90. A steady climb, with a right-hand turn near the top, just before Brentwood station.

The bank went on and on, seeming to never end as the steam pressure dropped every half mile. It was not until you climbed out of Brentwood on a long left-hand curve and reached the Three Arch bridge that the summit was reached. By that time the train had climbed about 500 feet. Then came the rapid drop into Shenfield at about 1 in 95. If the water was low in the glass as you barked under the bridge, trouble lay ahead. As the track went from uphill to downhill the water in the boiler would surge forward and, if its level was not deep enough to keep the top of the firebox covered, that's when the safety plug blew. It was then a case of stopping to throw the fire out before irreparable damage was done to the boiler.

With No. 9000 on the front on an eight-coach suburban set such things were just nightmares in a fireman's mind. We were before time at most stations and Brentwood Bank just seemed to make her steam more freely. It was while we had No. 9000 that we found out how fast we really went in keeping section times. The speedometer showed a regular 60 to 65 miles an hour between stations. Going down the Brentwood Bank, from Brentwood to Harold Wood, we would regularly clock 98 miles an hour. This came as quite a shock, especially as we would sometimes be passed on the up main by a 'B17', fast to London with the 'East Anglian'. They would have to be clocking about 110 miles an hour. We wondered if they knew! No wonder stations used to rattle as expresses thundered through. Four hundred tons of train travelling at that speed was quite impressive.

Driving at night was quite an experience, especially during the war in blackout conditions. I often wondered if passengers really understood how great was the element of fate in their safe journey. Engine headlamps were only codes for signalmen and did not light the way for footplate crews. Even the electric lamps on No. 9000 and the 'B1s', when they came out, were only for destination and train code working.

As the crew looked out of the cab they saw nothing but the darkness around them. All the houses along the lineside were invisible with their curtained or shuttered windows. The only lights to be seen were the signals and the subdued lighting on the stations. Even the latter were extinguished when the red alert came through. It was this situation which called for a full knowledge of the track and its surroundings.

We could tell the speed of the train by the sound of the wheels over the joints in the track. Their rhythmic clatter told you whether you were keeping time in the section or not. The driver would know, for instance, that once he passed the Romford inner home signal he could shut off steam and roll into the station. The clatter of the junction crossings would herald the platform's approach even though you could not see it. There would be the sudden enclosed roar as the brick wall of the signal box threw back the sound of the engine into the cab. A lesser roar told you that the ganger's hut had just been passed. That called for the first application of the Westinghouse brake. The senses had not let you down. The white painted edge of the platform loomed into sight. Suddenly things seemed to flash by. Another application of the brake and the train began to check its progress. By the time the platform end rolled into sight the train was stopping. A green light from the oil lamps of the station staff and it was off into the black void again.

Moonlit nights helped a lot but, on the average, it was driving by sounds, senses and the feel of the train behind you. The rumble over a bridge, the roar under a bridge, the sudden gasping, baffling echo of the engine's beat against the wall of a cutting . . . all these things were the sounds that told the engineman where he was at night. Moonlight nights were feared more than the blackness because enemy bombers could pick out railways more easily on such nights. Except on moonlit nights we never saw the track. It could reflect like dull silver ribbons in the lights of stations but that was all. We never really knew if it was there or not.

Typical of the shocks that could confront train crews was that experienced during a heavy air raid in the winter of 1942. As usual, it had been going on since sundown and dawn did not flush the grey skies till about eight the next morning. Bombing had been quite heavy in the Dagenham, Chadwell Heath and Goodmayes area. On the up main side of Chadwell Heath station were some oak trees that relieved the station's otherwise austere look. As the dawn light crept through the grey sky the station staff assessed the night's damage. They were horrified to see a German parachute caught in the oak trees, from whose slender cords dangled a land mine.

Trains had been running under it all night without knowing about the 500 1b. of explosives hanging there like the sword of Damocles above their heads. The vibration could have caused it to slip or drop, even trigger off the delicate fuse mechanism. God was on the railwaymen's side that night. The line was immediately closed and the bomb disposal men began their heroic and sometimes suicidal task of removal.

The one factor in our favour at night was the signalling system. If a bomb damaged the track it was also highly likely that it would damage the wires controlling the semaphore signals as they ran beside the track. This would cause the signals to drop to the danger position and give a red light. Even if the light went out that would be sufficient cause to stop the train and investigate as an absent light to train crews spelt danger at any time. Once again this was a good indication of the need for a thorough knowledge of the road by enginemen.

I never had a lot of time for railway management and the officers who carried out the decisions of management. They were a breed of their own, steeped in class distinction with no humanity in their souls when dealing with staff matters, whether the railwayman was at fault or just a victim of circumstances. They were the elite of the private companies who were running the railways into the ground, with the full knowledge that men were risking their lives on some of the engines.

They also knew that the taxpayer was going to be left with the impossible financial burden to pay after the war when revitalising the railways.

I well remember an incident involving Jim Tant and myself with the managerial elite. It was during the rush hour on a trip from Hertford to Liverpool Street with an eight-coach train full of city workers. No. 2633 was the engine, all polished up and steaming well. We stood on the up line at Clapton station. It was a station in a cutting and, when the train left for London, it immediately entered a tunnel of some length. The starting signal stood on a short post at the tunnel's mouth and, at the other end, was the advance starter, also operated by the Clapton signalman. When that was all clear it gave us the road to the Hackney Downs home signal. Hackney Downs was the junction with the Enfield line.

I was on the platform side. On receiving the porter's 'right away' signal I looked round to check that the starter was still in the 'off' position.

'Right away Jim,' I shouted above the panting Westinghouse pump and the roar of the blower. We were travelling bunker first. The 'N7' gripped the track with solid wheels and her 60 tons of living machinery surged forward. I went round the box with half shovels of cracked coal. The silvery glare through the trap door lit the cab like Southend pier as we entered the darkness of the tunnel.

The tunnel's roof restricted the blast of the engine's exhaust and the baffled beat reverberated round us as we gained speed. This way round the smoke and steam didn't worry us. It rolled over the train and the passengers would have their windows closed. Suddenly we broke into the morning light and Jim could see the advanced starter giving us the all clear to the Hackney Downs home signal. It was an uphill climb and No. 2633 barked along at a steady 40 miles an hour.

After passing the signal the track turned tightly to the left. This meant that Jim had his immediate vision cut off by the high sides of the bunker. The first thing he would see from his side would be the Enfield line and then the station platforms coming into view on the curve. The top of the climb had been reached, Jim was nearly in mid-gear with second port on the regulator. I could see further round the bend than Jim. I had just checked the waste water pipe to see that the feed was working properly. Looking up I saw the rear of another passenger train looming up in front of us! It was about 200 yards away, an eight-coach Westinghouse set that ran on the Chingford line.

'There's a train in front, Jim!' I bellowed.

Jim didn't doubt my word as some would have done. He gave the vacuum brake its full application, shut off steam and put the Westinghouse brake into emergency.

We pulled up in a heap and I suppose the passengers wondered what the hell was going on up front. We stopped about five yards from the rear coach of the Chingford train. If I hadn't seen the train in time on the bend we would have ploughed into the back of it at about 40 miles an hour. Splintered coaches in front, telescoped coaches behind us, the possibility of fire, death and injuries. It didn't bear thinking about. In the moments immediately after the stop, when Jim and I realised what could have been, we felt quite shaken.

'That was pure luck, Rob,' Jim mumbled. 'You did a good job son.'

There was an inquiry and the board found the Clapton signalman at fault. He admitted to pulling the advanced starter to the all clear before getting clearance from the signalman at Hackney Downs. Because he accepted guilt there was no need for us to attend the board hearing. They accepted Jim's written report as sufficient evidence. We never received one word of praise for our actions, thanks for our prompt attention in the cause of duty or acceptance of the fact that things could have gone the other way with substantial damage and compensation costs.

That was typical of the management behind their mahogany desks in the Victorian offices. They looked at operations through the cover of a manila folder which held a man's career history. The grime of the coal dust and oil never stained their carpets. The heat of the fires and the dust of endless miles without food and drink never worried their palates. But if a man slept in, or was late for his shift after his nine hours off between the last spell of 20 hours on the bucking footplate of a worn out crock, out would come the manila folder and disciplinary action would be worked out over the morning cup of tea and arrowroot biscuit.

I was quite bitter about it all but Jim would just shrug his stooped shoulders. 'Nothing you can do about it, Rob. There has to be discipline you know . . .'

I knew all right. I'd had discipline right through my life with an ex-army man as a father. I felt there should also be praise for a job well done. But praise was the last thing railwaymen received during the war, either from the boss, the government or the public.

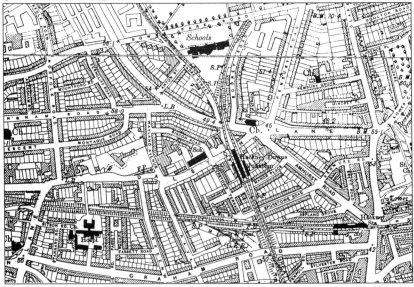

The near collision occurred on the line from Hertford via Clapton, approaching Hackney Downs station from the north east. Graham Road goods yard on the ex-North London Railway was where we used to have hot bacon sandwiches and syrupy tea for breakfast when we rolled in at about 4.0 am with the local goods. The local café catered for early workers. Fassett Square is adjacent to the goods yard, and has been restored to its true East End Splendour and is the set for the BBC soap 'Eastenders'.

Reproduced from the 6", 1920 Ordnance Survey Map

Chapter Twenty Seven

Discipline and Promotion

Discipline was more strict in the suburban links than any of the others. The only two tussles I had with the authorities came during my time in those links. Once I was booked on at 4.15 am. I caught the train that left Brentwood at 2.15 am. It was known as the railwaymen's train as we were the main ones to use it. It was due in Stratford at 3.15 am, giving me plenty of time before starting work.

There had been some heavy bombing that night and tracks were damaged. Due to late running the train did not arrive at Stratford until 4.20 am. It was a good 15 minutes walk to the loco. depot from the station. When I reached the Sign On room the big old clock on the wall showed 4.35 am. You were allowed 15 minutes. After that the absence was reported to the loco. running foreman.

I went to sign on but was not allowed to, even though it was enemy action that had caused the lateness of their own train service. Twenty minutes late for the shift and I was sent home. No 'sorry son, we understand.' Just a curt statement saying that I had failed to comply with the regulations. The result, a black mark on the records in the manila folder and loss of a day's pay.

The second event took place after the war and on a Sunday. I was working on the Shenfield line and had a full eight hour shift with passenger trains to and from Liverpool Street. On the run down to Shenfield, after about eight and a half hours on duty, we were to be relieved at Stratford.

When we ran into the platform the driver was there but no fireman. It didn't surprise me as many youngsters were suddenly becoming 'sick' at the weekends, with the war no longer wielding the big stick that demanded their regular attendance. I was told that relief would be available on the return trip. That would be two hours later. On the up trip, arriving at Stratford, still no relief. Work down to Stratford train control said, we'll see if relief can be arranged.

The next trip down was to Hertford via Stratford. By this time I had been on duty 14 hours. I had no food or drink. There was nowhere to buy any except Liverpool Street and my new driver said we didn't have time. When we ran into Stratford on the Hertford trip there was no fireman to be seen.

'Looks as though you're out of luck mate,' the driver said, still only halfway through his shift. I left the engine and went to the control box.

'Sorry mate, no relief. We'll remember you on the way back.'

That would be another two hours. I couldn't agree to 16 hours without food and drink.

'Well you have a train at the station until you find somebody,' I said.

'You can't stop there till relief comes!' they said.

'I'm not,' I told them, 'I'm going home.'

I grabbed my jacket and bag, told the driver I was leaving, and walked off the station. My train home was about 30 minutes away so I went to the railwayman's only haven at Stratford. On the corner of two grimy streets outside the station stood Jack's Cafe. It was really a converted terraced house from the Victorian era, still standing after Hitler had knocked the other end down, halfway up the street. It was condemned but, in true Cockney style, Jack didn't worry about things like that. In the room that was once somebody's pride and joy as a front parlour stood his counter with the ever boiling tea urn steaming away under the blackened ceiling.

Glass covered dishes held an assortment of cakes and pies, the contents of which we never questioned but ate eagerly to supplement the tight rationing at home. Day and night, seven days a week, raids or no raids, Jack was always open and round his six or seven tables you would find locomen and guards, sipping the stewed tea and waiting for the train home or time to start the next shift.

After I had walked off they soon found relief. They took a fireman from one of the shed shunting engines. That's how it was. Work till you cracked, then place the onus of bad management on you as the naughty boy. I had to attend an inquiry before some crow faced inspectors who had already made up their minds. I was suspended from duty for three days. In other words I lost three days' pay for refusing to work more than 14 hours without food and drink.

The wartime government of England also planned to treat us like slaves. It was their legislation that ruled we were in a reserved occupation, a service vital to the country's war effort. Men had tried to leave the railways and had actually joined the armed forces, only to be tracked down and returned to their depots.

I was called up and had my medical inspection for the army. I gave the army officer the special form given to me by the railway authorities which stated that I was in a reserved occupation. He just tossed it onto the desk in typical arrogant military fashion.

'You'll be in the army lad, no matter what they say,' he told me. He only revealed his ignorance of the situation. I was classified as reserved and remained at the Stratford depot.

As the war drew to a close the government announced that all men who had been in reserved occupations during the war would be called up to serve three years in the army of occupation. The landslide vote towards the Labour Party upset that idea and the decision was annulled. The unions made Attlee's government fully aware of the work done by railwaymen during the war, and could not support the policy of men being forced to work in the industry for six years and then give another three years forced labour to suit the whims of the government.

All good things come to an end and the relentless seniority movement through the links at Stratford eventually led to me leaving Jim Tant to go into the Main Line Goods link. It was a sad time for me as Jim was one of the few friends I had. It was also a strange period for a while, suddenly leaving the world of passenger trains and stepping back into the world of the slow, lumbering freight trains. They were main line trips and not just on the local goods in the London area. After quite a spell on trains averaging 60 miles an hour and strict timing in the sections, it seemed dreamtime to be clanking along at a steady 15 to 20 miles an hour. A further contrast was to be shunted into sidings, taking second place to passenger traffic.

The war was now over and passenger trains took preference over freight train. All that the cessation of hostilities meant to us was that the blackout was over and there was no need to search the skies for air attacks. The tin hat and gas mask could go into the cupboard. Apart from that things were the same. Food was still rationed, freight was still as heavy due to the need to supply the armies still overseas and industries now starting up at home with peacetime production. Raw materials were needed to rebuild the ravaged cities. The removal of bomb debris, trains fetching back evacuated school children, the movement of goods and people throughout the land now that restrictions had been lifted . . . all this became the railways' problem in an age when road transport was still practically non-existent due to the lack of vehicles and petrol.

If anything, the situation on the railways was worsening. The track was worn out, the locomotives were falling apart and the rolling stock was in bad order. This was not only the work of time but also a decision by the private railway companies to sit tight on their capital as it was obvious, with Labour now in power, that the railways would be nationalised.

This attitude disgusted railwaymen all over Britain. They realised that the Labour government was going to inherit a transport system that would be a financial loss from the start, purely because the companies had bled it dry by not replacing vital equipment and running down that which they had.

The locomotives used on the main line goods were like faithful old cart horses that had served their time, should have been put out to graze but were still in harness. The selection in our area was not great and included the Standard, or 'J39,' the 'J17' an 0-6-0 tender engine of vintage age, the 'K3', a powerful looking, three cylinder engine from the northern section of the LNER with a 2-8-0 wheel arrangement and a larger type which we called the 'Tango'. Its official classification was 'O2'. Its name came from the beat given by the three cylinders which powered it and also the way in which the thrust of those pistons into the cylinders would cause the cab to sway from side to side when on the run.

Now and then we would get passenger engines on the freight trains. They were no good for freight work, but we had them because freight locomotives were short and the passenger engines were waiting to go into the shops for repair, being under powered for the trains they should be hauling. The only time we had any decent locomotives on the main line goods was when we relieved in the country and found ourselves on an engine from some outstation such as Cambridge, Ipswich, Colchester or March. These engines were usually in good order as the outstations received the best Stratford could give them. In turn, with the limited crews using them the engines practically became their own and could be looked after in the same way that we had looked after the 'N7s'.

The only additions to heavy freight locomotives during the war on the LNER were two engines specifically designed as part of the war effort. One came from the British government and the other from the US as part of the lease-lend agreement. The British locomotive was the 'O7', known as the Austerity freight locomotive. It was a really solid design with the large boiler sitting high on a frame carried by 2-8-0 wheels. The driving wheels were the same size in diameter as the track gauge, 4 ft 8½ in. The two cylinders were placed outside the main frame for easy maintenance and repair. An unusual part of the boiler design was that the smokebox was slightly smaller in diameter than the boiler, so there was a slight tapering effect beneath the squat chimney.

It was superheated, had a boiler pressure of 225 lb. and was left-hand firing. There was plenty of room in the cab and this was needed when it came to cleaning the fire. The '07' was designed with a drop grate but half the time the grate would not work so it was a case of cleaning the 9 ft 4 in.-long box with the slice. It was heavy enough without the clinker on it and the blade took some angling out the cab doorway.

They steamed well and pulled heavy loads without trouble. We were told that they were originally designed for shipping to Russia for the Second Front but, due to the desperate situation at Stratford for a decent heavy freight locomotive, some were transferred to the depot for use on the coal trains from the Midlands. They were fitted with steam and vacuum brakes, the vacuum being for use when running on express freight trains or troop trains that had army equipment, like tanks or guns, as well as coaches for the troops.

The US engines were typical of the locomotives of that country. Everything seemed to be hanging on the outside and the engine seemed to be top-heavy when compared with the British counterpart. Its boiler sat above the outside motions of the two cylinders and the driving wheels would not have been more than four feet in diameter. Where the British locomotives had the footplate and boiler down to the wheels, over the axles, the Yankee job had the boiler that far in the air you could see over the wheels and straight through to the other side.

They were a powerful locomotive and good to work. They steamed with the slightest fire and were a fireman's delight when it came to disposal. The firebox was as wide as it was long and had a grate that was divided into four sections. The firebars were very different from the British design. They were something like the gas frets on pre-war gas stoves. The fixed sections of bars were attached to steel bars underneath which rocked when manipulated with the rocker bar from inside the cab, just in front of the firebox door. It was called the rocker grate.

A steel lever was placed in the apparatus in front of the firebox door and, as the fireman rocked the lever backward and forward, so the grates down one side of the firebox would rock diagonally on their fittings. The clinker would fall into the ashpan for disposal. After rocking one side of the box the live fire would be placed on the clean side and the clinker would be rocked into the ashpan again.

There were two cases, one on the GWR and one on the LNER, where the crown of the steel firebox of these locomotives collapsed due to a shortage of water in the boiler. These were officially found to have been caused by the crews' unfamiliarity with the water gauge and test cocks. Comprehensive instructions regarding the gauge were issued but a third firebox collapse occurred several months later, despite the enginemen having signed for these instructions. Again a shortage of water in the boiler caused the collapse and the official inquiry put this down to mismanagement on the part of the crew (who were killed).

I have known of occasions on British locomotives where the plug has melted due to lack of water but the firebox has not collapsed in such a fashion. I would say the situation with the US locos was a combination of lack of water and the fact that steel boiler stays were employed, rather than the copper ones used in Britain.

Chapter Twenty Eight

The Tale of Driver Smith

Although we were supposed to have the best engines available in the Main Line Goods link, it was not unusual to arrive at a marshalling yard to relieve a crew and find that the engine was the good old faithful 'J15'. It had replaced one of the more modern locomotives that had given up the ghost somewhere in the country. This happened to me on an occasion that has never left my memory.

One of the things that a fireman found out when getting into the Main Line Goods link, was that he didn't keep his regular driver for long. There was a constant call for experienced drivers in the express passenger links and you could report for work, expecting your regular mate to be there, only to find some stranger at the sign-on book. On this occasion I signed on at about 8.0 pm to find that my mate had been rostered elsewhere.

My new driver was one by the name of Smith. He was the demon driver of Stratford loco. and all young firemen had hair raising tales of his exploits. I had never been with him up till then but I had heard the tales that went around. Some were exaggerated but others were very true and he had the meetings with inspectors to prove them.

Like the time he worked one of the crack expresses down road and ended up with most people spilling their coffee in the dining car. Or the time he was on the Cambridge line with an express, failed to notice a speed restriction and thundered through a country station leaving a trail of debris as all the waiting room windows fell out.

He was one of the characters around the place. Not a great locomotive man but either possessing nerves of steel or being slightly mad. He was never seen in dirty overalls or cap. Very debonair with well laundered bib and brace overalls and jacket, ironed to perfection. He had a cap with an oil cloth top that shone like a lifeguard's helmet. From a distance he could have been taken for Errol Flynn and we sometimes thought he saw himself as that swashbuckling film star. A sabre would have looked better in his hand than an oil feeder.

Passenger to Goodmayes, freight train to Southend and return to Goodmayes was the diagram working. We would finish about five in the morning if we were lucky. We caught a suburban train to Goodmayes and walked across the tracks to the engine road. The rostered engine was a 'J39' which I thought would be hard enough to keep steam up with this driver on the regulator. When I saw the old 'J15' standing by the water column I could not check the gasp.

'A Little Goods on the Southend run,' I said.

'Don't let that worry you me boy. They used to run every freight train on the Great Eastern once.'

I knew that but what driver Smith didn't say was that the tonnages were only half that which we were pulling in 1945. The engine had been coaled and everything was ready for us. The train was not the usual mixed freight but a full load of aviation fuel for the Royal Air Force base at Rochford. My heart was in my boots by this time. Ordinary freight was bad enough but a train of loaded petrol tankers was not only heavy but needed special handling, not like the trip they were about to get.

We backed on to the solid black frame of the leading truck and I slipped the three link coupling over the drawbar hook. The only brakes on the train would be those on the engine and in the guard's brake. The Queen Mary type guard's van weighing 20 tons was a good anchorman in time of need.

I must say the old girl steamed well. I had a good fire on as we rolled slowly down the outlet loop, waiting for the starter to blink its green aspect to let us on to the down suburban. The coals were level with the firebox door lip at the door and a solid wedge to the front boiler plate. Feeds worked well and I kept the boiler level at the two-thirds old Bill Cole had told me, allowing for the lift when driver Smith took off.

The signal arm lowered and the paraffin lamp threw its golden glow against the green glass. Smith pushed the little regulator to first port and the 37 ton locomotive bit the rails with her six 4 ft 11 in. driving wheels. The beat from the tall chimney was crisp and clear. At least her valves were well set. The siderod clanked as it took up on the bushes and rang into the cool night air. The tankers followed us on the down suburban line and I acknowledged the guard's swinging green light with a toot on the whistle. Our train was complete.

We were now on the main track and the Chadwell Heath distant showed that we were clear to Romford. The regulator went over to second port. Cinders rocketed out of the Victorian chimney of the 'J15' like a firework display and the reversing wheel was wound up to nearly 50 per cent cut off. The Ross safety valves roared into action as the roaring inferno pushed the steam needle past the 160 mark on the gauge. It seemed she liked the rough treatment and I was glad because she was going to get a lot more!

The firebox door clattered on to the cab floor as I lifted the latch from the ratchet to fire up. My overalls gave off a smell of scorching as the heat came into the cab, white and brilliant. Door up and feed on, the pale flickering light from the rape oil in the gauge glass lamp showing that we still had two-thirds of a boiler full. I couldn't see much for a while. It was always like that after firing up at night. The sudden glare of the fire then nothing as you shut the door, except for two throbbing rays of gold stabbing at the night sky behind you as firelight escaped from the side of the door where it did not fit flush to the boiler frame. They were the telltale rays of light that led enemy bombers towards unsuspecting engine crews during night trips in the war. Even with the protective blinds up a certain amount of light still escaped.

The austere lights of Chadwell Heath station went by as our heavy beat thundered under the timber canopies of the platforms. The rhythmic click-clack of the tanker wheels over the rail joints punctuated the night air and seemed to disappear as we left the station behind us. The track was fairly level to Romford and, once having the train on the move, it did not take a lot of steam to keep it rolling.

We rumbled over the steel bridge that straddled Romford's main street and driver Smith shut the regulator for the first time since we had left Goodmayes.

The distant was on and Gidea Park's home signal was at danger. We felt the train run into us as the engine lost momentum. Then there was the double surge as the petrol in the tankers surged against the bulkheads. This was the danger when working any train that had a liquid load.

The load would slop about in the container and gain a movement of its own that had nothing to do with the forward movement of the train. In fact the weight of the surging liquid could be going the opposite way as it tried to find its own level. Being a loose-coupled train it meant that there was a double strain on those three steel links between each wagon. If the brake was applied too suddenly there would be a bunching of the wagons then, as they eased out, the liquid could force them together again. If this happened on a curve, buffer could jump buffer and then the wagons would become buffer-locked. This was sufficient to lift the wagon's wheels and cause a derailment.

The driver worked the steam brake in short bursts so that, as he collected the wagons as they ran into us, they did not bunch or snatch. Although quite an extrovert in his driving he rarely spoke during a journey. He stood in his corner, one shiny-booted foot up on the wooden locker on which most drivers sat, gazing out of the cab window as though his steely blue eyes would cause the red light to change to green. One hand held the steam brake, the other a cigarette. I used the time to fill the boiler and put a fire on ready for the bank ahead. We had nearly rolled to a stop when the signal changed to green.

The cause of the check had been a passenger train arriving at Gidea Park station from Harold Wood. They wanted to switch us on to the down main and, until the up suburban line was cleared, they could not switch us across.

Now we had green lights all the way. My mate let the wheel out and gave her the lot. Steam, smoke and cinders shrouded the station as we belched under the brick bridge that carried the road over the railway at the station. The train pulled heavily now as the gradient was against us and would not improve for the next five miles.

The fire was burning well and the old 'J15' was steaming better than many of her kind but, when working a train of such tonnage, a greater steam pressure than 160 lb. was needed so that there was something in reserve.

The bank between Harold Wood and Brentwood was as straight as a ruler, it was widened from two to four tracks by Irish labour during the depression before World War II. The labourers had no homes except the timber shanties they built themselves along the track side. Old drivers would tell us tales of the Irishmen's poverty. How they turned empty condensed milk tins into cups and steel lids off metal drums as plates. They lived and sometimes died along the track and their monument was the best piece of track in the London suburban service.

Looking ahead into the darkness of the night all I could see was a row of green lights coming from the automatic signals in front of us, like an emerald necklace climbing slowly toward heaven. There would be no stopping unless it was because of a shortage of steam. And many an engine crew had stopped on the bank for a 'blow-up' as it was known.

By the time Brentwood station was behind us the steam gauge was showing 100 lb. and there was about one third of a glass of water in the boiler. I couldn't put the boiler feed on because we were using steam as fast as she made it. We were well on time. In fact we had been going five miles an hour faster than was necessary, and that was the difference between a comfortable journey and scratching for steam as we were when we panted under the Seven Arch bridge.

Soon we could shut off steam and coast for miles and I would have all the time in the world to fill the boiler but, with only one-third of a glass, I knew that once we topped the bank the water would nearly disappear. On the level we would only have about a quarter of a boiler full but as we went down hill the water would go to the front of the boiler and the level would just about bubble in 'the nut'.

I could put the feed on but that would only lower the steam pressure further and it was the steam brake that was going to take all priorities when we started to roll down the bank towards Shenfield. The lower the steam pressure the weaker the brake to hold the unbraked train. I looked at driver Smith but his face was a mask of stoic acceptance of the inevitable.

At last we were there. The 'J15' began to chant her beat more rapidly between the weathered cement walls of the cutting. The regulator was shut and the wheel wound out ready for the 1 in 95 drop in gradient. The water in the glass disappeared and then came back with a surge. I put the feed on to bring the water to a safer level. There was a hefty nudge in the rear as the tankers ran into us, the law of gravity taking control of our liquid load.

Smith applied the steam brake and the train seemed to push harder. At least the tankers were together and we felt no snatch to show that they had pulled away from the engine. He made the maximum application and told me to screw the hand brake on hard on the tender. It went about eight turns. He released the steam brake to recharge the cylinder.

The steam gauge was quivering on 100, nowhere near the pressure needed to hold a train of surging aviation spirit. He applied the brake again. The steel brake blocks gave off an acrid smoke as they gripped the driving wheels that were now coasting over the silver ribbons of track turning towards the bridge before Shenfield junction. The electric signal against the smoke grimed brickwork glared a sullen red and I knew we had no chance of stopping at it.

Driver Smith never said a word. He pulled on the whistle chain and gave a cock-a-doodle-doo whistle repeatedly. It was the cry of a locomotive in distress and would let the guard know that we wanted him to apply the brake in his guard's van, if he hadn't already done so. We felt a slight pull in the rear and knew that he had responded, no doubt applying sand to the rail so that the brake would get a stronger hold.

We rumbled under the bridge with the signal still showing red. We were in the next section without authority. There could be a train standing in the station and we were rolling on remorselessly towards it. Fate only knew the outcome. In the darkness I could only imagine the 'J15' splintering the rear coaches, tankers rupturing behind us and Shenfield having its greatest night of terror as the station went up in flames. All because of my mate's love of speed.

He was still blowing the whistle. The steam pressure was coming up well and holding at 150. The difference was remarkable. We were gaining the upper hand over the sheer weight of the moving petrol. It looked as though we could stop at the station. We could see the station starter now on the gantry which had the down main starter and down main to Southend branch starter blazing red in the darkness. The danger was over. There was no train in the station platform. There would be no fire.

Suddenly the down main to Southend signal flashed to green. My driver acknowledged with a cheeky toot on the whistle and told me to release the hand brake. We clattered through the station at about 25 miles an hour, quite fast enough for a loose-coupled train of petrol tankers, rumbling over the steel bridge that crossed the road below and into the night again.

We found out later that the signals were at danger because the signalman had intended to let an up main express through before we crossed to the Southend line in front of him. On hearing our whistle of distress he found he could hold the express outside the station and give us a chance to cross to the Southend branch. After getting 'entering section' from Brentwood signal box he had underestimated my driver's ability for speed, even with a freight train and 19th century engine. Whether driver Smith was disciplined I don't know. I never had him as a driver again.

Chapter Twenty Nine

Working Heavy Freight from March

Most of my main line freight work was on the Cambridge line with coal trains from the Midlands via the huge marshalling yard at Whitemoor, and coal empties back. These trains were worked by crews from the railway depot at March. March was a railway town and served the Whitemoor marshalling complex with engine power.

There was no love lost between Stratford and March crews. Commonly known as Swede Bashers, Stratford men alleged that the March crews lived on that vegetable alone. Fact or fiction, we knew that they lived better than we did. On average the country people didn't starve during the war. It was only the Londoner who really knew the rigours of life on government rations and no extras.

The March crews would drag their time out so that we would relieve them in the country and so save them the horrors of sleeping at Stratford dormitory during the blitz. You couldn't blame them but it was galling to know that they could get relief almost at any time whereas, once we stepped on the footplate, we were there to stay.

The set pattern of operations in the main line link was to sign on at Stratford, get an engine from the shed that had been prepared by the shed staff, travel light to Temple Mills and pick up a train of empty coal trucks. Work the train towards Cambridge to cross a coal train coming from Whitemoor. Crews would then change footplates and we would work back to Stratford, they would go on to March.

On other occasions we would travel passenger to relieve on a train coming to Temple Mills from Whitemoor. Usually these were coal trains where the crew was originally rostered to work to Stratford and stay in the dormitory. Due to their late running we were sent to relieve them on the road and they would catch the train back to March.

The only joy we had from working these trains was that most of the engines were from the March depot and, as an outstation of Stratford, they were in good order. The March men used to complain at times about their poor mechanical ability but, when compared with the locomotives we had every day, a March engine was like the locomotive on the Royal Train. At least they had the capacity to do the job.

A good proportion of the time at Stratford we were working heavy freight trains with worn out passenger engines. The 'B12' and 'B17' were all right on a 12-coach passenger train but, put 50 to 70 freight wagons behind them and there was all the trouble in the world. The 6 ft 6 in. driving wheels of the 'B12', or the 6 ft 8 in. wheels of the 'B17' were too large to get the adhesive traction powers needed to haul badly maintained freight wagons from a standing start. They would slip and slide, even on a dry rail and, in wet weather, it could take 15 minutes to get the train rolling.

The braking system on passenger locomotives was also dangerous for freight

One of a pair built in 1903, class 'Y5' 0-4-0T No. 230 was in service stock by Grouping, being employed in the Stratford Carriage works for general shunting and brake testing. Before the war the engine was maintained in immaculate condition, appearing as the 'Coffee Pot' in annual railway exhibitions in the GE area. It is seen here by Chobham Farm box, shortly after its renumbering in December 1946 from No. 7230, well loaded with coal for the day's work. It was withdrawn in April 1948. *Photomatic*

The class 'Y4' 0-4-0Ts were employed in the Stratford area, mainly at Canning Town and Devonshire goods stations where tight curves abounded. No. 8127 rests at Stratford in about 1947; it was formerly GER No. 226, built in 1914, withdrawal came in 1956. *Photomatic*

This atmospheric view shows 'N7/3' class 0-6-2T No. 9726 reaching the top of Bethnal Green bank on a down through line train, composed of quintuple sets, heading for Romford and Shenfield on 2nd December, 1946. The signal gantry spans the six running lines into Liverpool Street. *H.C. Casserley*

An early British Railways period view of 'B12/3' class 4-6-0 No. E1530, note the regional prefix 'E' to the LNER running number applied in 1948. This was one of several 'B12s' to be used on ambulance train workings for the use of American forces in World War II, ideal engines in view of their light weight and restricted loading gauge. To clear the Southern structure gauge the footsteps have been cut back, hence the pierced backplate to the steps. *John Watling Collection*

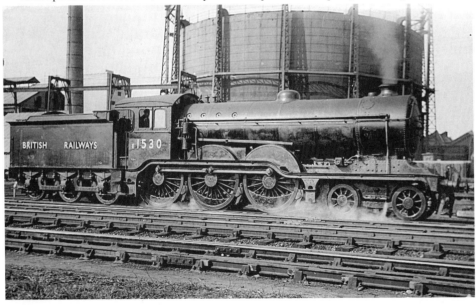

Many 'J15s' were pressed into traffic at weekends to handle excursion traffic. Here 'J15' class 0-6-0 No. 5446 heads an excursion from Enfield to Southend, passing Copper Mill Junction on 23rd July, 1949. The train consists of at least one quintuple set, perhaps two.   *Ken Nunn*

'N7' class 0-6-2T No. 69727 stands on the loop opposite the Bethnal Green station awaiting a path into Liverpool Street. The period is very early BR as the GER 8-coach Ilford suburban set still carries the LNER style lettering.   *N.E. Stead*

'N7/3' class 0-6-2T No. 69729 is seen leaving Gidea Park on the 12.48 up train to Liverpool Street on 5th October, 1949. The train consists of a GER 8-coach suburban set, soon to be displaced by the introduction of the Shenfield electric stock. *Ken Nunn*

'N7/3' 0-6-2T No. 9716, built as 2614 at Doncaster in 1928, rests at Shenfield on an up train in about 1950, consisting of a single quintuple suburban set. *John Watling Collection*

In latter days the whole of the 'J19' class was allocated to the GE Section, employed on a variety of goods duties. 'J19' class 0-6-0 No. 64649, built in 1913, is at Stratford on 19th August, 1950, with early BR lettering but still lacking the smokebox number plate. It was withdrawn in January 1959. *H.C. Casserley*

The North Woolwich to Palace Gates service brought trains onto the Cambridge main line between Loughton Junction and Seven Sisters. 'F5' class 2-4-2T No. 67210 is seen travelling northwards near Tottenham South Junction on 29th August, 1953, hauling a 4-coach set of Gresley's 1935 stock. *A.G. Ellis*

The up 'Norfolkman' train, introduced in 1948, at Bethnal Green headed by 'B1' class 4-6-0 No.61119, built by the North British Locomotive Co. in January 1947. Nearing the end of its journey from Norwich to Liverpool Street, in about 1950, the formation comprised 8 Gresley carriages.					*R.W. Beaton*

An early 1950s view of 'B17' class 4-6-0 No. 61606 *Audley End*, one of the original batch of 'Sandringhams', following its rebuilding to 'B17/6' in March 1950. The train, composed of Gresley stock, is ascending Brentwood bank on a down express. The carriages are in crimson and cream livery, note the presence of catch points on the 1 in 70 bank.				*R.W. Beaton*

'B1' class 4-6-0 No. 61005 *Bongo* heading the 'Day Continental' from Harwich and approaching Shenfield Junction. The two white boards denote it is an express train, 11th September, 1953.

British Railways

Seen at Stratford in the early 1950s, 'J15' class 0-6-0 No. 65432 was fitted with vacuum ejector in 1935 and a side window cab and tender weatherboards for working trains over the Colne Valley line.

J. Kirke

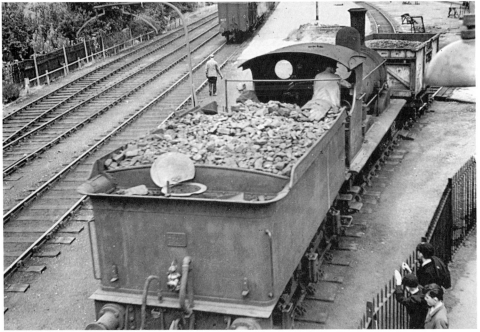

Although the Epping and Ongar line passenger services were now in the hands of London Transport as part of the Central line, goods trains were still steam hauled until the early 1960s. Here 'J15' class 0-6-0 No. 65455, built in 1906, shunts in Loughton coal yard on 17th October 1959, a few months before withdrawal.   *G. Pember*

A daily stores train running between Stratford and Leyton depot was a regular working for many years. 'J69/1' class 0-6-0T No. 68556 leaves Stratford station during the late 1950s, past the general offices and Old Works. The engine survived to the end of steam on the GE in September 1962.   *Lyn Brooks Collection*

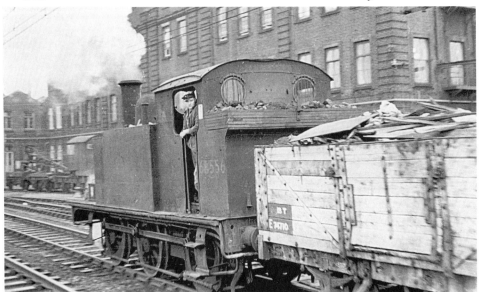

work. With only the Westinghouse brake on the engine the actions needed to stop unbraked, loose-coupled freight trains called on all the skills a driver could muster.

I remember working a freight train to Temple Mills from Cambridge with a 'B12' that was in a bad way. It was coming in for repairs and should have been worked light engine. Due to engine power shortage it was put on a freight train. Brake blocks were paper thin on the driving wheels, the smokebox was drawing air and both clacks were blowing. It seemed that when the boiler feeds were on, more water was running on the ground than being fed into the boiler. The water in the gauge glass never seemed to get above half full and my driver's opinion was that the boiler was so furred up that the lime deposit was absorbing most of the water we put in.

The most alarming fault of all was that the engine had been in a derailment and the main frame was buckled. The trailing driving wheel of a 'B12' was situated under the lockers in the cab on which the crew sat during the journey. The lockers were made of steel and came from the cab front to the doorway between cab and tender. Due to the buckled frame the trailing wheel of this engine had worked against the steel wall of the lockers and ground its way through so that the flange came into the cab on each rotation!

It was whipping round like a grindstone where the fireman's legs would be if he were silly enough to sit there. My driver thought it was a great joke, although he did admit that in all his years on the railway he had never seen an engine with its wheels in the cab. He found his pocket knife and proceeded to sharpen it on the wheel's flange as we went along.

The main engines we worked on the Whitemoor run were 'K3s' and 'O2s' with the War Department 'O7' coming into use quite frequently. I didn't mind the 'O2' or 'Tango' as we called it. Others hated it but had to admit that its 2-8-0 wheel arrangement, with 4 ft 8½ in. driving wheels, was the best formula for heavy freight loads. The three cylinders gave the extra punch up the banks.

The main trouble with the 'Tango' was its firebox. It was long and narrow. It also dropped at quite a sharp angle when compared with the 'B12' which had a firebox of similar length. The 'Tango' was also a left-hand firing engine. To get the coal up to the front of the box a rapid swing was needed in the restricted cab and the correct bounce of the blade on the side of the firebox door to get the coal to ricochet to the front corners. As if this was not difficult enough, the coal had to be on a flight path that would not collide with the leading edge of the brick arch. Due to the sharp angle by which the firebox dropped from back to front, the brick arch came that much lower than those we were used to in the standard fireboxes.

If the coal left the shovel at an angle that was too sharp, it hit the middle of the brick arch and dropped about 18 inches short of the front of the firebox. This created a situation where the fire built up high under the brick arch but did not cover the bare bars at the front boiler plate. With the bare grate just above the ashpan opening, cold air flowed against the boiler plate and soon the steam pressure dropped. The only answer to the problem was to get the slice off the tender tray and push the heaped fire under the brick arch down to the gap at the front. Working a slice over 10 feet of roaring fire was no welcome task.

Getting it back onto the tender was worse. So it paid to perfect the art of getting the coals right up to the front of the firebox without hitting the brick arch. Once there the old 'Tangos' would steam forever.

The engines were all black in colour, seldom cleaned and never off the road. I really enjoyed the Cambridge run with a 'Tango'. On the expresses you were too busy battling for steam and water to notice the countryside. With the freight trains going at their leisurely 20 or 30 miles an hour through the Home Counties you could see things in more detail.

I liked the countryside after the train had left Bishops Stortford behind. Between there and Cambridge was some of the most rustic scenery to be found in that part of the world. Shortly after leaving Bishops Stortford the track would begin to climb. The rising ground was known as the East Anglian Heights and it was steep enough to make the three cylinders of the 'Tango' let the farms and cottages in the valleys know that we were on our way.

Choof choof choof : . . choof choof choof . . . the exhaust would bark against the clear sky. As the cab rocked from side to side, following the thrust of the big ends and the silvery pistons flashing in and out of the black, greasy cylinders, the fireman would have his backside wedged against the seat, swinging the shovel with cracked coal into the brightness of the flames. The shovel would 'ting' with the heat after a while and the newly placed coal on its shining blade would start to smoke before it even made the firebox door. The eight driving wheels would grab the track with the tenacity of a rock climber and the rumbling coal empties would clickerty-clack over the joints behind us.

Working under pressure, the steam gauge would pass the 180 1b. and the welcome white feather of steam would wisp away from the safety valves in front of the cab and trail over the tender, mixed with the smoke and steam from the stumpy chimney. The boiler feed would sing as water rushed along the pipes and all was well with the world. The billy of tea would be lifted off the tray on the boiler front and driver and fireman would sip the hot beverage as it slopped in the enamel mug with the motion of the engine. They would find comfort in its syrupy flavour, and would be hoping that the kettle would be boiling where they crossed with the up train so that another brew could be made to see them back to war torn London.

When the top of the bank was reached it was a case of shutting off steam to the cylinders, winding the reversing wheel right out and rolling with the train to the next up gradient. The weight of the train would build up the speed and the steam brake would not only control the train's speed but also bunch the train together so that there was not too much surge and snatch as the train lost momentum and the engine gained power.

As the downhill run levelled out and the train was felt to stretch its couplings the driver would ease open the regulator and wind up the wheel to nearly 50 per cent cut-off. There would be just enough steam getting through the steam chest to maintain the required speed and the train would rumble on with the engine purring contentedly.

At times like this the crew would sit and watch around them. Freight trains usually ran when most people were in bed, either late at night, through the night or early mornings. Because of this engine crews saw the landscape as few others saw it. It was devoid of human beings. The roads were empty and only animals were the railwaymen's companions through the long and lonely shifts. Even stations were unattended. The only staff on duty were the signalmen in their solitary wooden fortresses some 20 feet in the air, at the end of station platforms or sometimes in the middle of nowhere, controlling a vital junction on a steel artery that linked London with its mineral lifeline.

Newport, Elsenham, Littlebury, Great Chesterford . . . the station name boards would drift by in the steam and smoke like monuments to a lost civilisation. The Victorian design of the brick stations stood silently in the morning sunlight or evening shadows. I always remember one country station on that line as I saw it on an autumn morning, nestled in a valley that had its trees dressed in their Jacob's coat of orange, yellow and brown. A little cottage stood against the darkness of the hawthorn hedgerow and from its crooked chimney came the light blue wisp of smoke that left the fire in some tidy country kitchen. Someone was getting breakfast and, standing on the hillside in the frosty grass with the slanting rays of the sun on their backs, stood two cart horses. They were also watching the smoke from the cottage. Perhaps their day was about to start.

We clattered by with siderods ringing and safety valves whistling like an old kitchen kettle on the hob. I thought how good it would be, to live there, away from the war torn city, dust and dirt. To get up at regular hours and go to bed at regular hours. Maybe have a weekend off now and then. We all had these dreams. The locals would have been surprised if they knew how intently we followed their lives.

Lineside gardens were of great interest to locomen. They were mostly gardeners themselves. They would see the cabbage plants put in by the old boy who lived two houses past Newport station on the down side. On the next shift it would be noted if the plants were doing any good, or if they were going ahead faster than the plants put in by the engine crew. Then there was that farm cottage just beyond the quarter mile peg on the other side of the Whittlesford loop. Had you ever seen such dirty washing on a clothes line? Slung between two elms with the spar of a tree as a prop. Perhaps it was because it hung there for three or four days. Our smoke wouldn't help! A great game was coming across some young thing hanging out her smalls. Waiting until she was about to peg up a pair of silk knickers and then give her a cheeky toot-toot on the whistle.

Whittlesford was well known by Stratford men. They spent many an hour in the siding waiting for the up train to lumber through Cambridge with coal for London. Another 'Tango' would clatter over the points and the Swede bashers would climb down. A few curt instructions and we would climb on to take the train to Temple Mills. At Northumberland Park we would be switched to one of the goods roads that ran parallel with the up main. It then became permissive working. We had to travel slowly because there could be another freight train in front of us, heading for the reception roads at Temple Mills.

It was a case of follow the leader. This was usually where we were relieved by a spare crew from Stratford Loco. Then it was a case of humping the bag and walking to the Mills, hoping to catch a light engine that would be going to

Stratford for disposal. If luck was out it was a walk all the way, about two miles over tracks and through sidings, come rain, sun or snow. Sign off and then study the roster for the next turn of duty. Maybe the train home had just left and it was into Jack's Cafe for a cuppa and a couple of his cakes.

Some would draw on the home made cigarette, with grease or coal dust still marking the tissue as it was rolled. They often relived some trip they had made, their thoughts revolving round the only world they really knew.

'Remember that night when old Joe Sutcliffe failed at Bow Junction? Blocked six tracks he did . . . well, I ask you, 500 tons with a 'Buck Jumper' . . .'

The situation in the Main Line Goods Link was hectic and we often experienced the case where we would have our nine hours off, sign on for another train to Whitemoor and find ourselves walking to Temple Mills to relieve men on the same engine that we had left there on the previous shift. It had taken them all that time to get to the yard, leave the train and get on the engine road for requirements. No wonder the old 'Tangos' looked dirty. They never saw a cleaner's rag or a fitter's piece of waste.

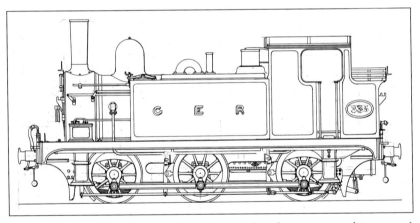

Another version of the 'Buck Jumper'. This one has the stove pipe chimney, and ramsbottom safety valves housed in front of the cab. The smallness of the bunker can be seen and it was against the steel railings that we would stack large lumps of coal to increase the bunker's capacity.   *Great Eastern Railway Society Collection*

Chapter Thirty

The Catch with Catch Points

I never worked an express freight train and, looking back, I don't think I missed much. The only difference between main line slow freight and the express freight was that the express had the first 9 to 12 wagons fitted with the vacuum brake. The rest of the train was still loose coupled with the three link coupling. A crew could have a 60 wagon train and, because the first 12 wagons were fitted with the continuous brake, their timetable moved to the express time bracket.

Admittedly the extra braking power was a help but not that much when it came to working the train through the long sections with semaphore signalling in the country districts. Problems arose in foggy weather when the advanced starter of a station had been passed and it was not possible to see whether the next distant signal was at caution or clear.

On clear days or nights, with the distant signal in sight, fast running could be maintained but when the fog came down over the Essex marshes and visibility was to the end of the engine's boiler the driver could not take the risk and hope that the next distant was off. Once again it was a case of knowing very inch of the track. Knowing, for instance, that the next distant signal was just past the mile peg after the stone bridge. And that, if the distant signal was at caution the home signal was where the row of pine trees began near the farm gate at Nine Mile Bottom. This was never learned from any departmental document or regulation but handed down from driver to fireman and then spare fireman to cleaner.

There was an improvement in the couplings of freight trains towards the end of the war when the three link coupling changed its design. As it was the three link coupling allowed too much play between wagons and on a long train there was much trouble with bunching and run outs over the gradients in the track. The engine would be fully extended in getting the train up a bank and the couplings would be taut as gravity held the trucks back. As the engine topped the bank and began the downhill run the train would stay taut because the bulk of the load was still on the up grade.

As the majority of the train's load breasted the peak of the hill the trucks would gather more speed than the engine and start to run into it. Sometimes the buffer faces of the wagons could be at least 12 inches apart, especially if the buffers were of an old design or not properly maintained. This meant that with 50 wagons on the train there could be a run in and run out of 50 feet. It was in a situation like this that, if the engine's brake was not applied in the proper manner, wagons could bunch and buffers would ride up on each other. Or the run in could make the loose coupling jump off the drawbar hook. If this happened, as the front of the train pulled away the uncoupled wagons would lose momentum and roll to a stop in the section. If it happened on an incline they would start to run backwards. This was known as a breakaway in the section.

The only thing that could stop them from running backwards into an oncoming train was the ability of the guard to check them with the brake in the guard's van. This was possible if the breakaway was noticed in time but, at night in the blackness of the van's interior, with only his oil burning handlamp to light his surroundings, it was sometimes minutes before the guard realised that he was going backwards and not forwards.

One way to reduce this play between wagon buffer faces was to shorten the coupling's length. On express freight trains this was done by screwing up the screw couplings on the vacuum brake wagons as far as they would go while the engine had the trucks pushed up against the stops or the guard's van with its brake on. The difference between the screw coupling and the three link coupling was that the screw coupling had two U-shaped steel links fitted on to a steel centre rod that was threaded so the shackles drew into the centre as the central rod was screwed up by the shunter.

The new three link coupling was designed with the central link being pear shaped, not elongated as the orthodox three link coupling. When lying horizontally, like a pear on its side, the link was as big as the normal link. When the train was eased up and the buffers were in their sleeves, the middle link was turned so that the bottom of the 'pear' was upmost and the top of the 'pear' pointed to the ground. This then became the shortened link and considerably reduced the pull and snatch on a loose-coupled train.

Knowing the ever present possibility of freight train breakaways, the railway companies devised a safety method on most major lines where inclines were steep. It was known as the catch point. There were quite a few up the Brentwood Bank. Basically they were a spring loaded set of points in the running track that always held an open position in the opposite direction to the normal movement of trains.

As the train ran over them in the correct direction, it was like running through a set of points. The point blades would close to complete the line. Once the vehicle had passed over the leading edge of the point's blade it would spring open so that, if the wagon should roll back, the wheels would be directed away from the main running track and on to the cess beside the track. It was an automatic derailer and stopped runaway trains from careering into oncoming traffic.

Although an essential part of the safety equipment they were also the hidden fear of locomen on freight trains at night, and sometimes passenger trains. Brentwood Bank held no fear for a crew with a normal loading and a locomotive that was in its prime. But that used to be the exception more than the rule. The panic situation was with the engine that was failing to maintain steam and losing tractive effort due to the loss of power.

Suddenly the wheels would find a greasy section where the night mist had condensed on the rail surface. The driving wheels would spin in an uncontrollable slip before the driver could shut the regulator. With the regulator shut, the steam brake would be applied to anchor those wheels while waiting with baited breath for the giant pull of the train that had been suddenly checked in its momentum and bunched up behind the tender. Would the couplings take the strain or would they snap like cotton and let the wagons roll back down the bank? The correct thing to do would be to release the steam brake and not apply it until the pull of the train was felt. This would reduce coupling and drawbar strain but would increase the length of the backward movement of the train while the braked engine acted as anchorman when the pull did come.

The driver didn't have that choice because he did not know how near he was to a set of catch points. The run back could derail his train, maybe in the middle of it. The crew would stand on the darkened footplate, the firelight casting golden rays towards the blackness of the sky, sometimes taking on a wispy beauty as the smoke blew back in the light.

There it was! A sudden yank that felt like a dentist pulling out a monster's tooth. Poor old guard. They hope he was sitting down! The thing to do was to let the back sanders run as the brake was released with the train running back off the greasy section. Then put the brake on, steadily. When the train stopped, open the front sanders and then regulator to first port. She should grip the sanded rail and start to move slowly forward with stifled exhaust as the pistons pushed painfully against the gravitational force of nature.

But the driver knows he dare not do this. The train is in the middle of a section and somewhere in that section is a set of catch points. In daylight they can be seen by the warning boards on the side of the bank but at night they are lost in the darkness. Is the train beyond them? Or are they somewhere under 50 or more wagons, just waiting for one to roll back another yard and be thrown off the track? There's only one thing to do.

The fireman lights a slush lamp and climbs down the steep steps from the cab on to the metal ballast between the down and up main lines. Like Wee Willie Winkie he walks alongside the train and looks for the catch points. Halfway along the train he hasn't found them but he can hear something in the quiet of the night. A metallic click, click . . . click, click . . .

A quick look over the shoulder and he picks out the two small white lights of the up main express that is bearing down on him. He's in the 'four foot' - a dead man's place at any time! He runs forward and scrambles in between two wagons. Not before time. Trains don't use much steam going down hill, just enough to cushion the valves as the pistons seem stationary in their frantic thrust in and out of the cylinders. He didn't hear the beat but he picked up the rhythmic clickerty, clack of the train's wheels as they drummed out their message over the joints in the track about a quarter of a mile away. Good job it was a quiet night!

With a thunderous roar the express flew by at a hundred miles an hour. They didn't know he was there. Carriage lights flickered on the grimy boards of the freight wagons like an old movie show and then it was darkness and quiet again. The red light on the last coach swayed and winked its way to London and his slush lamp had gone out in the suction of air behind the express.

The guard told him that the catch points were about 200 yards behind them. Thank God for that. Better than under the train. By the time the fireman reached the engine things were a lot better. The ten minute halt had allowed the engine to build up steam. The driver had built up the fire and the boiler was filling.

The steam brake was released. There was a gradual pulling back as the train went with nature. Front sanders open and regulator to first port. The engine locked its siderods on the straining axles and for a brief moment it was a tug-of-war between gravity and man. Then the 180 1b. steam pressure in the cylinders took the upper hand. Slowly the wheels gripped on the sand and the flanges ground forward.

There was a stilted 'chooof' from the chimney. Another quarter of a revolution of the 5 ft driving wheels and a stronger 'chooof'! They've won! The train is on the move, the engine is holding its grip and the catch points recede with their fears. In the signal box ahead the signalman looks at the slowly ticking clock on the wall and wonders what the hell they're up to. He'll have to switch them to the down suburban or they will check the Hook of Holland boat train coming rapidly up behind them. Then it would be a 'please explain'!

I had been in worse situations than that. Times such as when the previous crew hadn't bothered to check the sand in the boxes and the engine had started to slip on a curve up a bank. No good pulling on sand levers when the boxes are empty. It's a case of getting down with the shovel and trickling dirt, ash or any fine soil on the rail top so that the driving wheels can get a grip. Sometimes it means walking a mile with the train but at least it keeps it moving. Sometimes it meant a soaking in the rain or snow but there was no choice. When you got back into the cab the fire would be in poor shape because you had the shovel and the driver could only throw the coal on with his hands.

Chapter Thirty One

The End of the Line

The Express Passenger Link was the ultimate aim of every fireman and driver. Fate stepped in and denied me that great honour. Seven years of life in war torn London had left their mark and in 1948 I was dismissed from the locomotive department due to poor health. However I did enjoy the thrill of working fast passenger trains on a few occasions. This came about during relief in the express links from main line goods, when on spare shifts.

Express drivers were the untouchables in the pecking order at Stratford. To have a wartime fireman rostered with them was bordering on to racial discrimination. They saw my kind as the dregs of the labour pool, to be abolished as soon as the cease fire was achieved.

After overcoming the initial fear of the express runs and wondering if one could master the art, it was quite a relief to find that, on the whole, express trains were the easiest to work. They had the best of engines, the best of rolling stock and priority on the track. After battling for hundreds of miles with worn out locomotives, disintegrating rolling stock and being put into numerous sidings across East Anglia to make way for the boys in the express links, it was like leaving serfdom to ride with kings.

I seem to remember it being expected that crews wore neat looking overalls on these runs because they were working with the elite in the passenger world. Did they really believe the public studied us that much? The only people who really paid us any attention were the train spotters and little boys who longed to step into the cab 'just to have a look mister, please'. The average passenger, suburban or main line, never gave a second thought for the crew on the front and the disdain was obvious on most of their faces as they lined the platform edge during rush hours.

Just a sea of features flashing by as you ran in. Fat, thin, heavy jowled, angular and bald headed, heavy with make-up or lined with age, their wide, narrow, slit or oval eyes would give a fleeting glance at the engine. If you happened to catch one's eye and give a smile the face immediately froze into a mask.

They worked nine till five, enjoyed all weekends off and were back for the 8.15 to the office next Monday morning. If you were running five minutes late the cry went up 'What a railway!'. They didn't know, neither would they have cared, that it was ten days since the crew had a day off, that the engine was a wreck and that the 100 pounds on the steam gauge was doing far more than Stephenson had ever intended.

I always remember my first trip on the expresses. We went passenger to Colchester to pick up a train coming from Norwich. The driver was a regular express man and not too pleased in being given a supernumerary fireman. We never spoke from Liverpool Street to Colchester. Crossing to the up platform at that dreary station on a dreary day he asked, 'Ever fired to a 1500?'

'Only on the local goods,' I said and he knew what that meant. He never spoke again and we stood at the London end of the up platform, just waiting.

She steamed in ten minutes late.

It was a beautifully maintained 'B12'. Obviously not a Stratford engine. The apple green livery was highlighted by the black bands round the boiler, lined with cream. The blower roared away the smoke in a thin veil of blue as the engine stopped in front of us. The Ross valves were wisping with steam and the motions gave off that special smell of hot oil and lubricants that hung around the underside of the hot boiler.

The Colchester crew stepped off and we climbed aboard. Little was said. They didn't have to, it was all on the cab front. Steam gauge needle steady on 180, water in the glass see-sawing at three-quarters full and the vacuum brake gauge showing 19 inches. The coal was damped down, footplate spotless and steaming from the recent hose down with the pep pipe. The feed my side was singing as it fed water into the boiler. The firebox door was partly open showing the flames dancing under the blower's draught. My driver was studying his departmental watch. I looked back along a train of 12 glistening wooden coaches in the traditional Great Eastern teak finish and saw the station staff putting the last of the parcels in the guard's van.

The green flag waved and a porter's arm shot up.

'Right away!' sang out the East Anglian voices . . . so very different from the easy going Cockney that I heard every day of my working life.

'Right!' I told my driver. The strong, sturdy regulator that came from the centre of the boiler was pulled to first port. The beat came clear and loud from the flower pot chimney, shining with its recent coat of smokebox jelly.

Four rhythmic barks followed each other in beautiful unison. No faulty valves here but an engine in the prime of condition. No steam weeping from poorly packed glands around the pistons. I looked back. Everything was coming correctly. No doors swinging open or just held by the safety catch. For a change I had a right-hand firing locomotive and she was rapidly getting into her stride. The regulator was full second port now and the reversing wheel was nearly at mid-gear. Like a thoroughbred racehorse, her 6 ft 6 in. driving wheels were gripping the rails and every part of her 70 tons was working like clockwork. It was a joy to be on the living creature.

The firebox door was in two sections on the 'B12', square in design and opening by one lever which was about centre of the boiler when the doors were closed. To open, it was pulled towards the fireman's side. This caused the doors to slide open from the centre outwards, revealing the large oval mouth in the boiler front.

There were no doors to the cab of a 'B12'. Being an inside motion design the footplate did not oscillate like the three cylinder or two cylinder outside motion express engines. Nevertheless when speed was high there was a good amount of bucking and swaying and it paid to get a good foothold while firing or you could get tossed out of the side!

We were non-stop to Chelmsford and then Liverpool Street. I pulled the firebox door open and had a look round. Ten feet of roaring golden fire, thick under the door and trailing to dancing embers under the front boiler plate. Going round the box on a 'B12' was no light task. In fact it seemed never ending after the compact box of the 'N7'. I sighed with relief as I found I had mastered the art of bouncing the blade to get the coal up the front without hitting the brick arch. I had no desire to juggle around with a slice at 90 miles an hour.

The needle on the steam gauge barely moved from the red line and I began to wonder if it was stuck. It was obvious that nothing as fragile as the needle on the steam gauge would stick on that bucking, heaving, rolling footplate but I had never had such a good steamer. The driver just looked steadfastly ahead, noting the mileage pegs as they flashed by and knowing he was on time. In fact we were gaining time and, as we rolled into Chelmsford, we had made up eight minutes.

Right away again, this time non-stop to Liverpool Street. I started to get a good fire on ready for the climb into Shenfield after we had gone through sleepy Ingatestone. We had expected a signal check at Shenfield. It was not often you went through that junction without a caution light. This time the green lights of the electric signals beamed their welcome message from under the black hoods that sheltered the lamp glass from the sun's rays. The regulator was wide open and the reversing wheel at 25 per cent cut-off. She was purring up the bank with unbelievable ease. My mind went back to the times when I had struggled up there with a Harwich fish train. Full regulator and full wheel, praying there would be enough water in the glass when we topped the bank after Shenfield station.

The driver gave a long pull on the whistle as the station rapidly came into view. It was mandatory and ordered by the whistle board that stood on the embankment some distance from the station. Shenfield station was on a sharp curve and, if anyone was on the track at the other end, they would not see us until we were on top of them. Crossing points clattered under the bogie as it led the nose of the 'B12' into the bend. Driving wheels shuddered as they hit the frogs and the tender clickerty, clacked rapidly with its six rigid wheels as we roared through the station. Engine and train leaned hard to the left as it travelled over the eight inch canted rail and we did our regulation 80 miles an hour.

In seconds Shenfield was no more and we snarled under the brick bridge that dared to stand in our way, with London only 20 miles away. I put some more fire on. I didn't want to be standing up as we went down Brentwood Bank. As we neared the top of the bank the driver eased the wheel right back to nearly mid-gear. Just enough steam to cushion the valves as they shuttled their message to the steam chest. One hundred miles an hour down the bank, with the front of the 'B12' dancing over the bogies as they measured each joint that flashed beneath them.

In no time we seemed to be coasting towards Stratford. We had rolled without steam for the last five miles due to signal checks. Our momentum kept the train moving. Now Bow Junction's distant pointed to the smoky air over the city. We had a clear run to Bethnal Green. I fired up and it was the first time the driver had spoken to me during the trip.

'Not too much boy, we don't want to be blowing off in the station.'

I looked at the fire. It was very light in places. If I didn't put some on it would be out up at the front end when we stopped at platform 11. We had a good run into the Street and came to a gentle stop before the buffers of number 11 platform with the tender in the right place for water. The blower was eased off and there was no smoke from the chimney.

We were relieved by a local crew who were working empty carriage stock down before getting the engine ready again for a night train back to the Fen country. I was quietly pleased with my efforts and thought that, if that was express working, I'd do it any day.

At this time in my career I was beginning to experience a weariness that could not be dispelled by sleep. I would get home, have a meal and then go to bed and sleep for 10 hours without waking, only to get up and feel that I had never been to bed. I was having dizzy spells on the footplate and that wasn't good. A dizzy spell while moving at 50 miles an hour, and standing on the edge of the footplate to see if the feed was picking up the water, could spell disaster.

The end came after a night shift on the Whitemoor coal trains. I had a cup of tea in the Stratford canteen and then caught an all stations train home to Brentwood. It was about nine in the morning and I was going in the opposite direction to most people so I had a compartment to myself. I stretched out on the seat and went to sleep. I remembered the train stopping at Brentwood but a kind of black cloud seemed to engulf me as I went to get up. The next memory was being found on the floor of the compartment by two amazed porters at Shenfield.

They dragged me out and sat me on a platform seat. I was groggy, as white as a sheet and had no idea of the time. I caught the next train back to Brentwood and walked the three miles to home. People in the street gave me funny looks and when I reached home I could see why. Falling on the floor I had blackened my face on one side. No one had bothered to tell me so I walked through the town with a black and white face.

The trip to the doctor told the story. He called it vertigo and it was later described as a complete physical and nervous breakdown due to stress. Oh yes, after a long period of rest I would be all right, but it would be light duties and day work for some time. I took this advice to the running shed offices at Stratford and had visions of being a day labourer as many had in the past. I was told to come back in a week's time after a decision had been made. It was quite brief. Dismissal.

It was obvious that I could not stay on the footplate and they would not allow me to be near any moving vehicles. Quite a logical decision as I see it now but, at the time, I thought it was the end of my world. In the mists of time I had seen myself on the driver's side of the cab, hand on the regulator and eyes squinting for the distant signal to my future. But that was not to be and I suppose I should be grateful for those years that I did enjoy on the footplate, doing what most boys of my generation dreamed of doing but never achieved.

The background to my bill of health was the conditions of war in a beleaguered land. Nine years of rationing and limited diet was too much. The rations in wartime England were never great. Four ounces of bacon, four ounces of butter, eight ounces of sugar, two ounces of tea, one ounce of cheese and one shilling and twopence worth of fresh meat was all that my ration book gave me a week for shifting 20 tons of coal a day or working on an insatiable steam engine for ten to 20 hours at a time, seven days a week.

The government did give us a bit of consideration at one stage and increased a railwayman's cheese ration to four ounces a week. We also had an extra tea ration but, other than the odd sausage that could only be bought by queuing for hours at a butcher's shop, life was as grim as the air raids and the blackout.

Chapter Thirty Two

Living with the 'V1' and 'V2'

Apart from the purely physical problems during wartime railwaymen had to endure much which could be classed as psychological torment and anguish. Many men suffered in many ways during the war, fighting losing battles or on to victory, losing mates and being away from home for many years. In a way they were lucky because they were not in the front line all the time. They would be pulled back for relief, or the action would leave their area.

There were the highs and lows in their traumatic tensions and at no time did they have to worry about their surroundings. Whatever the devastation, it was not their homeland. No matter how appalled they may have been by the dead and injured in the streets, the shattered buildings, the refugees . . . they were detached. It was not part of them or their land. They knew when they left it that it would eventually fade like a bad dream.

Not so the London railwaymen. They not only worked in the bombed cities but they also lived there, day in and day out. They went to work not knowing if their homes would be standing when they came back, or whether they would even come back. They saw relatives and their families killed and maimed and it was work as usual. There was no relief until the final siren in 1945.

Even after all these years I can still remember those vivid experiences when men shared danger with grim silence, and a despair which made them wonder if they could face another shift. The night, for instance, when I worked a train of 500 lb. high explosive bombs from North London to the docks at Canning Town. It was one of those trip shifts and I was with my regular driver in the Local Goods Link. There wasn't much of him. About 45 years old, six feet tall and weighing about ten stone. One of the thin, wiry Cockneys who lived in the smoke-grimed terraced houses ringing the East End suburbs.

We had the job because he knew the road over the LMS lines from Kentish Town to the junction with the London to Cambridge line at South Tottenham. We relieved the LMS crew at Kentish Town and were surprised to find the 'J39' working tender first with its lethal load. It was about eight at night in the winter and the air raid had been going since six. He told me he'd made sure that his wife and children would sleep in the Anderson shelter that night. It stood in their small back yard.

The going was slow and hot. We had blackout curtains up and the cab windows were closed so that the fire's glow was curbed as much as possible from the night sky. The only light in the cab came from the gauge glass lamp hanging on the sooty boiler. The cloud ceiling was about 4,000 feet. Searchlights were constantly sweeping them in most suburbs. The erratic crump . . . crump . . . berwoof . . . berwoof . . . of the anti-aircraft guns and shells filled the air with their reverberations, and angry red blobs would glow above the clouds when shells exploded. Now and then we could see a fat barrage balloon against the clouds as a stick of bombs would light up the darkness a few miles away.

We reached the junction at Tottenham and had the road to Temple Mills. One thing about the old paraffin oil lamps sitting high on the timber signal gantries, they never went out. Power failures due to bombing never affected our Victorian era signals. At least the going was easy for me. With first port on the regulator and the wheel at 25 per cent cut-off the old girl wasn't using too much steam. Our speed was only about 10 miles an hour. It was a case of being ready for the rapid stop in case the track suddenly disappeared.

We were lumbering by the Hackney Marshes when a string of flares drifted down from the heavy sky. Some German bomber was deciding to have a closer look. It was obvious they were after Temple Mills. The flares drifted down in brilliant array, like giant Roman Candles, only death stalked above them. The Bofor guns on the marshes began to chatter fiercely in an effort to blast them out of the sky. Then we could feel the tremor of high explosive bombs as they ripped into the houses that we knew stood on the hills to our left.

My driver stepped over to my side and pulled the blackout curtain to one side.

'That's my home, Rob,' he said. 'That's where I live. I hope to Christ they've missed us . . .'

He went back to the driver's side. The Lea Bridge home signal was at danger. Over towards Hackney a dull red glow increased to a glaring gold as fires got out of hand after a Molotov breadbasket emptied its load of incendiary bombs over the city. I made up the fire ready for the pull when we had the road and climbed into the tender to drag some coal forward. The drone of aircraft was everywhere. There was the crack of the AA guns that ringed Temple Mills on waste ground and the dull thud of distant bombs. Shrapnel from bursting shells whined through the air on its downward fall.

The red turned to green and we rolled through the deserted station, a gentle beat leaving the chimney and the siderods clanking rhythmically as the greasy wheels of the scruffy looking Standard took us slowly but surely to the London Docks. The marshalling yard was in complete darkness and no work was in progress. They were waiting for the lull that would come. The Germans were very methodical. They worked to a better timetable than we did.

When we reached the signal box near the yardmaster's office my driver stopped the train and went up the steep wooden stairs to where a faint glimmer showed the signalman at the frame. He wanted to know what it was like at Leyton. Where had the bombs fallen that we had seen across the marshes? He was told that his street had been hit. No news yet but they would keep him informed. No, he couldn't be relieved to go home. Yes, they knew he'd been on duty for nine hours but there was no relief. There was no proof that his house was damaged. No, he'd have to keep going. They would bear us in mind when relief was available.

He climbed back into the cab and we eased out the couplings on the trucks of bombs. When we felt the strain he gave her first port and the joints clattered slowly under the driving wheels as we steamed through the war torn night. He told me this conversation with Train Control as we swayed erratically over crossing points through the Temple Mills complex. As his home was receding in the background, crossed searchlights in the distance showed us where the docks hid in the blackness.

He lit a hand-rolled cigarette and the sudden flare of his match etched his drawn face on my mind for all time. Under the peaked cap I saw the grime of the coal dust, collected from the tender as we travelled tender first. There were rivulets where his tears had cut a channel to his chin. The match went out and he was back to his personal sorrow. We never got relief. We rolled on to the Stratford disposal pits four hours later. He went home and I went to the canteen for a cup of wishy tea and a talk to anyone who happened to be there.

'Poor old Alf', they told me, talking about my mate, 'direct hit they say. What swine, eh?'

And it went through my mind, what soldier had to experience all that and still report for duty after burying his family?

The air raids were bad enough but I believe the flying bombs and rockets were much worse. With the air raids the wail of the siren prepared you for the worst. Like it or not, you knew that death was your companion until the 'all clear'. Then you could relax. Due to the strength of England's air defences in daylight, raids between sunrise and sunset were rare and occurred mainly on cloudy days. Even then they were light fighter-bombers and not the lumbering Heinkels or Junkers.

The flying bomb was different. It came day and night and you could nearly always pick out the one that might have your name on it. Not like the high flying bomber that released its stick of bombs way up in the darkness and left you with the customary whistle as they fell towards their target. You knew that once the plane had passed over you were safe till the next one.

The flying bomb's official name was Vergeltungswaffe Eins or, in English, Reprisal Weapon One. It was specifically designed to break the morale of the people in the London area and surrounding districts. It had no pilot, was completely automatic and was nothing more than a bomb with wings and a jet engine. Its wing span was 17 feet, its overall length 25 feet and the engine was 11 feet long. Its gross weight was 4,700 1b. and in the nose was 2,2041 lb. of high explosive.

The bomb had three fuses. The main one was a sensitive impact fuse which caused the bomb to explode on immediate impact, thus giving the maximum blast effect above the surface. If the sensitive fuse failed to act because the bomb had glided to the ground instead of diving, as intended, a universal mechanical fuse exploded the bomb. If neither fuse worked the third fuse, a clock fuse, would explode the bomb two hours after landing.

It travelled at 400 miles an hour, at between 800 and 2,500 feet. Between June 1944, when they were first used, and September of that year, 8,070 flying bombs were launched against the London area. After that, due to the allied advance into France, they became spasmodic and the rockets took over. During their reign of terror 23,000 houses were destroyed in south-eastern England and more than one million were damaged. When the peak of the offensive was reached 200 flying bombs were aimed at the Greater London area each day.

This was the background to life in 1944 when Hitler's new weapon was not just a novelty but one that nearly destroyed the will power of the people living in the area under attack. I was on duty at Stratford loco. depot the night the first one fell in London. We were on the disposal pits when the air raid warning sounded. It was four in the morning and we were beginning to get that weary feeling that comes round at that time on a night shift. The sirens changed all that.

As we steamed quietly up to the coal stage we could here the approaching plane. It seemed to be moving very fast. We thought it must be an FW 190, one of the fighter bombers that were being used frequently to bomb the railway tracks and then machine gun trains. The anti-aircraft guns were banging away and then, suddenly, the engine stopped.

'They've hit the swine!' my mate shouted with much jubilation. Minutes later there was a heavy explosion behind the Bryant & May match factory near Bow Junction. By the time we made the mess room the news was all over Stratford.

A German plane had been shot down and it had crashed next to the bridge at the Liverpool Street end of Coborn Road station. It must have had its bomb load on board because there was one hell of a mess. A row of houses demolished, the bridge was down and the lines into Liverpool Street were closed. That was 4.15 am on 13th June, 1944.

Although British intelligence officers knew the flying bomb existed they never let the public know. But the old Cockney began to get suspicious when it was discovered that the plane's engine was not like a normal plane's engine and they never found the crew. Then we were told. This new method of attack greatly changed the air raid warning system. If London were to be on the same red alert with the 'V1', or 'Doodlebug' as it was soon named, as it was when bomber squadrons came over, there would be no work done.

The main difference between the ordinary air raid and flying bomb attacks was that, with planes, they could alter course at any time. The flying bomb was set on a course from France or Holland and it would not deviate unless shot down. So a general alert was sounded when observers knew the direction of approach by the bombs. When the bomb neared the London area a local alert was given so that workers could take shelter in case the bomb came down.

This was the nerve wracking part. The 'V1' had a strong reverberating sound with an erratic beat. Its approach could be heard miles away and then it would be seen, about 1,000 feet up, its flaming tail sending it forward with grim determination. There would be no faltering engine note at the end. The engine would suddenly cut out and an ominous silence would replace the shattering roar of the jet.

It would then do one of two things. It would either drop its nose vertically and come down like an ordinary bomb, or it would glide to earth. It could glide for nearly four miles under the right circumstances. I remember one train crew on the suburban services looking out of the cab to find a 'Doodlebug' gliding alongside the train, about 200 feet up. Rough on the passengers or not, there was an emergency stop that day!

Normally they came one at a time but in the early part of the campaign it was not unusual to see groups of three and four. I remember being in the engine road at Temple Mills one evening in July, getting water with a 'J15'. The local alert was on. I happened to look over the top of a road bridge that stood behind the engine and was amazed to see a group of flying bombs bearing down on me.

They seemed to be flying in vee formation, just as though they had pilots. I counted seven and then decided it was time to take cover. The 'J15' tender was not that high from the ground and I jumped without troubling to use the steel steps down the back. They roared overhead and continued towards Tottenham where they eventually came down over a wide area.

The Germans were uncannily efficient with their remote controlled weapons and overall they scored more hits on military targets with the 'V1' and 'V2' than they did with orthodox bombing. We began to wonder if they had spies in the area doing some target spotting for the bomb crews across the Channel.

My worst shift at that time was on the Stores Pilot as they called it. It was a day shift, 11.0 am to 7.0 pm with a 'Buckjumper' that shuttled back and forth from the Stratford depot to the railway stores sidings at Temple Mills, about a quarter of a mile from Leyton station. We would take coal empties to the sidings and come back with more coal or oil, maybe steel for the workshops or sand for the sand furnace, to be dried for engine sand boxes.

It was about midday and we had picked up a train from the sidings at the Leyton end of Temple Mills and worked it to the sidings that stretched between the offices and carriage sheds at Stratford loco. depot. The klaxon went to let us know that a flying bomb was heading our way. Shortly afterwards came the familiar roar of the jet engine and we picked it up, coming from the direction of Bow Junction. It was about 1,000 feet up and didn't seem to be going that fast.

Suddenly the engine stopped and so did my heart! It was right above Stratford station and heading our way. But it didn't dive. It started a slow glide and drifted towards Leyton. Then it did the unexpected. As though a pilot were sitting in the cockpit, it slowly began to bank to the left. It had reached the junction of the Leyton line with the main and was coming back! Losing height all the time, it glided silently over the repair shops beside the Channelsea loop line that led to the low level station at Stratford and banked towards the Jubilee Shed.

By this time everyone was clammy with the sweat of fear and yet we just stood and watched. It skimmed over the shed at about 200 feet. I could see every detail. The green and brown camouflage paintwork on the wings and body, the German lettering on the fuselage and the air vents on the front of the engine. Still turning it drifted on its way, just missing the brick road bridge that spanned the tracks leading to Temple Mills and landed in the stores sidings - right where I had been 30 minutes beforehand!

The explosion was ear shattering and took the breath away. Debris went high and wide. Half the yard was wiped out but the great relief among those of us watching was that it had missed Leyton and all the houses that huddled so close to the railway. Another 200 yards and the death toll would have been high. By the end of that shift I had seen eight 'V1s' come down within a half mile radius of the Stratford shed. Jerry was not far off his target.

As the allied armies advanced into Europe so the flying bombs reduced in numbers but that didn't mean the war was over for Londoners. Vergeltungswaffe number two was on the launching pad. The rocket was more devastating, physically and morally, than any other weapon. Known as the 'V2' it was a rocket fired from deeper in Europe, beyond the advancing armies and against which there was no defence.

Due to the set course of the 'V1', its loss rate was high once the RAF fighters had mastered a technique to bring them down. The AA guns also had their share of victories but with the 'V2' it was impossible to halt its approach once it left the launch pad.

The ironic part about it all was that the weapon that was about to kill and maim thousands in the Greater London area was designed by a German scientist who, after the war, was accepted by the Americans with open arms. He became the main scientist behind their space programme. Such was the interest in the ordinary individual by the warlords. They praised his rocketry precision and overlooked the murder of men, women and children in the name of scientific advancement. Other Germans who had acted in the more orthodox way with their brutality, were classed as war criminals and sentenced according to their crimes against humanity.

The 'V2' carried a ton of explosives in its warhead. It was propelled into the stratosphere to a height of about 60 miles from where it then dropped to targets in the London area. The first arrived about September 1944, not that we were told anything about them. The first reports spoke about gas mains exploding in Chiswick. Then another gas main exploded at a school in Dagenham. But people in the area knew that gas mains did not have tail fins and other pieces of sophisticated equipment.

By this time the Cockney's sense of humour was running out and no colloquial name was given to this instrument of sudden death. The main characteristic and terror of the 'V2' was its space age approach to orthodox warfare. It travelled much faster than the speed of sound and arrived at the target before anyone knew or heard it. There was no chance of shooting it down. The first thing known was the huge explosion. As the reverberations died away there would be a second, smaller explosion in the sky. It was the sound of the rocket entering the atmosphere and breaking the sound barrier. Then you would hear it coming down. This all happened AFTER the weapon had exploded!

One morning I was walking from Stratford station to the Jubilee Shed for a three o'clock start. It was dark with low cloud and the buildings around me seemed to melt into the blackness as I followed the goods road that led from Temple Mills to the docks via Fork Junction and Stratford Low Level station. Suddenly the place was alight, as though the running sheds had been hit by lightning. I instinctively dropped to the ground and put my hands over my head. The tin hat that hung by my side clattered to the ground. There was no time to put it on. The ground seemed to come up to meet me with the roar of the explosion.

A 'V2' had fallen on vacant ground between the repair shops and the running road that dissected the running shed roads from the loop line through Channelsea. Another 300 yards my way and it would have been the end of the Stratford shed and about 200 engines. I looked up. In the glare of the explosion I could see freight wagons hurtling towards the sky like toys being tossed aside by a giant. Wheels and tangled track seemed to hang in slow motion in the angry red light and then drop back to earth. Clods of earth, bricks and ash fell round me. It was all over. I went to see the crater. It was about 50 feet deep and

200 yards across.

On another occasion I was working a semi-fast train from Liverpool Street to Southend. We had just left Stratford on the down main and the next stop was Ilford. The 'B12' was picking up speed as we barked through Maryland Point with eight coaches of corridor stock. It was midday. The distant was off for Forest Gate and we were reaching 60 miles an hour. Suddenly Forest Gate station disappeared. Our view between the concrete walls of the cutting was nothing but grey dust and black smoke. My mate made an emergency stop and, as the haze cleared, we saw that a rocket had exploded in the street to the right of the station. Debris from the explosion had fallen on the station as well as causing part of the building to collapse onto the track. Being in a shallow cutting we had escaped the main blast.

My most harrowing experience with the 'V2' was on an early shift at Stratford depot. I was in the Main Line Goods Link at the time. We had been rostered on at 2.0 am to relieve a troop train in Channelsea Loop, coming from East Anglia and bound for the south-east coast of England. Traffic control advised that it was running about two hours late so we sat in the crib room talking railways with other crews. There was always a cup of tea going and it was handy to pick up the latest facts on speed orders or revised train workings.

The running foreman came in about four o'clock and told us our train had arrived and was waiting at the Channelsea starter for relief. That meant a walk round the back of the shed and across the sluggish River Lea by footbridge. Ten minutes and we'd be there. I went to the ever boiling urn and made a billy of tea. My driver said he didn't know when we would get the next chance. Suddenly the whole building shook like a jelly on a plate. We heard the sound of broken glass as some windows fell out. We instinctively ducked. Another rocket.

'That wasn't far off,' someone muttered.

'The old Swede bashers won't want a call boy this morning!' said another, referring to the March men in the dormitory above the crib room.

We collected our bags and billy of tea and made our way to the train that waited for us. As we picked our way through the sidings it was obvious that the rocket had landed nearby. Great lumps of earth and clay were scattered all over the place. We crossed the river and saw the silhouette of the troop train against the lights of a factory on the other side of the tracks. Something seemed grotesque. Handlamps were bobbing around the scene, throwing the puny lights on the remains of a 'J17'.

The 45 ton engine was leaning heavily to one side, severed from its tender. The train, which was made up of eight flat tops with heavy tanks chained on each and two coaches at the rear with their crews, didn't seem the worse for wear in the half light. This was our train. There was no sign of the mates we were to relieve. All that could be found was a boot belonging to the fireman.

The rocket had landed beside the engine about 100 yards away. I believe they found parts of the crew round the sidings as day broke. The old goods engine whimpered with escaping steam. I felt sick and neither of us could speak. We knew the driver and fireman well. If the train had been on time it would not have happened. If it had arrived a little earlier we would have been on the footplate and not them . . .

Chapter Thirty Three

Mateship

Having lived in the wonderful world of steam railways I suppose it could be expected that one should have some special memories of moments that would be good to relive. Such is not my case. Admittedly I'd go for miles just to get a ride on a swaying footplate and feel the smoke and steam on my face, the heat of the fire against my legs. To smell the wooden floor, freshly washed down with the hose and the hot oil working in the steam lubricator. But all those sensations belong to the engines themselves, not to any special circumstances or slot of time in a perpetual calendar which marked the end of a shift and the start of another.

The lasting memories I have of those brief years are fashioned by the men that I worked with and the conditions under which we worked. As I said earlier, we were social outcasts. Our shifts never allowed us to join the hobbies and pastimes that the majority of the community enjoyed. There was no getting together at weekends with friends or family when most people were free. We would be casting our shadows across the countryside somewhere with a train snaking behind the fantasies of steam against the skyline.

Within the industry itself we were also outcasts. Due to the historic background of the footplate section within the railway structure, fitters, boilerwashers, labourers and the like round the sheds worked with us but never joined us as part of a united force. Very few guards, shunters or station staff mixed with the 'Loco'. The Indian caste system had nothing on the class structure of the railway industry.

On the other side of the workforce was the company's elite. Foremen, inspectors, superintendents and departmental heads. They never left their ivory castles. Even when inspectors boarded an engine on a train to travel a section of the line there would never be any conversation unless the engine had a defect and then notes would be taken. Locomotive men lived in their own world which, in turn, was based on the nucleus of two men working together in a restricted work place for most of their working life.

It was in this restricted society that I learned the basics of trade unionism and what it was all about. The enginemen's union was a strong organisation and a great help to its members. I am talking of times when there was no such thing as sick pay and other frills to pamper the employee. It was the grim time when workers had to band together to help themselves and their families. Looking back, I think they might have been the best times. They bred an independence of thought and action and a society that was not made selfish by the featherbedding of social services.

We had a sick benefits club where all members paid a set amount and, when sickness hit them, they received weekly payments that helped to make the National Health sick payment a sum that could be lived on. There were also funeral benefits which gave a considerable lump sum to the widow if her footplate husband passed away. Also through the union movement there were educational schemes whereby shift workers such as ourselves, who could not attend night schools, could study by correspondence.

It was against this background of brotherhood that my memories were shaped in those war years. My two most vivid recollections are of men and not machines. One concerns a lad who started with me on the same day at Stratford; he also lived at Brentwood. We were both in our teens but he was not the typical Brentwood lad. He was a true Cockney and his family had moved to Brentwood early during the war to get away from the East End and the constant bombing. He had the cheek of the devil and was a real live wire, always telling jokes and keeping us generally amused.

He had a rolling gait, like a sailor, and a big moon face as red as a radish. There was always a cigarette hanging from the bottom lip. We travelled together while cleaning but, as the shifts came along and we went through the various links, it was rarely that we met in later years. Most of our meetings were in Jack's Cafe or the railway canteen while waiting to start work or catch a train home. He would take me through his eventful life . . . all the girls he had taken out, the films he had seen, the money he had won at cards.

He was the first to get married and they lived at home with his parents in a terraced house that overlooked the railway yards at Brentwood. Then he proudly told me he was going to be a father. At the time I could not understand people getting married, let alone having children with the war dragging on and death all around us.

He said I was a misery. Why didn't I find myself a girl and start to live? The night I bumped into him in the dimly lit subway under Stratford station he told me it was only a month to his baby's birth. He still had the cheeky grin, the cigarette in the corner of the mouth and a sparkle in his blue eyes. He was going home and I was on at 11.0 pm with a local goods job.

'Can't stop Rob, want to catch the Southend!' he said.

He went on his way with his jaunty walk. The train was semi-fast and he would be home with his wife in 40 minutes. I remember thinking half his luck, as I started a shift that would end when he was having breakfast. In 30 minutes he was dead.

It was a cold, foggy night and trains were running off course. The down Southend was on time but the Liverpool Street to Ipswich express was late out of London due to the late arrival of engine power. The Southend train was Stratford-Ilford-Romford and all stations to Southend and its normal running was down main to Ilford and then on to the down suburban to Shenfield. This left the down main clear for the Ipswich express which left Liverpool Street later but was fast to Shenfield.

On the night that he caught the Southend home they kept the train on the down main until Gidea Park. It was intended to switch over to the down suburban at that station. After the Southend train had left the Romford signalman's section he put his distant at caution, his home signal off but his starter at danger because the Southend train was approaching Gidea Park and, in the fog it was a requirement to keep two sections clear between trains.

The Ipswich train was thundering towards Romford, trying to make up time, and a horrified signalman saw the dark shape flash past his box, the golden glow from the cab sending a halo of light into the fog. The bright haze marked the train's progress through the station. It failed to stop at the starter with its red warning light glaring towards the cab. The signalman realised that the driver had either missed the distant or had taken it to be off and thought he had the road to Gidea Park.

The peace of Gidea Park was shattered as the roaring express belched under the road bridge and ploughed into the back of the stationary Southend train. The down main and up suburban were blocked for the rest of that murky night and many hours later they pulled the bodies out of the rear coaches. My friend was one of them. He always travelled in the rear coach because it was nearest to the stairway at Brentwood when leaving the station.

The news travelled like wildfire at the depot but nobody knew who the victims were at that stage. I found out the next day and the loss of that cheeky chappie had a profound effect on me. The union said his widow would naturally receive compensation but I wondered how much that would mean to a fatherless child. Then complications started to rear their technical heads. This was before the days when compensation laws covered a man travelling to and from his work. The only compensation my friend's wife would get would be that as a widow of one killed in a railway accident but I knew then, with knowledge gained through union activities, that this could be touch and go.

Those of us who lived in an area outside a certain radius from Stratford had to pay our fares to travel to work. It was called a privilege pass and operated like a season ticket. There was a reduction in fare and also a reduction in legal liabilities for the company. They could pay compensation but they didn't have to. However, the refusal to pay compensation came from another quarter.

When I had met him in the subway it was 10 o'clock that evening and he had just arrived at the depot from a suburban passenger shift where the final job was light engine to Stratford. He and his mate had done disposal work on the engine in the carriage siding while waiting for release to Stratford. When they arrived at the depot they went straight to the coal road with the engine and left it for the shed gang to place. They were entitled to claim one hour for disposal duties and, having arrived at the depot at 10 o'clock, this entitled them to sign off at 11 o'clock.

Thirty minutes before he had signed off, according to the time book, he was dead at Gidea Park. The powers that be ruled that he had falsified his time sheet and therefore, under the regulations, should face disciplinary action. For this alleged false entry, even though the work had been done that entitled him to claim the extra 60 minutes, it was ruled that he was outside the legal scope for compensation claims for next of kin.

This move shocked us because it was something we all did at sometime or other. It had always been accepted by the company because it was in their interests as much as the crews. It often released an engine for work well before they would otherwise get it. It was also typical of a management that expected its staff to break every rule in the book to keep the trains on time and yet crack the disciplinary whip when the odd occasion went against the employer.

I made inquiries through the union to see what could be done. I was told nothing could be done. To me this was unacceptable. Within a small group that had known him well we started a collection for his wife and unborn child. We did quite well in the depot with an occasional knock-back from the pre-war oldies. The eventual count was nearly £100, quite a sum of money in the forties.

It became my task, as instigator of the idea, to take it to his wife. I had never done anything like it before and had butterflies in the stomach as I walked down the working class street beside the embankment at Brentwood. It would have been about a month after the accident and the day was as grey as my task. I walked up the hearthstoned steps and knocked with the solid brass knocker on the front door. It was quite a surprise when she opened the door. After all his talk of the dazzling women he had known she came as plain as you would find them. I gave her the notebooks with all the signatures of those who had given from their weekly pay packets and the envelope with the green notes just showing. I mumbled something about a gesture from his mates in her time of grief and left her standing there. I was afraid she might cry and I couldn't stand that because I had a lump in my throat at the thought of him and the good times we had enjoyed under those grim conditions at Stratford. He had been a great mate and it was the least we could do for him.

My other memory is not so much of men I knew but of men who represented our forgotten breed and were treated with less respect than animals. It was during the latter years of the war when the German air force was more of a nuisance value than a real threat to life. The mass raids had finished, the all-night bombings were few and far between and the new strategy was the fast fighter-bomber attack. They came in low over the coast to dodge radar, but kept out of the London area because of the barrage balloons and the steel curtain of cables.

The moon was just about in the first quarter. Not enough light to show up the countryside below but enough to show a pilot the telltale strip of silver ribbon that snaked over the landscape in the form of a railway. This must have been how the pilot of the FW 190 picked up the London to Ipswich main line as it cut through the fields between Shenfield and Ingatestone the night he dropped his 500 1b. high explosive bomb on the track.

It was about 15 minutes before the Liverpool Street to Ipswich semi-fast pulled into Shenfield station. The electric signals that had been winking from the darkness down the line suddenly went out. The signalman knew that something had gone wrong and he linked it with the explosion that had rattled the signal box windows. It wasn't a power failure. Something had disrupted the power lines beside the track.

He put the starter at danger and contacted traffic control. It was felt that the track should be inspected before any train went over it. The eight coach Ipswich train was held at the platform while the local permanent way ganger walked ahead to find out what had happened. Each signal post had a telephone attached and he could ring in at any time.

After a quarter of an hour had passed with no advice from the ganger the control centre began to get fidgety. The precious minutes were ticking by and the train was late. The signalman was instructed to tell the driver to proceed with caution. Slowly the train pulled out of the station with the regulator just off the face as it was a downhill gradient for about three miles. How did you 'proceed with caution' with about 500 tons in the dark, with no headlights, and be prepared to stop as soon as something suspicious loomed ahead?

The train rumbled by the horrified ganger. They did not see him in the dark. It wasn't long after that when the 'B12' fell into the mammoth crater gouged out of the embankment by the FW 190's bomb. Track, signalling cables and ballast had gone sky high. The engine dug its nose into the crater's side. The tender jumped on top of the cab and the first two coaches followed. I forget how many died but it was a long time before they dug the crew out from under the wreckage.

Many years later the next of kin of the driver and fireman were still fighting for compensation. The company argued that it was an act of war and not in the course of their duty. The head train controller received an OBE after the war for services rendered. People say I'm a cynic when I say I've never met a good boss yet. Perhaps I'm unlucky but, for all that, railways are in my blood and I'd go back on the footplate tomorrow if they'd have me.